An Australasian Beekeeping Bibliography

Peter Barrett

An Australasian Beekeeping Bibliography
© Peter Barrett

All rights reserved. No part of this publication may be reproduced, stored in a retrieval system, transmitted in any form or by any means electronic, mechanical, including photocopying, recording or otherwise without prior consent of the copyright holders.

ISBN 978-1-904846-85-7

Published by Northern Bee Books, 2011
Scout Bottom Farm
Mytholmroyd
Hebden Bridge
HX7 5JS (UK)

An Australasian Beekeeping Bibliography

Peter Barrett

An Australasian Beekeeping Bibliography

Peter Barrett

Third Edition, April 2011

This book is copyright. Apart from fair dealing for the purposes of private study, research, criticism or review, as permitted under the Copyright Act, no part (those parts having been originally authored by Peter Barrett) may be reproduced by any process without written permission. Inquiries regarding any form of reproduction beyond the above permissions, should be directed to the author:

Peter Barrett
33 Osprey Street, Caloundra 4551 Qld., Australia
Phone 07 5491 1204 or Overseas +61 7 5491 1204
email barrpete@bigpond.net.au

Author of

The Immigrant Bees 1788 to 1898, Volume I (1995)
An Australian Beekeeping Bibliography (1996, 1999)
William Charles Cotton, Grand Bee Master of NZ, 1842-1847 (1997)
The Immigrant Bees 1788 to 1898, Volume II (1999)
The Immigrant Bees 1788 to 1898, Volume III (2006)
The Immigrant Bees 1788 to 1898, Volume IV (2010)
The Immigrant Bees 1788 to 1898, Volume V (2011, manuscript)

This work is dedicated to the memory of Tarlton Rayment's phenomenal output of works on Australian bees and beekeeping, both published and unpublished.

Typeset in 12 and 11 point Times New Roman.

Title page illustration: "Advance Australia", frontispiece from Albert Gale's 1912 *Australian Bee Lore and Bee Culture*

Foreword

This work provides a significantly updated catalogue of Australian works on bees and beekeeping. Some New Zealand works have been included as they were heavily used by both NZ and Australian beekeepers. Within Great Britain there are extensive lists of beekeeping works held by the British Beekeepers' Association, Walker's *Descriptive Catalogue of Bee-books* and the IBRA's *British Bee Books, A Bibliography 1500-1976* (1979). New Zealand has its *Bibliography of New Zealand Apiculture* (1988) by Reid, Matheson and Walton; and in the U.S.A., courtesy of T. S. K. & M. P. Johanssen is *Apicultural Literature Published in Canada and the United States* (1972).

I hope my bibliography makes a worthwhile contribution to this family of books about bee books. It commenced life as a catalogue of my humble beekeeping library, then progressed into a book targeted at beekeepers interested in bee books – such beings do exist! The 2nd edition was published in England in 1999. I was pleased to find just recently that three Australian libraries each held a copy.

Some early 20th Century Australian works stand with the best from overseas. To name but two I find those left by Rayment and Gale a delight. The illustrator in Albert Gale's book has added some whimsical and humourous components, visible only to the sharp eyed. Rayment's books often have a touch of literary magic about them. These and others have remained unappreciated for too long.

In addition, Australia's earliest works on beekeeping are entitled to join company with the rarest books in the world. Four late 19th century books exist – only two copies of each – in public or governmental libraries. Two copies are known to exist for a fifth work, one public and one in a private collection. For a sixth and seventh there are no known copies - maybe some exist in a private library, either treasured or forgotten. Rare copies do surface from time to time, possibly as a result of estate clearances. A copy of Chambers *The Colonial Beekeeper* (1888) appeared on the retail market in 1996 and Mackay's *Beekeeping as a Business in Australia* (1895) bubbled up recently in early 2010 – the only extant known copy !

An Australian Beekeeping Bibliography, 1875 to 2010, addresses Australian books on beekeeping published since 1875. None are known to have existed before this. I've grouped the catalogue into three sections: 1875 to 1918, 1919 to 1945 and Post 1945, alphabetically sequenced by author name. Other publications such as pamphlets and Departmental bulletins, beekeeping journals, catalogues and ephemera are also covered but to a lesser extent. A detailed index is also provided along with many illustrations, including woodcuts from books now over 100 years old.

This work is more than a Ferguson style catalogue. Firstly, some beekeeper-author biographical details are presented including those of Fred Beuhne (pronounced "Boyna") of Victoria (to 1933), James Carroll of Brisbane (1870s – 1880s), L.T. Chambers of Melbourne (1880s), R.J. Cribb of Brisbane (1880s – 1890s), Albert Gale of Sydney (to 1915), Angus Mackay of Brisbane and Sydney (to 1910) and Tarlton Rayment of New South Wales (to 1960s). Some notes on Henry Hacker of the Queensland Museum are also presented. These authors receive specific entries in my Table of Contents, while all authors appear alphabetically within each time zone I've chosen.

Secondly, some late 19th century book reviews have also been reproduced; estimates of some rare book prices are shown; and chapter headings from many books are listed.

Thirdly, endearing components of some quirky books are highlighted. For example, the engraver who worked on Albert Gale's *Australian Bee Lore and Bee Culture* (1912) had a whimsical sense of humour. The magnified image above forms less than 5% of one full page illustration on the components of a Langstroth hive. (p.221) What can you see? Think photography - a magnifying glass may help. This was not the engraver's only reward for future vigilant readers. Another example: Several illustrations in Angus Mackay's *The Elements of Australian Agriculture* (1885), I lately discovered, were "lifted" from an April 1881 issue of the New York publication *Harper's Weekly*. The joke was on me for I'd reproduced several in some of my works thinking they were original Australian woodcuts.

One of my favourites comes from Kylie Tennant's autobiography: "Because I am not very accurate I write everything down in a notebook and double check. When I was getting the material for *The Honey Flow*, [1956] I was a pest to the friendly apiarists, the brothers Koina and Brogan, with whom I travelled. 'What's wrong with the girl! We told you that yesterday!' 'And "Bimble Box".' [a species of eucalypt] 'How would you distinguish Bimble Box?' Bill Koina gave a scowl and the perfect answer: 'It's bimbley, of course.' "

As this work is to be published in the U.K., I've included some anecdotes about William Charles Cotton, some true and some not so true – but make up your own mind as to their veracity. These were unearthed using Google's Book Search facility and their appearance in print ranges between 1842 and 1903. This edition covers those works held by public and university libraries, both overseas and in Australia, as well as some private collections. I welcome details of books not described herein. Please enjoy.   Peter Barrett, Caloundra, Queensland

Table of Contents

FOREWORD 4
ACKNOWLEDGEMENTS 8
BOOKS TO 1918 10
    FRED BEUHNE 11
    A.E. BONNEY 17
    JAMES CARROLL 22
    LEONARD CHAMBERS 35
    ALBERT GALE 83
    ISAAC HOPKINS 99
    ANGUS MACKAY 117
    TARLTON RAYMENT 143
BOOKS 1919 - 1945 157
    HENRY HACKER 160
    TARLTON RAYMENT 165
BOOKS - POST 1945 174
    HENRY LEWIS JONES 194
JOURNALS 234
OTHER PUBLICATIONS 248
    PAMPHLETS & BULLETINS & COURSE NOTES 248
    CATALOGUES & EPHEMERA 252
    ARTICLES IN OTHER WORKS 253
BIBLIOGRAPHY 254
INDEX 257
ABBREVIATIONS 264

Acknowledgements

I have pleasure in acknowledging the assistance of the following for their replies and/or contributions to my latest volume.

| Courtney Moran | Fryer Library, University of Queensland |
| Gina Tom | Client Services, State Library of Queensland |

The Bee Hive

The beehive stirs at break of day,
Before first light, workers on their way.
Removing rubbish on outward flight,
To clean debris from the night.

Pollen collecting, from the flowers,
Filled pollen baskets within the hour.
In cells, this protein food they store,
before flying off and collecting more.

Nectar gatherers find the flow,
Countless bees, out they go.
Visiting lots of flowers in turn,
With full nectar sacs, they return.

Ripening nectar in the hive,
Converting nectar to honey, all strive.
before white wax cap, on they pop
Filling each cell to the top.

Water carriers also muster,
To evaporate and cool the cluster.
Guard bees watch the to and fro,
As their sisters come and go.

(from *Milk to Honey via the Sea* (1997, limited edition),
Norman Rice, M.B.E

Books to 1918

Apiarian Society of Victoria. ***Rules and by-laws of the Apiarian Society of Victoria.*** 1861. pp.8 Copy at SLV. The Society was formed in Feb. 1861. Refer *The Sydney Morning Herald*, 13 February 1861 (p.2). Also see *The Mercury*, Hobart, 14 February 1861 (p.2). "BEE BREEDING. - In accordance with the resolution arrived at by the gentlemen who, on Monday week last, met at the Clarence Hotel for the purpose of initiating a society for the cultivation of the science of bee-breeding, to be called the Apiarian Society of Victoria, a second meeting was held yesterday evening, at the Bush Inn, to give a definite shape to the association. The assemblage was not numerous, nor could it have been expected to be so, for the science has not been largely cultivated in Victoria; but those who were present seemed decidedly in earnest. Mr. Veevers having been appointed to the chair, Mr. Falstead lamented that a wider interest was not exhibited. Little was known, he was sure, of the ease with which ladies, and children even, might not only keep bees but, by joining the society, aid in the good work of establishing that which might be the means to a very good end. Mr. Joshua Snowball moved that the meeting be adjourned till Monday next but it was the general opinion that business should be proceeded with at once, and the motion was not seconded. Mr. Search proposed - "That this meeting is of opinion that the establishment of a society, through which the knowledge of the habits of the honey-bee and its management would be disseminated, is desirable." Mr. Richardson seconded the resolution, which was unanimously carried. Mr. Richardson moved, and Mr. Round seconded - "That a society be now formed, to be called the Apiarian Society of Victoria." This, too, was carried unanimously. A committee of five, three to form a quorum, was appointed, consisting of Messrs. J. Sayce, M'Millan, Veevers, Search, and Falstead; and Mr. M'Millan was requested to act as secretary pro tem. after which the meeting was adjourned to Monday next, at the same place, proceedings to commence at 7 o'clock sharp. We are requested to state that the secretary, whose residence is No. 6O, Elizabeth-street, will be happy to receive communications on behalf of the society.-*Argus*." A letter from J. Sayce, President of the Apiarian Society of Victoria, appeared in the *Journal of Horticulture, Cottage Gardener, and Country Gentleman*, 18 March 1862, p.508; also 14 July 1863, p.40; 20 June 1865, p.468.

APIARIST (pseudonym) ***South Australian Amateur Beekeeper***, 1891, Adelaide: Whillas & Ormiston, Printers. pp.36, illus, Ferguson #6048, SLSA (catlg. 638.1 A642 Mortlock Pamphlets)

The Australasian, Staff Members ***The Australasian Farmer***, c1890, compiled by the staff of *The Australasian* Contains many topics on farming including a section on beekeeping

Fred Beuhne

BEUHNE, F. R. ***The Bee-Keeping Industry in Victoria, Australia***, 1915, pp.8, Bulletin no. 29. Copy held at Cornell University Library. Gives beekeeping statistics for the 1912-13 season. Honey sold for 3d (pence) per lb., beeswax 14d. Full text may be found at

http://www.archive.org/stream/cu31924003053943#page/n2/mode/1up

BEUHNE, F. R. ***Bee-Keeping in Victoria***, 1915 hardbound green cloth, 25 chapters, pp.128, 43 illus, Beuhne named as author; 1916, pp.128; 1925, pp.170, illus, index, price one shilling, 1/1 post paid, Beuhne author. Reviewed in *ABK* May

1916, p.216. Library Holdings: UWSH, ML. Collection of articles from *Journal of Agriculture* Jan 1912 to April 1915. Published as Vic. Department of Agriculture, Bulletin no. 31. Beuhne (Ed. note: I understand it to be pronounced "Boyna".) was an Inspector of Bee Diseases and later became Government Apiculturist within the Dept of Agriculture. <u>Chapters</u>: Locations, The Bees, Races of Bees, Hives, How to Make a Start, Transferring Bees, Spring Management, Swarming, Honey, Uncapping, Treatment of Honey, Comb Honey, Rearing Queen Bees, Nuclei, Introducing Queens, Robber Bees, Feeding Bees, Wintering Bees, Diseases of Bees, Enemies of Bees, Beeswax, Comb Foundation, The Use of Comb Foundation, Water for Bees, Bees & the Fertilisation of Flowers .$35 to $40

Just outside of Kilmore, at the intersection of the Northern Highway and the old Hume Highway, (Broadford Road) Kilmore, Vic. 3764, is the Frederick Beuhne memorial. [1]

Biographical: The following biography provided by Laurie Braybrook in 1995: Frederick Richard Beuhne (1859-1933). Apiarist, Inventor & Author. He was born Dresden, Germany on 11 January 1859. He arrived in Melbourne aboard the *S.S. Cuzco* in 1880, and in spite of his knowledge of German, Latin & French, he had no English, but he soon learnt to read, write and speak English fluently. He gained employment in the poultry industry at Garfield where he met W Garnet, an advanced beekeeper. Frederick soon started keeping bees and was responsible for the establishment of the Victorian Apiarists' Association in 1892. The Beuhne family settled at Tooborac in 1896 and purchased three acres of land on the edge of the State Forest. In 1900 severe drought wiped out many bee colonies and lead to his study of bee nutrition and honeybee flora. In 1908 he was deputized by the Department of Agriculture to investigate bee losses due to seasonal conditions. He traveled to Germany, England and America and returned with updated scientific knowledge on beekeeping. In 1909 he was a key participant in a conference on bee diseases and was subsequently appointed Inspector of Bee Diseases. Later he became Government Apiculturist with the Department of Agriculture. He wrote the first version of *Beekeeping in Victoria* as a bulletin in 1912 [2] and expanded it into a book in 1916. This was revised several times

---

[1] Image from monumentaustralia.org.au/monument_display.php?id=31812&image=1   Photograph supplied by Kent Watson
[2] The full text of Bulletin No. 31, 1915, may be found at http://www.archive.org/stream/cu31924003053935#page/n9/mode/1up
The original is held by the Cornell University Library.

until his death in 1933. His other work *Honey Flora of Victoria* ran into several volumes.

[note: The preface to his *Beekeeping in Victoria*, Bulletin no. 31, states: "This Bulletin, into which are collected the articles on Bee-Keeping which have appeared in the Journal of Agriculture from January 1912, to April 1915, is not intended to take the place of a text book of Bee Culture, but as a guide that should enable the reader to employ profitably such of the information as is contained in the standard works of other parts of the world, and has been approved of as suitable by the practical experience of Australian apiarists."]

Beuhne was something of a mechanical genius and produced a number of devices, some of which he patented, for the bee industry including an improved telescopic hive cover, the Beuhne honeycomb cappings reducer, wax press, honey heater, belt driven honey extractor and designed a foundation making plant. His experiments into the clarification of honey through correct processing and blending without heat damage were very successful. He also initiated the analysis of honey for mineral content and the search for a pollen substitute.

He had hives of pure Italian and Carniolan bees sent to various islands adjacent to Australia for the purpose of establishing pure strains. Frederick was a member of many organisations including the Victorian Beekeepers' Association, Victorian Apiarists' Association, a delegate to the Victorian Farmers'

Annual Convention, Victorian Field Naturalist Club, Victoria Forest League, and Chamber of Agriculture. He was editor of the *Victorian Bee Journal* which was initially a quarterly journal, but was to later become a monthly magazine. Beuhne was well known as a honey judge at Royal Melbourne Show and other agricultural shows.

A plantation of honey flora consisting of *Eucalyptus Botryoides* (Southern Mahogany) and *Hakea Laurina* was planted on 11 August 1939 on the intersection of the Northern Highway and Broadford-Kilmore Road (Hume Highway) by Len Wills, Jim Eagland and others. This was followed by a stone cairn and a brass plaque which was erected to his memory and was unveiled by Victorian Apiarists' Association President, George Loft on 24 June 1949. The inscription read "Beuhne Memorial. This plaque marks an avenue of trees planted by the Victorian Apiarists' Association in appreciation and commemoration of the life of Frederick Richard Beuhne in the interest of apiculture." In 1973 a beekeeping pavilion was located in the McIvor Range Park at Tooborac near the Beuhne home. The plaque on the Kilmore cairn was removed in the early 1980s when the Northern Highway was being realigned and has since been affixed in Old Sandhurst Town at Bendigo where a display of the Victorian Apiarists' Association is located. Beuhne is regarded as the Father of Victorian Beekeeping.

References:
- *Biographical Register of Kilmore and District People*
- *Tooborac 1837-1969* (1969)
- *Australian Bee Journal*, September 1933 (memorial number), Nov. 1984 pp.8-10
- personal communication Mrs Dorothy Cunningham

Personal communications from Laurie Braybrook (Apr. & Dec. 1995) provided me the above biographical notes; he also advised that Sandhurst Town, a tourist village, had since closed due to a lack of finance. Laurie was then a member of a committee whose intention was to upgrade the Beuhne Memorial at Kilmore. Laurie also wrote that Beuhne was the first member of the Victorian Department of Agriculture, Apiary Branch. "He was absolutely dedicated to bees and the welfare of Victorian beekeepers. He was the first author of *Beekeeping in Victoria*, a book still published which had a profound influence on beekeeping throughout Australasia. Beuhne was so highly regarded that following his death in the thirties, Victorian beekeepers subscribed and lobbied for the establishment of a memorial plantation to the memory of F.R.B. The plantation is still there today. It was further remembered in the late forties or early fifties when beekeepers again rallied to erect a stone cairn and bronze plaque in the plantation to his memory. Many years later when that part of the highway became a back road, caring beekeepers quietly removed the plaque for safe storage. The cairn is still in place in the plantation."

Laurie provided an anecdote about Beuhne's antics at one Victorian Apiarists' Association Conference "F.R.B. was under some stress and agitation. His daughter was in hospital awaiting the birth of her first child. F.R. kept on marching out of the room to phone and enquire re progress. At last he came back with that big smile and announced to the conference 'Flossie has cast a swarm' "

The Beuhne memorial cairn was re-dedicated on 9 November 1997. In Laurie's words, a group of beekeepers assembled to "again honour the name and work of a truly great and kind man." Laurie recalled Jim Eagland, Beuhne's assistant at the Dept. Agriculture, who, though a hard man to impress, had enormous respect and admiration for Beuhne. Eagland spoke of Beuhne's dedication, his sacrifices for the good of the bees and the beekeepers of Victoria. Jim requested Laurie to make an effort to see that Beuhne and his achievements were never forgotten. "I think that speaks for itself about the man we are honouring today." Of the memorial and its surrounding plantation "Just remember and keep this special place. I know Jim will be pleased." Laurie quoted a tribute to Beuhne which appeared in the *Australian Bee Journal* for September 1933 "He had a beautiful nature and endeared himself to all; and one can think of him as did the little scout in *The Keeper of the Bees* 'And when God decided that he should go to sleep in the night, and there wouldn't be any more pain in his side, I bet all the harps and all the trumpets in Heaven went *Zoom! Zoom!* and all the angels came flocking when the Bee Master went through the gates'."

In the Adelaide *Advertiser*, 1 June 1916 "Mr. F.R. Beuhne, the Government Apiculturist of Victoria, has issued a new bulletin on the subject of beekeeping in that State, and from a beekeeper's point of view it would be difficult to find a publication more interesting and instructive. Mr. Beuhne goes into the subject in a most thorough manner, and the pages of the issue are profusely illustrated with blocks of a highly educational character. ..." (p.5)

A.E. Bonney

BONNEY, A.E. ***Modern beekeeping: a paper***, 1884, Adelaide, W.K. Thomas & Co. pp.8, Ferguson no. 7186, Cover title "Reprinted from the *Adelaide Observer*, February 16, 1884", "Read before the S.A. Chamber of Manufactures on February 8, 1883." Copies: NLA, SLSA (catlg. 638.1 B717 Rare Books).

For all his achievements in the field of beekeeping and his intense involvement in the introduction of Ligurian bees into South Australia and especially Kangaroo Island since 1883, one might think A.E. Bonney was a full time beekeeper, but this was not the case. The Adelaide *Advertiser*, 24 December 1883, described him as "an accomplished and experienced apiarian." The *Maitland Mercury*, 16 October 1884, carried an article headed Bee-keeping in South Australia (from the *Australasian*), in which he was labeled "a skilled manipulator of bees". By 1886, Bonney, who "began with four hives, [had] increased to 21 hives and 35 nucleus-boxes, reared more than 100 queens, and took 820 lb. of honey." [3]

Bees were his passion rather than his vocation. From *The First Ten Years*, being Chapter One of *A history of South Australia's Central Agricultural Bureau from 1888*. [4] "Beekeeping was particularly encouraged, to the extent that lecture tours were arranged. In October 1888 Mr A. E. Bonney spoke on the subject at Clarendon, Willunga, Meadows, Macclesfield, Strathalbyn and Mt Barker. He continued for several months, spreading practical information in the hope that farmers would take up this useful occupation." (p.16)

In 1889 he was President of the South Australian Beekeepers' Association and a Government lecturer on bee-keeping. [5] In 1905, along with fellow beekeeper J. H. Weidenhofer, Bonney was an apiary section judge at the Autumn Show of the Royal Agricultural and Horticultural Society. [6] There were other occasions on which his judging skills were sought in the Bees, Honey and Appliances Division at the RAHS Show, [7] as in 1909, with his partner judge F. R. Beuhne, president of the

---

[3] The South Australian Advertiser, 9 July 1886, page 3
[4] pir.sa.gov.au/__data/assets/pdf_file/0008/62747/100yrs-chapter1.pdf
[5] The Brisbane *Courier*, 17 January 1889, (p.4) The *South Australian Advertiser*, 8 April 1886 (p.7) announced his resignation as Secretary, so he must have again taken up the office.
[6] The Adelaide *Advertiser*, 2 March 1905, p.9
[7] The Adelaide *Advertiser*, 27 February 1909, p.14

Victorian Agricultural [Apiarists' ?] Association; or again in 1910, this time the adjudication was shared with F. A. Joyner.[8]

"An apiary owned by Frederick Joyner, 1888."
Image held by State Library South Australia.

The National Library of Australia holds a cartographic work [9] of his titled "Part (as finished to date) of the general plan of the province of South Australia," created for the Surveyor General's Office at Adelaide in 1871. He is listed in the 1903 *Public Service List of South Australia* as Chief Draughtsman, Railway Engineering Staff, Engineer-in-Chief's Department. (p.72) He was still employed there in 1908. These professional activities thus account for 37 years of his working life.

His advertisement headed "BEES" appeared in the Adelaide *Advertiser*, 14 July 1906 "Several good colonies Italian Bees, also Beekeeping Appliances, and Queen-Hearing Hives. - A. E. Bonney, Burnside." (p.7) This appeared immediately following another: "BEES. - To arrive direct from Italy, best Italian Queens it is possible for money to buy. Orders now booked.

---

[8] The Adelaide *Advertiser*, 3 March 1910, p.14
[9] trove.nla.gov.au/work/25733572?q=a.+e.+bonney&c=map

Illustrated price-list of appliances on application.- J. Drage, East Adelaide." After almost 23 years involving himself with Ligurian bees and queen bee breeding, it's possible he was easing himself out of one hobby, freeing up time for others. [10]

Possibly nearing retirement Bonney and his wife holidayed between the end of March [11] and September 1908 [12] pursuing "a Continental round which occupied a month and enabled them to see a good deal of Northern Italy, Switzerland, and Paris. Arriving in London last week, Mr. and Mrs. Bonney have been hard at work sightseeing, but presently they repair to Devonshire and Cornwall, where Mr. Bonney hopes for three weeks to freely indulge his penchant for golf and fishing. Whilst in London Mr. Bonney is visiting as many as possible of the important railway, sewerage, and other works under construction. Wherever he has gone he has met with most courteous treatment, and our railway companies, having discovered his connection with the South Australian railways, are offering him substantial concessions in travelling. Mr. Bonney's health has greatly improved during his wanderings."

There's ample evidence of the couple's love of golf at the Adelaide Golf Club in the Adelaide *Advertiser* for 1910. [13] Given the little I could locate about his life, I was still surprised I could not identify his first name.

One of Bonney's beekeeping associates, John Weidenhofer, experienced the vicissitudes of antipodean beekeeping. An article titled "Families Washed Out" appeared in the *Chronicle*, 20 April 1889 "In April 1889 heavy rains in the hills had the effect of swelling all the creeks that flowed across the Adelaide

---

[10] The Adelaide *Advertiser*, 21 July 1908 (p.10)
[11] The Adelaide *Advertiser*, 28 March 1908, p.8
[12] The Adelaide *Advertiser*, 17 September 1908, p.6
[13] eg., 4 May, p.12; 10 May, p.7; 14 June, p.12; 2 September, p.10;

plains and form tributaries to the River Torrens. In those places where the water had a free course it did only small damage but where the watercourse became obstructed with debris washed down by the flood waters considerable damage resulted. ... Mr Weidenhofer's property was entirely submerged and his garden bore the appearance of a lake. ... an inspection revealed that the flood did great damage to five properties in Kent Town. The water was still rushing through Mr J.H. Weidenhofer's property, but had partially subsided. He was a heavy sufferer for all his bee hives were washed away and his loss was estimated at £400." (p.9b) [14]

Mr. and Mrs. John Henry Weidenhofer (1850-1908) [15] and his wife Kathleen of Adelaide at the races, circa 1908. Weidenhofer was a well known auctioneer [and beekeeper] of 20 Currie Street, Adelaide
Image from State Library of South Australia [16]

---

[14] http://www.slsa.sa.gov.au/manning/pn/k/k3.htm
[15] Obituary in the Adelaide *Advertiser*, 28 October 1908, p.6

James Carroll

CARROLL, James. *My Little Bee Book: being a practical treatise on bees, their management and culture, in Australia,* 1875. Brisbane, Courier General Machine Printing Office. Originally sold for 1 shilling. The first known beekeeping book in Australia. Sometimes described as a pamphlet. One copy only known to exist world wide. *Google Book Search* reveals two hits, one at the Fryer Library, [17] University of Queensland, and via *Worldcat.org* lists an 1874 edition is held at the State Library of Queensland, catalogued as "My Little Book". The SLQ copy held within its John Oxley Library was incorrectly catalogued in April 2010 as "My Little Book". The Fryer Library [18] copy is an original copy while both SLQ and the library of the Department of Primary Industries (DPI) have only a photocopy. The Fryer Library catalogue has a note which states there is a picture of a bee in place of the word "bee" on the cover title, hence the likely reason for the SLQ cataloging error: the picture was not translated into the word "bee".

In *Boxes to Bar Hives*, Weatherhead (1986) states "It has been said that the first book on beekeeping written in Australia was *My Little Bee Book* by James Carroll in 1875. The contents of this book first appeared as articles by Carroll in *The Queenslander* newspaper beginning on 19 September 1874. [19]

---

[16] http://images.slsa.sa.gov.au/searcy/11/PRG280_1_11_420.htm
[17] catlg: SF523 .C38 1874), 17 cm long. (6.7") ill.
[18] Pers. comm., 14 May 2010, Courtney Moran, Fryer Library
[19] Carroll's column "The Honey Bee" appeared in the *Queenslander* as early as 5 November 1870, and possibly before this date. In April 2010 this newspaper was undergoing digitization by the NLA *Australian Newspapers* project, so, in time, prior examples may surface.

The articles there were reproduced word perfect in Carroll's book with a few additions. [20]

The articles from *The Queenslander* were [again] reproduced word perfect in a book called *The Semi-tropical Agriculturist and Colonists' Guide* by Angus Mackay in 1875. I am not sure which book was published first, Carroll's or Mackay's." [21] (p.28)

There was the possibility of a bee book by Carroll from 1871, but time constraints must have prevented him. He was a busy beekeeper building, promoting and sustaining his business, as well as writing "The Honey Bee" column for the *Queenslander*. Hence Carroll wrote in the Brisbane *Courier*, 7 October 1871 "My Manual on the Hive and Honey Bee in Queensland will be published in February next." (p.6) Such a book was not to be, yet. Just over two years later in the *Queenslander*, 20 December 1873 "Mr Carroll has not published a collected work." (p.2). A year later the *Queenslander*, 9 January 1875 announced *Carroll's Little Bee Book* - "This work - fully illustrated - gives full particulars concerning the Bee as it is in this country." (p.1) The laurel must go to Carroll's *My Little Bee Book* as the first of its kind in Australia.

The *Queenslander*, 17 July 1875, gave the correct title *My Little Bee Book* - "a practical treatise on bees, their management and culture in Australia; with illustrations. price 1 shilling." (p.1) His book continued to be advertised as late as 11 January 1890 (p.51) in the *Queenslander*.

In Sim's 1999 thesis titled *Designed Landscapes in Queensland, 1859-1939*, she observed: "The 19th century practice of

---

[20] I've not yet identified what these additions are.

[21] A second edition of the *Semi-tropical Agriculturist* appeared in 1890 and a third in 1897, both slightly re-titled, but neither had any content on bees.

serialising essays in periodicals that were later published as a book is acknowledged by Mackay [22] in this prefatory remark: 'The work, as a whole, goes to show the immense amount of information placed before the public by the Press – all the papers here published appeared in *The Queenslander* during the year from March 1874, to March 1875, in addition to the contents of a popular newspaper.' " Here then is definitive proof that Carroll's book came first, followed just over two and a half months later by Mackay's.

In the advertising section of *The Queenslander* for 20 March 1875, as on many previous Saturdays, it was declared that Mackay's *Semi-tropical Agriculturist* "will be published in March." Seven days later the replacement advertisement announced "This new work, by Angus Mackay …" was available in Brisbane, Sydney, Melbourne and Adelaide for 10 shillings and sixpence, postage 1 shilling. Immediately below is Carroll's standing illustrated advertisement for his bee book and improved bar frame hive.

Having sighted an 1875 copy of Mackay in early 2010 and compared it to the five articles in *The Queenslander*, I find Weatherhead's description confirmed. In Mackay 1875 on pages 153-160 I found the series of articles, complete with illustrations from *The Queenslander*, presented under the heading "The Honey Bee in Australia." To complicate matters a little, this chapter also appears in Mackay's 1885 *Elements of Australian Agriculture*, revised and enhanced with additional text including a slightly lengthier description of the Italian bee and another nineteen illustrations.

---

[22] *The Semi-Tropical Agriculturalist and Colonists' Guide* (1875)

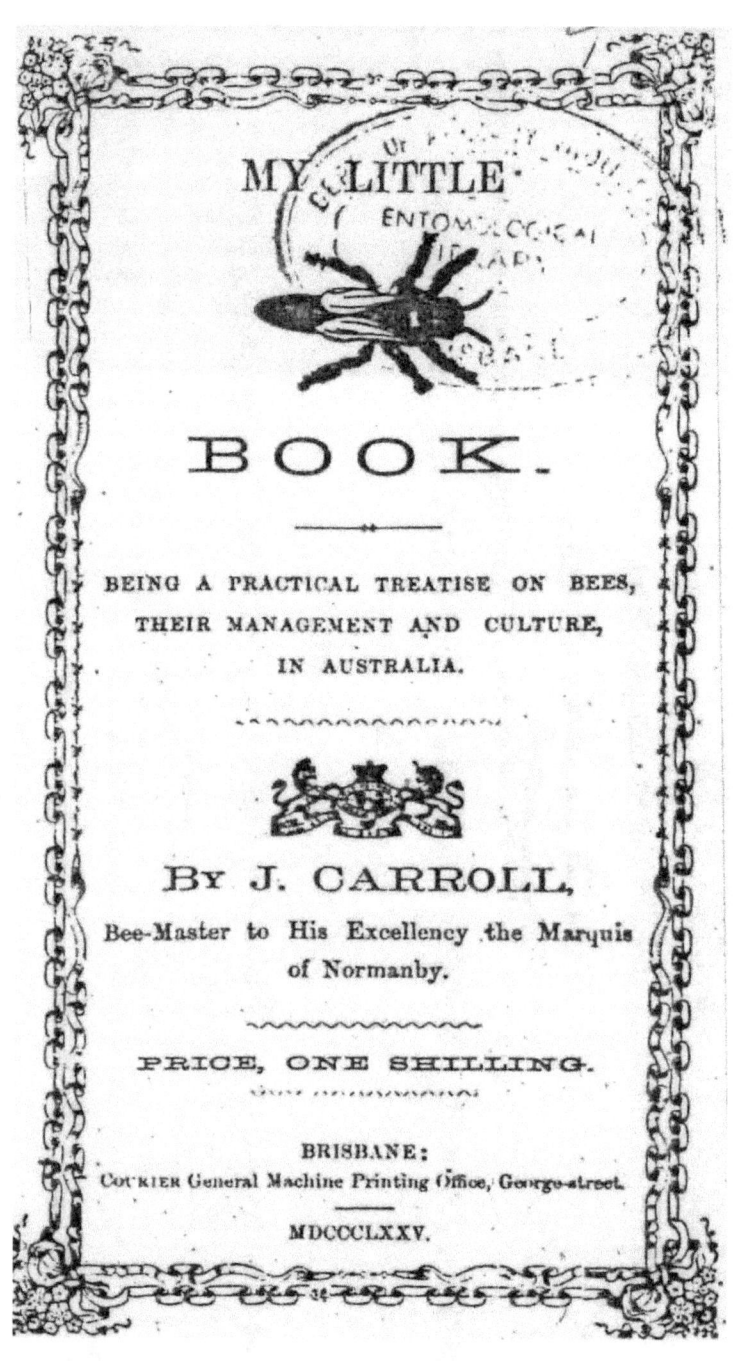

Illustration below: sale of the property *Lizzy Lee*, *Brisbane Courier*, 12 April 1884 (p.8) [23]

---

[23] The supporting text is creatively written, possibly a piece of literature

LIZZY LEE—The old Residence and Grounds of Angus Mackay, Esq.

LIZZY LEE—The present Residence of J. Carroll, Esq.

LIZZY LEE—Go and See the Views.

LIZZY LEE—The Purest Air near Brisbane.

LIZZY LEE—No Fevers, no Illness.

LIZZY LEE—A Rural Retreat in the heart of the Suburbs.

LIZZY LEE—A MAGNIFICENT SPOT TO GROW HEALTHY LITTLE ONES.

L I Z Z Y   L E E—

The Grandest Sites near Brisbane, and on the way to the One-Tree Hill Public Park.

Also,

MR. CARROLL'S RESIDENCE

AND

ONE ACRE OF LAND.

Weatherhead's observation of the duplicity of content between Carroll's and Mackay's 1875 books might have added another query: "Who really was the author of the second Australian bee book?" Mackay and Carroll were close friends - Carroll had his apiary at Mackay's former residence named *Lizzie lee* near Brisbane. Carroll thus ran his *Lizzie lee* apiary there, and it was for Carroll that Mackay procured a hive of Ligurian bees from California in 1877. [24] It's possible Carroll shared in some of the royalties on Mackay's books, given the former authored the basis of the articles that appeared in Mackay's subsequent books, ie., his 1875, 1885 [25] and 1895 [26] works. Mackay was in a position to ensure this happened for he had been general editor of *The Queenslander* since 1866 [27]

The first essay in *The Queenslander* is titled "Bee Farming - I". [28] The next line unequivocally declares the author with the by-line "by J. Carroll. Beemaster." The essay opens "I do not intend to write a lengthy treatise on bees, but a short, easy, and comprehensive summary on the insect as it is in Australia, which I trust will enable all who desire to obtain a quick insight into the nature of the honey bee." The same sentence opens the third paragraph in Mackay's 1875 chapter titled "The Honey Bee in Australia", except the "I" has been replaced with "We". Presumably written by Mackay alone, a two paragraph "preface"

---

[24] Carroll and Mackay knew each other at least as early as October 1872. See Brisbane *Courier* 23 October, p.2, where they were present at the East Moreton Agricultural Society's show.
[25] *Elements of Australian Agriculture*
[26] *Beekeeping as a Business in Australia*
[27] Sim (1999) pp.110-112
[28] The second bears the heading "The Honey Bee, Australian Experience; the third through the fifth continue that titling theme with "The Honey Bee, Australian Experience III", followed by "IV" and "V".

preceding the reproduction of the first of five *Queenslander* articles [29] contains the statement "The object of our essay is to show [how bees may be] easily managed in hives – in bar-frame or moveable hives especially ... with certainty, comfort and profit." Does the royal collective "our" mean both Carroll and Mackay contributed to the "short, easy, and comprehensive summary" that followed? Or does it simply refer to the staff of *The Queenslander*? I think the latter.

The Honey Bee chapter in Mackay, on first inspection, does not appear in Mackay's Table of Contents – actually an index – but the List of Illustrations does contain the bee items under the entry "Bees". Paging forward one finds the "Honey Bee" entries sandwiched between those on the "Horse" and "Homestead." Strict alphabetical sequencing does not appear to have been a priority.

Carroll was acknowledged by Angus Mackay as "amongst the first practical bee masters in the colonies". An illustration of the former demonstrating bar-frames and hive appears in Mackay 1885. The 1875 Carroll at UQ appears to be unique while copies of Mackay 1875 are rare.

Part V contains Carroll's section on the honey extractor: "This machine has been used by American bee-keepers for some time. I imported one in 1873, and found it to be a rather rough affair, the maker not having hit upon what he was aiming at - the application of centrifugal force. He made the body of his machine revolve around a centre-shaft. Mr. Mackay of *The Queenslander* promptly remedied the defect, and supplied plans for the machines I am now making - the best, probably, that have been invented for extracting honey from the comb." This

---

[29] The series of five articles appeared in *The Queenslander* in weekly instalments between 19 September and 17 October 1874, complete with illustrations.

section in Mackay 1875 appears unaltered, so that, rather than Carroll referring to Mackay's assistance, Mackay refers to Mackay's!

A short review of Carroll's *My Little Bee Book* appeared in the *Australian Bee Bulletin*, 1904. An incomplete extract is provided via Google Book Search; "... the earliest of its kind in Australia ... some facts connected with the author ... in it ... a principal treatise on bees, their management and culture, in Australia ..." (Vol. 13, p.74) Unfortunately, according to *Worldcat*, the four holding libraries for this 1904 *Australian Bee Bulletin* are either in Canada or the United States, so obtaining a full extract would be difficult.

Biographical: In 1869 Carroll was employed as a bee master by the Marquess of Normanby at Mulgrave Castle. There he used frame hives and Ligurian bees. Carroll may have taken opportunity to emigrate to Queensland given notice of his employer's possible move there to take up the post of Governor. By early July 1870 Carroll was established in Brisbane with working hives of bees. [30] He attended agricultural shows such as the East Moreton Farmers' Association where he displayed bees and beekeeping appliances. He attended the tenth annual exhibition of the Brisbane Poultry Club which was covered by the Brisbane *Courier*, 3 August 1870 (p.2) "Mr. Carroll is exhibiting some of his humane bee hives, which attract much attention. For the information of timid visitors, we may state that the bees can't get out of their' glass houses. He also shows a bar of comb, part of which was made in an ordinary hive, and the remainder in one of his patents. The difference between the two, and the marked superiority of the latter, are very striking."

---

[30] The *Queenslander*, 30 July 1870, p.5; Brisbane *Courier*, 1 August 1870 (p2)

In 1872 Carroll was again supporting the apiary of his former employer. From the Brisbane *Courier*, 12 December 1872 "His Excellency the Marquis of Normanby's hive is now working ten surplus boxes, and if the season proves good until the end of January twenty seven may be taken from it."

At this time he resided at *Bee Hive Cottage* on Milton Road. [31] His roving displays of bees, frame and glass hives at agricultural shows provided the opportunity to advertise his business and skills, promote modern beekeeping practices, build a potential customer base and, presumably, sell bees, bee hives and appliances. It can safely be stated that he was the introducer of the modern frame hive into Queensland. He was good at his craft and quickly built a solid reputation. He freely assisted beekeepers, advising them on how to construct hives, sometimes visiting their apiaries in order to solve problems. A letter from Mark Blasdale of Long Pocket, Indooroopilly, dated 28 November, appeared in the Brisbane *Courier*, 12 December 1872. In part, it stated of Carroll: "I must say he does not let the fact of his obtaining his livelihood by the sale of hives and bees have the slightest weight with him, for he freely gives practical information to any person, purchaser or non purchaser, that asks it, and from my own experience I have found his advice rigidly truthful and exceedingly useful" (p.4)

"The Honey Bee" column he edited and contributed to in the *Queenslander* commenced around November 1870. It ran to at least May 1889 and Carroll's editorship lasted until 1884. [32] By 1872 he was dispatching hives north and south by steamer from Brisbane to destinations such as Sydney, Maryborough, Rockhampton, Cardwell and Bowen. He developed a special

---

[31] The Brisbane *Courier*, 9 December 1871 (p.6)
[32] NLA's digitization of Australian newspapers is ongoing and an extension to these dates is possible.

small hive that could be carried, singly or in multiples, on horseback once landed. [33] The Brisbane *Courier*, 12 December 1872, stated "I have great pleasure in stating that I have sent hives stocked with bees to all parts of the colony and to New South Wales, Victoria, and the Fiji Islands, with the greatest success." (p.4)

It would appear from Carroll's presence in the Queensland press that his livelihood centred entirely upon his bees. Carroll was, in fact, a cattle farmer. His letter dated 15 October 1877 to *Gleanings in Bee Culture* appeared in the January 1878 issue. "It is a long time since I wrote you, and I am sorry to say that I have no good news to send you. The whole country is parched up by a drought, and when it will end, God only knows. Thousands have already been ruined by it. Cattle and sheep are dying in hundreds of thousands. It is a sight to travel through this country at this present moment; hardly a blade of grass is to be seen; and the water holes filled with dead and dying cattle. I am one of the suffering ones, and unless it breaks up very shortly, I see nothing but ruin for me and my family.

What puzzles me more than all the rest, is where the bees are getting honey from. I have never had more honey from my bees than I have had during the drought. So you see friend Novice that bees are to be depended upon, when many other things fail. I am sorry that I have not more of them. They beat cattle keeping in every way that I know of; in fact they have supported my cattle to a considerable extent." (p.8)

At some time he relocated to Angus Mackay's former property at Enoggera, *Lizzie lee*, which was later up for sale in April 1884, then still containing his residence and his *Lizzie lee* apiary. [34] From the *Queenslander*, 27 March 1886: "The long-

---

[33] See *Immigrant Bees, Vol. V*
[34] *Brisbane Courier*, 12 April 1884 (p.8)

established *Sweet Home* Apiary of the pioneer bee-master of Queensland, Mr. J. Carroll, is prettily situated upon one of those wooded hills between Rosalie and the One-tree Hill Range. There is a road which leads from Milton, round by Ithaca Greek, and coming out by the Toowong Cemetery, which is one of the prettiest roads for an afternoon or moonlight ride possible, and it is on this road that Mr. Carroll's apiary has now been established for over twenty years. [35]

Carroll advertised in *The Queenslander*, 7 February 1885, (p.221) under the banner "Sweet Home Apiary. HEAD QUARTERS for ITALIAN BEES and Beekeepers' Supplies."

---

[35] Working back this means he should have arrived in Brisbane by 1866 but he was still in England in 1869, so maybe his apiary had been there for a lesser time, say 16 or 17 years.

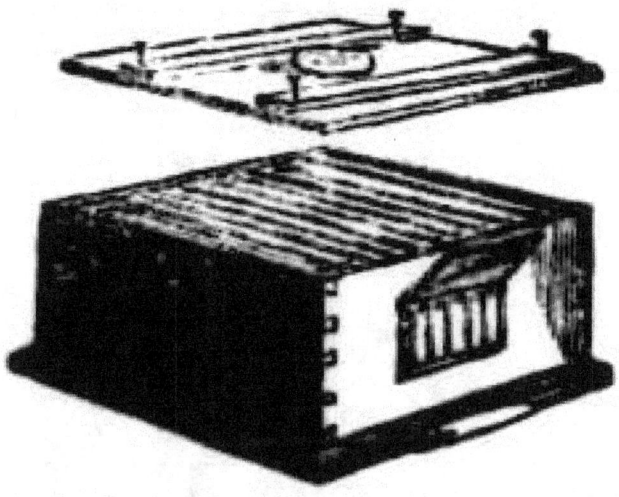

Above: An advertisement for Carroll's book in the *Queenslander*, 9 January 1875, (p.1)

From this spot hives of bees have been sent to every corner of Australia, and Mr. Carroll's name has become as a household word among bee keepers." Carroll retired from selling bees and hives as a business around 1884 [36] when he sold out to RJ Cribb, along with the rights to his bee book. He can rightly be described as Queensland's first bee master.

HANDLING BAR-FRAMES.

Jas. Carroll

---

[36] The *Brisbane Courier*, 21 August 1884, p.4. Inferred by Cribb from Milton having exhibited a honey extractor at the Brisbane Exhibition.

Phillip V. M. Filleul, 19th century beekeeping author and one time Tasmanian resident

My interest in Phillip [37] Valpy Mourant Filleul is not because he authored an Australian work on beekeeping during his stay in Tasmania between 1853 and 1857, but in honour of his overall contribution to books on beekeeping both before and after his Tasmanian residency. Under the title *The Cottage Bee Keeper:* [38] *or suggestions for the practical management of amateur, cottage, and farm apiaries, on scientific principles, with an appendix of notes, chiefly illustrative*, his book was published in 1851 in New York. That same year in London it was published as *The English bee-keeper ...* under the pseudonym of "A Country Curate". [39] Tasmania was his home between the years 1853 and 1858. Before he had visited Van Diemen's Land, Filleul made comment on matters beekeeping in the Illawarra region of New South Wales.

"While in America or Australia, it is almost incredible of how large an apiary one hive may become the parent in a very few years; in England, a similar hive may stand year after year, without change, apparently strong, yet unproductive in either swarms or honey, perhaps in both together. A stock, at the time of purchase, may have had a three or four-year-old queen, (an evil which is seldom acknowledged, and still more seldom guarded against,) who dies some time in our long winter before there is a brood wherewith to replace her; the winter may be mild and the spring cold and late, and no honey gathered till the end of May, whence proceeds the death from starvation of many a colony of bees, (which might be saved by a judicious and

---

[37] Spellings of his first name also appear as Philip and Philippe
[38] Full text may be found at books.google.com.au
Another edition published in 1854
[39] Published London, F. & J. Rivington

timely supply of food,) or its productiveness for the current season destroyed. A rainy summer, too, may follow, or a very dry one, neither of which yields much honey; in short, a thousand are the casualties to be feared in this fitful climate, with which the more fortunate bee keeper of other countries is happily unacquainted." (p.5) His footnote on hive performance in Australia states "In a late work on New South Wales, I read the following astonishing account of the produce of a single stock of bees: - "In the district Illawarra, near Sydney, one hive has been known to multiply itself to 300 (!!) in the course of *three* years!" (p.5)

Filleul undoubtedly sourced his footnote from Joseph Phipps Townsend's (1849) *Rambles & Observations in New South Wales*. Townsend provided a lengthier report: "The English bee has been introduced into Illawarra within the last few years, and with much success. The power this insect has of producing its own species, appears to be much increased in this climate, where there is no pinching winter. The produce of one hive gave, in three years, three hundred hives; besides those that had escaped into the bush, and become wild. This statement may appear extraordinary at first sight, but a reference to figures will attest its truth; and it must be recollected that the parent hive, and each of its swarms, with their produce again, and so on, are all continually increasing. ... Some of the housewives manufacture from honey a most excellent wine, which, the longer it is kept, the better it is; and much honey is sent to Sydney for sale and export. By referring to a local paper, I am enabled to give some particulars of the honey trade. One settler sent to England the produce of forty hives, which yielded about 1000 lbs. of rough comb, and in taking the honey, not a single hive of the bees was lost. The net produce was 7 cwt. and 10 lbs. of honey, and 34 lbs. of wax. This was sold in England for 20 guineas; but brokerages, duty, &c, had to be deducted, leaving only 16*l.* 9*s.* 5*d.* [16 pounds 9 shillings and 5 pence] I learn from the same source, that another settler sent to England a ton of honey and 4 cwt. of wax; and, of course, the larger the export, the less, in proportion, will be the expenses." (pp.138-139)

Samuel *Sidney's Emigrant Journal, Information, advice, and amusement for emigrants and colonizers*, 1849, [40] similarly borrowed the following: "Illawarra - ... The produce of one *hive* gave in three years *300 hives*, besides those that had escaped into the hush, and become wild." The most likely candidate for such a sizeable commercial beekeeping activity was David Berry. He'd arrived in the colony in July 1836, accompanied by two brothers and sisters. Shortly after their arrival in Sydney they joined their eldest brother Alexander Berry at his estate *Coolangatta*, situated close by the entrance of the Shoalhaven River on the south coast of New South Wales. [41]

P.V.M. Filleul was born around the year 1825 in St Aubins, Jersey, Channel Islands. [42] He graduated from the University of Oxford with an M.A. in 1847. [43] Aged 26 he'd written his book on beekeeping and two years later he was a world away in Van Diemen's Land. The Shipping News in the Hobart *Courier* announced his arrival on 5 December 1853 in Tasmania. [44] on the 337 ton steamer *Yarra Yarra* [45] from Port Phillip, Victoria,

---

[40] London, W.S. Orr and Co., 1849
[41] The *Sydney Morning Herald*, 24 September 1889, p.8
[42] Rev. Philip Filleul, M.A., Vice-Dean of Jersey, and Rector of S. Helier, Jersey is mentioned in James Bertrand Payne's (1859) *Armorial of Jersey : being an account, heraldic and antiquarian, of its chief native families, with pedigrees, biographical notices, and illustrative data; to which are added a brief history of heraldry, and remarks on the mediaeval antiquities of the island.*
[43] http://www.rootsweb.ancestry.com/~austas/Longford.htm
[44] The Hobart *Courier*, 7 December 1853, page 2.
[45] 337 tons. Lbd: 166'5" x 25' x 13'. Iron paddle steamer
Refer http://www.flotilla-australia.com/hrsn.htm#asn

to take up his post as Warden at Christ's College,[46] Bishopsbourne.[47]

His accomplishments, supported by his M.A. qualification, were soon after recognised by the Royal Society of Van Diemen's Land by his election to membership of that body in February 1854.[48] The Royal Society of Van Diemen's Land was "the first Royal Society established outside the United Kingdom. ... It was set up by Sir John Eardley-Wilmot in 1843 to administer the Colonial Gardens in Hobart, and a body of enthusiastic amateurs soon established a museum and a library. The Royal title was conferred in 1844. The Society contacted numerous international bodies and countless individuals, both at home and abroad, arranging for the exchange of items and soliciting donations. Its activities were broader in scope than any other colonial scientific body in the mid and late nineteenth century because of its museum and gardens and because it published a regular journal, in which overseas contributions appeared as

---

[46] The Hobart *Courier*, 3 June 1853, page 2.
From *Wikipediai*: "Christ's College ... is the oldest tertiary institution in Australia ... it was opened on 1 October 1846 with the hope that it would develop along the lines of an Oxbridge college and provide the basis for university education in Tasmania. It was also intended to prepare men for the priesthood. The Hutchins School and Launceston Church Grammar School were founded at the same time to act as feeder schools to the College. The College's first ten years (1846–1856) were at Bishopsbourne ... However, it never really developed as its founders hoped, and a depression in the colony, the remote site, and financial problems led to its closure in 1856."
[47] From *Wikipediai*: "Bishopsbourne is a farming community in northern Tasmania. It has a population of fewer than 200. It has a church, graveyard and recreation ground. Nearby towns include Carrick, Bracknell and Longford. Almost all the houses and farms are located on Bishopsbourne Road and there are a few back roads."
[48] The Hobart *Courier*, 11 February 1854, page 2.

well as articles by local authors, informing people about Tasmania's natural history and scientific endeavours. ... The Society's broad scope meant that it also involved local people: as visitors, or donors, if not as speakers at the regular monthly meetings, which were both practical as well as scientific. Members' interests included: meteorology, industrial development, tourism, immigration, public health, agriculture, mapping, land surveying, fisheries and scenery and wildlife preservation as well as science." [49] "The Royal Society was then and is today one of the world's most prestigious scientific societies" [50]

Given his strong interest in beekeeping it's not surprising he took advantage of Tasmania's favourable clime and indulged his apiarian interest. In the Hobart *Mercury*, 24 August 1933, an article appeared titled *BEE-KEEPING Important Tasmanian Industry Its Early History. Article 1.* "We now come to beekeeping In the 50's in Tasmania, and, although things have considerably improved since then, and the production of honey has greatly increased, an article by the Rev. P. V. M. Filleul, M.A., written on July 28, 1858, and reproduced in *The Tasmanian Mail* of 12 June 1919, gives a good insight into the industry:

---

[49] Gillian Winter, '*The foundation years of the Royal Society of Tasmania, 1843 – 86'*, PPRST 127, 1993.
utas.edu.au/library/companion_to_tasmanian_history/R/Royal%20Society.htm
See also Guy Green
utas.edu.au/library/companion_to_tasmanian_history/T/Tas%20creativity.htm
Ros Haynes
utas.edu.au/library/companion_to_tasmanian_history/V/VDL.htm
[50] utas.edu.au/library/companion_to_tasmanian_history/V/VDL.htm

Bees are not natives of the southern hemisphere, yet, so abundantly have they multiplied since the time when an Englishman (Dr. Wilson), about 40 years ago, [51] brought out the first hive from England, that they are to be found naturalised all over the various colonies of Australasia. Tasmania is no exception, for there they thrive so marvellously that the woods and forests are full of them, from which issue such a multitude of swarms every year, that any of the settlers may commence beekeeping or restore their failing apiaries in any season, without looking beyond the limits of their own homesteads and gardens.

It was my good fortune to find 'the lines fallen unto me' in a pleasant place, so far as the richness of the land and the productiveness of a large 30 years-established orchard and garden were concerned. At the back of our residence was a plain of considerable extent, backed by a range of mountains, whose highest 'bluffs' or 'tiers' rose about 4,000ft. from the level of the plain. These mountains, bare at their summits, were clothed at their bases, and for two or three thousand feet, with magnificent forests, more or less thinned by the hand of man. So rich is the soil here - they say more than 20ft. deep of alluvial deposit - that it is inexhaustible. It is covered everywhere with the Dutch, or white, clover for many miles, and being for the most part meadow land (or 'swamp,' as it is unpleasantly called), it retains its moisture, and consequent luxuriousness, long after the drier parts of the country are burnt up.

Owing to the great abundance of white clover, not to speak of gorse and sweet briar, all of which spreads over the country with great rapidity, as if they liked the soil, there is a vast quantity of honey annually spread out by the bountiful hand of nature for

---

[51] This is a reference to the year 1818. The correct year is 1831, 27 years previous to Filleul's date of writing.

the feast of the bees, and you may be sure our little busy friends are not slow to avail themselves of the treasure thus placed before them, especially as the great amount of sun in that splendid climate enables them to work with at least five times the success of English bees. There is also a great abundance of apple, peach, plum, and other fruit blossoms, in all the cultivated districts of Tasmania, owing to the extent and productiveness of the settlers' orchards and gardens. In these districts, therefore, where the native trees also produce honey, there are usually two honey harvests. The first, extending over tho months of November, December, January and February, and the latter over March and April. The honey collected during the former period is similar to the finest of our English honey - very pure and delicate in colour and flavour.

But the autumn season, which begins towards the end of March, found the bees collecting a totally different kind of honey, highly aromatic, and dark coloured. The flavour of this honey, being not so palatable as the other was always left for the bees. Their first harvest I invariably plundered towards the end of February, leaving the bees to replace their store before winter. This second harvest was never so large as the first, and in very rainy seasons in great measure failed, yet nowhere did the bees fail to thrive and collect a plentiful supply of honey.

Bee management in Tasmania is still rude and unscientific, although a few gentlemen bestow a great deal of attention op their apiaries. In general, bees are little cared for, and most unsightly were the corners of gardens or the sheds allotted to the bees. Any odd box, rail, barrel, or straw skep, large or small, well or ill-constructed, was made to serve the purpose of a beehive. I have often wondered to behold a swarm located in a huge tea-chest, or still larger candle-chest.

Soon after my arrival in December, 1853, I became the possessor of a swarm of three weeks' standing in a small candle-box, capable of holding three pecks of wheat. Owing to a considerable portion of the comb falling out during the removal to my garden, it barely recovered itself sufficiently to survive the following winter (1854). In August, however, the hive was very active, pollen, and even honey, being collected. So forward did the hive become, that, on October 19, drones being about in considerable numbers, I forced a swarm to issue artificially by driving. The new hive took the place of the old one, and did very well. In fact, it threw off a natural swarm about two months later (December 16), and, becoming vert strong again, in about a fortnight was compelled to give another swarm, by driving, on December 27. The natural swarm, not being very large, was joined to a hive containing a small stray swarm, which settled in my garden or December 7. My honey harvest this year, the result of all these experiments and pieces of luck, yielded me 871 lb. of the purest honeycomb, besides a weight of about 60 lb. net left in the four stocks for my next year's supply.

The next season (1854-5) was not so propitious. Only one stray swarm settled in our grounds, which barely compensated for the escape of one of my own, while two at least of the stocks that had survived the winter did little or nothing, so that my honey harvest did not exceed a weight of 22 lb. net honeycomb.

At the commencement of the summer of 1856, in November, I found my stock of hives reduced to one, which was subsequently strengthened by the addition of a stray swarm on November 20. The latter did so well (without warming) that I obtained from it alone 70 ½ lb. [numerics smudged] of super-excellent honeycomb leaving a sufficiency for the winter nutriment of the bees. The old hive, too, yielded me good profit, namely, five swarms and 108 ¾ lb. of honeycomb over and above their winter supply. In all my experience I never before heard of a stock becoming the great grand parent of a swarm in one and the same season - in other words, of one queen leading forth three successive swarms in one year."

The contributor ended with the comment "Mr. Filleul left Tasmania in 1857, after distributing his stocks of bees among his friends." (p.10)

s.s.s. *Royal Shepherd*

After three and a half years in the colony Filleul's return to England came about in July 1857. [52] The Melbourne *Argus* reported his arrival as saloon passenger aboard the *Royal Shepherd* [53] on the 10th from Launceston, along with "lady and family," having departed there on 15th June. In June 1858 the *Hobart Town Daily* [54] subsequently announced his Ecclesiastical Preferment "The Revd. V. M. Filleul, late Warden of Christ's

---

[52] The Melbourne *Argus*, 18 July 1857, page 4.
[53] Single screw steamship, 265 gross tons, 184 net. Lbd: 148'1" x 19'8" x 10'5". Refer http://www.flotilla-australia.com/adsteam.htm
Service speed of 10 knots on 22 tons of coal. Passenger vessel accomodating 60.
[54] The *Hobart Town Daily*, 15 June 1858, page 3. The Hobart *Courier*, 30 April 1858, page 3

College, Tasmania, has been presented by the Bishop of London to the Rectory of Biddesham, Somersetshire."

His interest in beekeeping continued for his *Profitable Beekeeping on Improved Principles: Chiefly Designed for the Use of Cottagers* [55] was published in 1867 and again in 1868 and 1883. In 1870 he continued to be Rector of Biddisham [56] and eleven years later he was still resident there. [57] At age 76 he died at Upway, Dorset, [58] on 17 April 1901. [59] (His wife followed 12 years later on 23 November 1913.)

---

[55] Published under the direction of the Committee of General Literature and Education, Appointed by the Society for Promoting Christian Knowledge. London
[56] The Melbourne *Argus*, 28 September 1870, p.4
[57] http://www.gurganus.org/ourfamily/browse.cfm/Marianne-Girdlestone/p265925
[58] http://worldconnect.rootsweb.ancestry.com/cgi-bin/igm.cgi?op=GET&db=karenwal1&id=P2762777137
[59] http://catalogue.statelibrary.tas.gov.au/item/?id=PH30-1-7010

Grave stone of Phillip V.M. Filleul; 4 years warden of Christ College, Tasmania, died Upway U.K. April 17 1901 - aged 76 years [60]

Leonard Chambers

CHAMBERS, L.T. *The Colonial Bee-keeper*, 1st ed. 1888, Melbourne, pp.44, adv, s/c, illus, ML, SLVic. 3rd ed. revised. J.C. Stephens, printer, Melbourne, 1893, pp.71, illus. price 1s. 2d. Copy at NLA, Np 638.1 C444-3. Copy at Deakin Univ Library, 638.1 Cha/Cbk 1893. Copy at SLVic, RARE LTP 638.1 C35C, Ferguson 8071. Another ed., 52 pages, cited by *Australian Bee Bulletin* in 1895, 4th ?; 7th ed 1902; 7th ed. Rev. 1905, J. C. Stephens, printer, Melbourne, , 71 pages. Copy at SLNSW, 638.1/18 "Mitchell Library copy from the Lynette Young collection". Copy at NLA, N 638.1 C444-7. NLA copy

---

[60] http://catalogue.statelibrary.tas.gov.au/item/?id=PH30-1-7010

contains an advertisement for the Beekeepers' Supply Co., 128 Franklin Street, Melbourne, c1888; another amongst several in *The Australian Bee Bulletin*, Sept. 1895, described booklet as "a handy primer for beginners." In the same issue "We acknowledge receipt from Mr. Leonard Chambers, of the Melbourne Supply Co., of what is termed a Circular and Price List, but is really a very complete book of some 52 pages." (p.158a)

A copy of the 27 page Beekeepers' Supply Co. catalogue is held at the library of the National Museum of Australia (catlg: PAM 381.10294 BEE) Chambers advertised in a range of New Zealand newspapers in 1891 and 1892. The example below appeared in the *Bush Advocate*, 28 February 1891 (p.8).

Chapters: Bees in Boxes, The Bar Frame Hive, Transferring Bees & Comb from Box Hives, Spring & Summer Management, Queens & Queen Rearing, How to Cut Out Comb with Eggs, Introduction of Queens, Foul Brood, Autumn & Winter Fixings, Marketing Honey, Section Honey, Hives & Fittings, Stings, Feeding, Robbing - How Avoided & Cured, Drones, Drone Laying, Queens & Laying Workers, Moving Bees, Beeswax. Possible earlier editions to 1875, 8th ed. in 1910.

Possibly created by Chambers was the following, announced in the *South Australian Advertiser*, 11 September 1884 "We have received from the South Australian Beekeepers' Supplies Company their catalogue of articles connected with the industry of bee-culture. The catalogue embraces almost every requisite of modern bee-culture, including hives of several kinds, extractors, section boxes, smokers, comb foundation, frames, and bee books, with the prices attached to the articles. Now that bee-culture is developing into an industry in this colony, this catalogue will be very useful to those who have already embarked in it, or are about to do so." (p.7)

A lengthy obituary appeared in The *Australasian Beekeeper*, 15 March 1918: "Very many of the readers of this journal will learn regretfully of the death of Mr. Chambers after a short illness last October, for to nearly all of maturer age, who have been engaged in beekeeping in Victoria and to many in the other States as well, the familiar initials L.T.C were those of a good friend, a gentleman in business dealings and of a leader in the agricultural matters of some years ago - a leader whose personal advice and written help led many an aspirant over the first difficulties of the pursuit till in the fair way to success.

The writer well remembers those first interviews of a Sunday afternoon in the eighties he used to have with the deceased gentleman as L.T.C. used to walk home from teaching a class in the Protestant Orphanage at Middle Brighton to his home, a mile or so distant, where a goodly number of hives and some experimental strawberry beds were to him, as a sheer novice almost, of very surprising interest.

About this time appeared his booklet the *Colonial Beekeeper*, the pages of which were pursued again and again, the last page being always reached long before the bee-fever stricken reader desired it. Then came the early catalogue as our friend developed his bee-supply business in Franklin Street, where a long flight of stairs, difficult to one out of health, had to be faced first, but by facing which one was rewarded by the keen interest of frames and joints and smokers and the fragrance of newly wrought pine and tissue-clad comb foundation. here, too, one saw the activities of a business-like man engaged with seeming pleasure in business hours in helping others - not only by supplying their wants of bee-material, but often by friendly counsel, brief and to the point, on the deeper matters of life, temperance or religion. One mutual friend refers fittingly to "his business habits, his untiring energy, his mechanical ability, his temperance and religious views, and, above all, his unquenchable optimism." Speaking personally, it was a treat, after a year or two away back on the bee-farm, to drop in for a short chat with and look around the work of our late friend.

In conjunction with the earlier Bee Association of Victoria and its Secretary, and assisted by the late Mr. Ellery, Astronomer Royal of Victoria and his bee-magazine, the bee calling fast advanced. When, as a result, honey came in and over-flooded the market as it did in a few years, export under bonus was tried, and to Mr. Chambers was given the supervision of the trade. It fell through for lack of demand and of supervision on the other side; and, in spite of £10 a ton bonus, some beekeepers had to make up deficiencies on their account sales.

Since the formation of the present apiarists' Association of Victoria, Mr. Chambers has had less to do with our beemen, and though he at times attended the Annual Conferences, and handed over to the present body the balance of funds of the old one, and gave the benefit of his advice on questions under discussion, one has seen very little of him as compared to those earlier years of beekeeping. Up to lately he still, I believe, had a personal liking for and kept some bees at his country residence at Fern Tree Gully. As an employer his men held him in esteem. One of these, of 17 years' service with him, "never had a harsh or angry word," a testimony by the way to both master and man. ... It is fitting that the pages of that Journal, which, of late years has so ably taken up the beekeepers interests, should convey at least to all its readers a tribute in the way of esteem and respect for Mr. Chambers the pioneer in this State in developing beekeeping from a hobby to a reliable and useful business and calling and livelihood. T. Bolton, Lambruck, Victoria." (pp.179-181) [61]

Chambers began making bee hives in Adelaide in 1880 and by 1886 in Melbourne [62] he was making them in the thousands. In 1888 he adopted and promoted the system of hanging frames in place of the standing frame. Chambers "did not manufacture bee supplies other than what a beekeeper needed and refrained from handling lines that, in his idea, were made to sell and did not give results. ... Although other makers came on the market with a cheaper hive he would not adopt it, as his policy was 'the best always.' "

In January 1886 Chambers was still resident in South Australia. His election to membership of the South Australian Beekeepers' Association was recorded in the *South Australian Advertiser*, 8 January 1886 (p.4). He was still there two months later - at the

---

[61] Further details are provided on Chambers' Cyclone Wire Fence Company.
[62] In March 1886 Chambers was still in Adelaide. See the *South Australian Advertiser*, 13 March 1886, page 7

Agricultural Society's Autumn Exhibition in March 1886, he obtained the first award for his movable comb hive.[63]

Chambers' letter dated "Middle Brighton, Aus., Nov. 6, 1887", appeared in *Gleanings in Bee Culture* for 15 January 1888. It gives his first hand account of his reasons for moving from South Australia to Victoria. "Since writing you last. I have packed up my traps and removed from the colony of South Australia to this, the adjoining colony. The distance of the capitals from each other Adelaide and Melbourne, is 500 miles; the route is either by water or rail, 40 hours in one case and 18 in the other. …

> BEES. BEES. BEES. BEES. BEES. BEES. BEES. BEES. BEES. BEES. We do not pretend to supply purebred stock at ridiculous prices, nor do we call a handful of bees a swarm, but we do supply carefully bred and selected Queens, in colonies of bees, in swarms, or on combs, guaranteeing whatever we sell to be according to specification. We have had many years' experience, and have a large business as our guarantee. Send to us for a copy of the Colonial Beekeeper, 1 ½ post, and our illustrated catalogue of supplies free. The Beekeepers' Supply Co., Franklin-st., Melbourne.

Advertisement from the Melbourne *Argus*,
1 December 1902 (p.3)

While South Australia has been passing through a severe time of financial depression, which I suppose is inseparable from young colonies with large borrowing powers and still larger wants, Victoria has fast been pushing ahead, developing her resources, opening up every inch of country by rail and otherwise,

---

[63] *South Australian Advertiser*, 12 March 1886, p.6.

attracting capital from all parts, increasing her population, and is now in a state of "goaheadiness" which is a pleasure to see. …

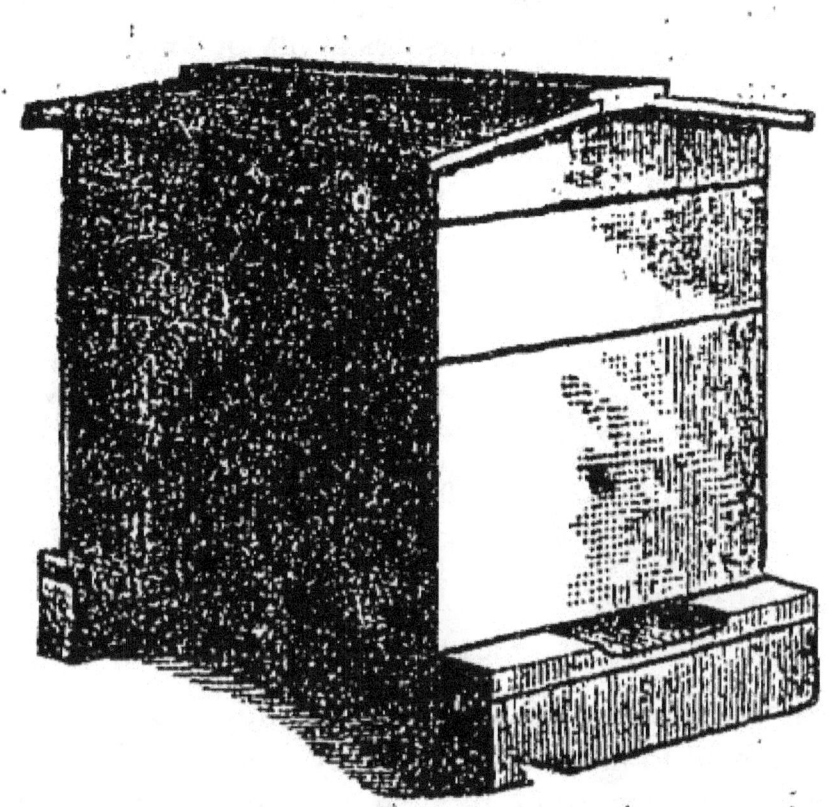

BEEKEEPERS.   ATTENTION.
Langstroth Frame Hives, Comb foundation, Smokers, Section boxes, Honey and Wax Extractors, and all apiarian requisites.
Ligurian bees and queens securely packed for transit to any part of the colonies. The "A.B.C. of Bee Culture," new edition, 37th thousand, 400 pages, 300 illustrations; price, 7s. 6d. posted. "The Colonial Beekeeper," by L. T. Chambers, price, 1s. 2d. posted. Send for illustrated catalogue. Free.
THE BEEKEEPERS' SUPPLY COMPANY,
Franklin street, Melbourne.

From NZ's the *Bush Advocate*, 28 February 1891 (p.8).

some means, smothered. The others lost very heavily in bees, and were thrown back a good deal, but have since increased at a fair rate, so that at the present time I count over 100 colonies, with every prospect of there being many more, although I am checking swarming as much as lies in my power.

Steamer *Adelaide*

I have been heartily welcomed by all interested in bee culture, who were glad to have an opportunity to supply their wants, and have every prospect of doing well, as I and my business become known. The honey yield is good, though little is yet known of the frame hive, and the newspapers still refer to matters pertaining thereto as a novelty.

Here, as in all these colonies, the honey harvest is to a great extent variable, one good yield and one light one; but the good one is a good one. I find that the bee-men calculate 80 to 100 hives of bees equal to 5 to 7 tons of honey, and this without any care bestowed upon them other than taking the honey, and this from a degenerate race of blacks. What may be accomplished under better management, and with better bees, is yet to be seen. It is my intention to send 50 good colonies into the country for the season now opening, and see what I can do. I fear I live too near town to secure any harvest, although up to the present my bees have been booming in spite of an exceptionally wet spring. Honey brings 4 ½ to 6 [pence] in bulk; 1-lb. sections, 9 to 10 wholesale, and no end to the demand at the present time, or likely to be for some time to come. ...

You will remember that, by a short act of parliament, the government of South Australia set apart Kangaroo Island as a spot for breeding Ligurians only. We are now about to reap the benefit of this, as one of our most experienced bee-masters, Mr. Fiebig, is now busy packing his first orders from there; and as he has had many years' experience in Germany, as well as here, we are pretty sure of getting the best-bred bees procurable, at a medium price, to commence with. Leonard T. Chambers." (pp.52-53)

The following announcement appeared in the *Alexandra and Yea Standard, Gobur, Thornton and Acheron Express*, 23 September 1887 "A Beekeepers' Supply Company has opened at 18 Franklin street, Melbourne. All requisites of the apiary can be obtained at the company's stores, as hives are made to order in any size, style, or shape required. All hives are made in dovetail parts, making a perfectly true hive body. Special attention is paid to the manufacture of comb foundation, great precautions bring taken to destroy any germs of disease which may have been in the wax, which is a frequent cause of transmission. Bees for the coming season can be supplied at prices varying with the purity of the different breed. The company has just issued a small catalogue with list of prices of the goods for sale, copies of which will be posted free to applicants by writing to the manager, Mr. L. T. Chambers". (p.5)

The following entry appeared in *The Cyclopedia of Victoria, Vol. II* (1904) Edited by James Smith. The Cyclopedia Company, Melbourne. "The CYCLONE WOVEN WIRE FENCE COMPANY and BEE-KEEPERS' SUPPLY near town to secure any harvest, although up to the present my bees have been booming in spite of an exceptionally wet spring. Honey brings 4 ½ to 6 [pence] in bulk; 1-lb. sections, 9 to 10 wholesale, and no end to the demand at the present time, or likely to be for some time to come. ...

You will remember that, by a short act of parliament, the government of South Australia set apart Kangaroo Island as a spot for breeding Ligurians only. We are now about to reap the benefit of this, as one of our most experienced bee-masters, Mr. Fiebig, is now busy packing his first orders from there; and as he has had many years' experience in Germany, as well as here, we are pretty sure of getting the best-bred bees procurable, at a medium price, to commence with. Leonard T. Chambers." (pp.52-53)

The following announcement appeared in the *Alexandra and Yea Standard, Gobur, Thornton and Acheron Express*, 23 September 1887 "A Beekeepers' Supply Company has opened at 18 Franklin street, Melbourne. All requisites of the apiary can be obtained at the company's stores, as hives are made to order in any size, style, or shape required. All hives are made in dovetail parts, making a perfectly true hive body. Special attention is paid to the manufacture of comb foundation, great precautions bring taken to destroy any germs of disease which may have been in the wax, which is a frequent cause of transmission. Bees for the coming season can be supplied at prices varying with the purity of the different breed. The company has just issued a small catalogue with list of prices of the goods for sale, copies of which will be posted free to applicants by writing to the manager, Mr. L. T. Chambers". (p.5)

The following entry appeared in *The Cyclopedia of Victoria, Vol. II* (1904) Edited by James Smith. The Cyclopedia Company, Melbourne. "The CYCLONE WOVEN WIRE FENCE COMPANY and BEE-KEEPERS' SUPPLY

COMPANY. Messrs. L. T. Chambers and W. A. Thompson, proprietors), 128 - 130 Franklin Street, Melbourne, with branches in Sydney, Brisbane, and Adelaide. This business was originally established in 1877 by Mr. L.T. Chambers, under the style of the Bee-keepers' Supply Company and carried on by him for seven years. Commencing in a small way as manufacturers of bee-keepers' supplies, the business increased so rapidly that it soon became necessary for Mr. Chambers to secure assistance, and he accordingly took into partnership Mr. W. A. Thompson. ..."

Preface by Robt. L. J. Ellery, Melbourne Observatory, 1888: "The great impetus that has been given to the Bee-keeping Industry in the southern parts of Australia in the last year or two, and more especially in Victoria, which hitherto had been somewhat behind her sisters, South Australia, New South Wales, and Queensland in particular, has brought about a widespread enquiry concerning the modern methods of bee management, the use of Frame Hives, the mode of securing comb honey by supering, of pure honey by extracting, and generally how to obtain the best results and most profit from the industry."

I found in the *Journal of agriculture and industry of South Australia, Vol. V, August 1901 to July 1902* (1902) published by the South Australian Dept. of Agriculture, under the agricultural editorship of Albert Molineux: "In selecting bees I should recommend the Italians, as they are the best breed and are not so aggressive as the native black bees. [65] ... My object in taking up this subject is to show that I believe every farmer and fruit grower should have his colony of bees, and to the beginner I should say get Doolittle's work on *Queen-rearing* and *The Colonial Beekeeper*. The former is a valuable work and can be

---

[65] I believe this refers to the introduced English "black" bee *Apis m. mellifera*

obtained for 5s, and the latter for 1s. In these books you will find the course you have to pursue, not forgetting the fact that you must learn the locality you place yourself in. ..." (p.406, Nov. 1901) [66] The inference is clear – Molineux couldn't wholly recommend the latter.

In the 1899 *Journal of the Department of Agriculture of Western Australia, Volumes 1-2*, headed "Beginners' Book on Bees": "By last week's mail the Editor received from Mr. LT Chambers, of Melbourne, a copy of *The Colonial Beekeeper*, a small book giving the art of bee-keeping in … " (p.18) Unfortunately, Google Book Search only provided this short "snippet."

Imagine my disappointment when in 1996 I was offered a 4th ed., 1902 copy by a bookshop for $75. I forwarded payment for this rare item, only to have my cheque returned as the shop had accidentally sold it to a walk in customer! Does lightening strike the same spot twice? In 1998 this same bookshop offered me another rarity, a pre-1910 Anthony Horderns catalogue titled *Eggs and Honey*, only to whisk it off to a book fair in Melbourne the next day and sell it there.

---

[66] Original held by National Library of Australia

William Charles Cottton

Cotton, William Charles (1813-1879 *A Manual for New Zealand Beekeepers,* R. Stokes, at the Spectator Office, Wellington, N.Z. 1848. Copies SLNSW, SLV, ANU. Full text is available via Google Book Search. Books.google.com.au Reprinted 1976, Wellington, N.Z., Newrick Associates. Limited ed. of 850 numbered copies. Facsimile of first edition. Another reprint Papakura, N.Z., Southern Reprints, 1987. An original copy of Cotton's *Manual* located retail in March 2011, listed at £450 (AUD$730), signed and dated by the author, 1854. The only retail copy I've come across in 15 years.

Two Cotton biographies have been published: Barrett, Peter (1997) *William Charles Cotton, Grand Bee Master of NZ, 1842-1847.* Smith, Arthur R. (2006) *William Charles Cotton MA 1813 - 1879 Priest, Missionary and Bee Master.*

My reader may ask why is Cotton included in this bibliography? No books of his were written or published in Australia. His series of articles titled *Hints on the Management of Bees*, authored in New Zealand, were widely circulated in NZ newspapers and later published as his *A Manual for New Zealand Beekeepers*. But his audience was not just NZ based - Australian newspapers also carried his beekeeping series [67] and his book was available, and undoubtedly avidly read, in Australia.

---

[67] See the *Sydney Chronicle* in 1847 and 1848.

> **JUST PUBLISHED,**
> **THE BEE-KEEPER'S MANUAL,**
> by the Rev. W. C. Cotton.
> Also,
> **A LEAF FROM THE NATURAL HISTORY OF NEW ZEALAND,** or a Vocabulary of its different productions, &c., &c., with their native names, by the Rev. Richard Taylor.
> 8454
> **W. AND F. FORD.**

From *The Sydney Morning Herald*, 17 November 1849 (p.1) [68]

During his layover in Sydney during April - May 1842, before proceeding to NZ with Bishop Selwyn, Cotton visited prominent Sydney residents who were also beekeepers, even opening some of their hives and handling the bees. On that basis, and as this is my book, he's in, and the opportunity to include some anecdotes about him is presented. Generated between 1842 and 1903, some are believable, others not quite so. But first, some evidence of Cotton's presence among several prominent Sydney beekeepers in 1842.

Visits to Sydney beekeepers, April-May 1842

The Bishop's Sydney host was senior Sydney merchant, Robert Campbell of Campbell's Wharf, behind which stood before Campbell's Wharf House with its own grounds and garden, dove cote and bee house. Campbell's Cove snuggles on the north western shore of Circular Quay, just south of the southern footings of Sydney Harbour Bridge. Stone warehouses remain but the Campbell house is long since demolished. In 1864,

---

[68] *The Sydney Morning Herald*, 25 February 1851, listed a range of "New Books - Just Landed" available from W. R. Piddington, Bookseller and Stationer, 485 George-street

Robert's eldest son, John, recalled Cotton's foray upon one of their apiaries.

A view of the garden adjacent *Wharf House*.
Note the dovecote at centre. There's no obvious sign of beehives.

The antiquarian bee book *Bee-Keeping, by "The Times" Bee-Master* was authored by Dr. John Cumming. At its rear are a series of correspondence from beekeepers, one of which is simply signed "An Australian. London 12th August, 1864". In part it reads "Our chief guide in the management was a book written by the Rev. Mr. Cotton, called 'My Bee-Book' and it may be interesting to mention, that when in after years that gentleman accompanied the Bishop of New Zealand to that country, via Australia, he was my father's guest. [69] … From

---

[69] Campbell's chronology is a little off here for *My Bee Book* was published in 1842. He may have, however, been referring to Cotton's

early childhood I shared my father's interest in his pets; and at one time I could have counted upwards of ninety hives in the two apiaries which he kept for his own amusement, and for the encouragement of those who were willing to keep bees. Everyone was welcome to a swarm who cared to ask for one. ...Mr. Cotton's delight at finding his favourites so appreciated was only equaled by our pleasure in meeting the author of 'My Bee-Book' ..."

Campbell described his apiaries: "Bees have many enemies in Australia; the greatest is probably the sugar-ant. To protect them from these intruders, we had the hives ranged on shelves, the supports of which stood in wide vessels of water, alike a protection against other foes. The apiaries were built open in front and ends, against a wall, with thatched roof and overhanging eaves; and there was a space between the shelf on which the hives stood and the wall, where one could sit or stand and watch them; for most of our hives were square, made of wood, with glass slides and wooden shutters; and the bees were so accustomed to be looked at, that they kept their side of the glass quite clean, and generally built a smooth surface of comb next to the glass, leaving space to move between the comb and the glass; and I have often seen the queen, surrounded by her admiring subjects (exactly as you describe) making her progress across the comb, each attendant bee with its head next her majesty, fanning with its wings, and one could hear a *purr* of satisfaction."

Picture below: another view of the grounds about Wharf House (approx.. centre view) where Cotton worked Campbell's hives.

1837 and 1838 letters to cottagers, both of which were included in *My Bee Book*

Cotton's acclaimed mastery over bees was somewhat dented for John humorously recounted "... sad to say, our bees conceived a dislike to their visitor; and upon his exhibiting his fearlessness in handling bees, he was stung (much to the amusement of some small bystanders) by two wicked bees ... "

During Cotton's short Sydney residence and his search for bee hive donors he also visited Alexander Macleay, prominent Sydney citizen, most likely at his Elizabeth Bay residence, whose garden, famous for its rare specimens of plants, was described as a "botanist's paradise." In Cotton's letter home dated April 1843 "I met Mr MacClay [sic.] ... Bees were first brought for his daughter. ... I paid a visit to Mrs [Elizabeth] McArthur at [Elizabeth Farm] Parramatta who has a capital apiary, and to Mr [Gregory] Blaxland." *Brush Farm,* Blaxland's property was close to Parramatta.

Elizabeth's nephew, Hannibal Hawkins Macarthur of *Vineyard House*, lived alongside the north bank of the Parramatta River. Emmeline Macarthur, Hannibal's daughter, described her home "A large property 15 miles from Sydney bounded one side by a tidal river, navigable for small steamers & on the other side extensive forests, chiefly composed of gum trees, & a good sized farm house with cultivated fields, and outbuildings ¾ of a mile from the house. Large gardens & in the heart of the forest, a semi-circular terraced vineyard, with a stream at the foot, bordered with ferns & mimosa, a lovely spot." Emmeline's recollections appear in *My Dear Miss Macarthur, The Recollections of Emmeline Maria Macarthur (1828-1911)* [70] "In 1841 [71] Bishop Selwyn, the first Bishop of New Zealand, arrived with his chaplain Mr. Cotton, who was delighted to find my

---

[70] de Falbe, Jean (1988) *My dear Miss Macarthur, The Recollections of Emmeline Maria Macarthur (1828-1911)*, Kangaroo Press
[71] It was actually in 1842

Father as enthusiastic about bees as he was. He wrote 'My Bee Book'. I remember his putting a small star of tin foil on the Queen Bee's back, so that he could watch her at work through the glass sides of the hive."

Cotton also attended Revd Thomas Steele's apiary near St. Peter's church: "I send you herewith, that is by the same ship, a bottle of Australian honey, which is so very nice, to my taste at least. It was made at Cooks River, near Botany Bay, by the bees belonging to Mr Steele the Parson of the place. The bees are English bees They do exceptionally here."

Frances Maria Spark

Another potential donor was the merchant gentleman, Alexander Spark and his wife Frances at *Tempe*, close by the banks of Cook's River, which flows into Botany Bay. Almost twelve months later Cotton wrote home [72] on 21 April 1843 "My Dear Arthur, my brother and my Godson. ... I hope to have some

---

[72] letter held at the Auckland Institute & Museum, New Zealand.

bees sent over to me from friends in Sydney, where they prosper, as I wrote to you before, most wonderfully." Despite promises no bees were then forthcoming. Some nine weeks later he noted in his journal on Friday, 7 July 1843 "I also sent a note to Mrs McArthur of Parramatta begging her to fulfil her promise of sending me some Bees."

Cotton's apiary visits and resulting promises finally bore results following his friend James Busby's visit to Sydney in July 1843. Cotton recorded in his journal for Thursday 3 August, under the page heading Bees Arrive "During the morning I had a letter from Mr Busby dated of this Day at sea, and bringing the joyful intelligence that he had his hives of Bees for me, one from D Steele's, the other from Mrs Sparke." The following day "Many thanks to them."

An alleged stinging encounter in Melbourne, 1842

In an 1881 edition of *The British Almanac of the Society for the Diffusion of Useful Knowledge for the year*, there is an article on apiculture in New Zealand. "… the people are more given to commerce than agricultural pursuits, hence it has been much neglected, for bees were introduced to South Australia many years before Mr. Cotton sailed with his living freight with Dr. Selwyn. When the party called at Melbourne on their way to the new diocese Mr. Cotton, seeing a colony of bees busy at work wished to show his friends and shipmates ... [his] skill in their management, but on taking the hive up, he found that the hot climate had made them much more fierce than his Oxford bees, and he was severely stung." (p.134) My understanding is that the *Tomatin* sailed direct to Sydney from Plymouth, so this mention of a visit to Melbourne is an anomaly.

"in a previous state of existence [he'd] been a queen bee himself", 1859

The following account from an 1859 book on pets [73] all but attributes Cotton having bee-like qualities: "I refer to bees, in which many take great pleasure and interest, like Cotton, who has written an amusing little pamphlet about them called the *Conservative Bee Keeper*, and he seems to know the inmost thoughts, politics and arrangements of his bees as well as if he had in a previous state of existence been a queen bee himself." The October 1874 issue of the *American Bee Journal* referred to Cotton's bees as his pets. "The Rev. Mr. Cotton accompanied the first Bishop of New Zealand in his missionary work, but he found time to introduce his pet bees among the islands of the Pacific ..." (p.228) [74]

A pains-taking industrious clergyman, 1857

Charles Hursthouse jun. came to New Zealand on the *Thomas Sparks* in 1843. He returned to England ca. 1849 but visited NZ again in 1854 aboard the *Joseph Fletcher*. From the New Zealand National Register of Archives and Manuscripts web site [75] "On separate return visits to England he published *An Account of the Settlement of New Plymouth* in 1849 and *New Zealand, the Britain of the South* in 1857." His 1857 comments on Cotton indicate the latter's notoriety. In the Chapter titled "Agriculture and Horticulture", Hursthouse commented unsympathetically on bees and their protagonists: "Most English flowering plants become larger in New Zealand, blossom more profusely, and lose none of their beauty or fragrance. Alluding to flowers, I may remark that bees bid fair to become a considerable nuisance

---

[73] Leigh (1859)
[74] The article was provided by a D. C. Millett of Holmesburg, Pa.
[75] nram.govt.nz/record.php?holderid=73&id=5944&parent=ncindex

in New Zealand. **A pains-taking, industrious clergyman,** [76] **who seems to have believed in bees, actually wrote, and then published a book on New Zealand bees;** [77] and some enthusiastic honey-eaters have gravely set down honey as a New Zealand export. If bees and honey could be exported together, once for all, the country, I think, would be well quit of both; but in deference to popular opinion and the prejudices of my readers, I must admit that the 'bee statistics' of New Zealand border on what Mr. Nutt [78] and enthusiastic bee-fanciers would term, prodigious -- one hive is said to have produced, in the course of four years, nearly one ton of honey!

Bumble bees for New Zealand, 1871

In *The Queenslander*, 17 June 1871 "The Rev. W. C. Cotton, of Frodsham, is making efforts to procure some bumble bees for New Zealand, and as soon as fine weather sets in he will doubtless have some ready for shipment." (p.6) The *Wellington Independent*, 21 June 1871, gave a fuller report: "The Rev. W.C. Cotton addresses *Land and Water* on the subject of the exportation of bumble bees to New Zealand. In the summer of 1871 he commenced to prepare a colony of those bees for transport, and he describes at length the method, which he adopted. Having secured the nest in a case and covered it with sods, he left England about the end of July for a holiday, not having been able to hear of anyone going out to New Zealand willing and competent to take charge of the case. On his return

---

[76] The commentator is clearly being sarcastic, his references to "pains-taking" – as in sting effected, and "industrious", both imply attributes of the bee upon the clergyman

[77] I read the word "*actually*" as if it is italicized - Hursthouse is astounded that someone would bother to believe in and then write about bees. This is obviously a reference to William Charles Cotton, who in 1848 published his *Manual for New Zealand Bee Keepers.*

[78] "Nott" should read "Nutt", the proponent of the collateral hive.

home in September, however, he found the nest deserted. "Nothing discouraged by this failure," Mr Cotton writes, "I am ready to try again to prepare a nest, or rather half-a-dozen, if I can find them, for transport in an active condition." Mr Cotton makes the following remarks with regard to the preparation of female bees for carriage to New Zealand whilst in a state of winter torpor:- "It may be possible to capture them just as they are leaving their nests, and by placing them in a box with mould and turf induce them to bury themselves, when they may be transported without disturbance, but sleep on in the ice-house of a steamer, so that their waking up may be under the influence of a bright New Zealand sun. Any which I may turn up, when digging in the winter, I will treat in the same manner giving them the chance of burying themselves again. Whether they will do so, I know not; but I can hardly think that all the female bees who are awakened before their proper time by an unusually bright day in March or April inevitably perish, when a prematurely bright shiny day is followed by cold winds or frosty mornings." " (p.2)

In the Bruce Herald, 23 August 1871, under the heading "The Bumble Bee and the Spread of Clover:" The Rev. Mr Cotton, Vicar of Frodsham, in England, in a letter to 'Land and Water,' writes:- "I was glad to see the enquiry in 'Land and Water' as to the best method of carrying my dear old friend the bumble bee to New Zealand, and naturalising him there. They would be a most valuable race of colonists. For whilst the ordinary honeybee does its work there, as here in the fertilisation of white clover, the red clover still remains "without the assistance of that species of bee whose longer proboscis enables it to reach the nectaries inaccessible, to the shorter one of the Apis mellifica.

Every lover of accurate observations in natural history must remember that excellent passage in Darwin's Origin of Species,' pages 73 and 74, in which he shows the intimate connection between the number of cats in a given district, and the yield of red clover seed. Cats are the natural enemies of mice, and mice the devourers of bumble bees, so that the increase of the first involves the decrease of the second, the consequent increase of the third, and the subsequent abundant fertilisation of red clover seed. Now, in New Zealand, cats are plenty, and mice, too, have introduced themselves. The former is there, as in England, "a domestic necessary cat," but many have gone wild in the bush, and, in lack of an abundance of mice, have learned to live upon lizards. I ascertained the fact by a post-mortem on a feline carcase, which the Maoris, with whom I was travelling, hunted down and were preparing to cook, as we were on very short commons.

The honey-bee lives from year to year as a member of a social republic; that of the bumble bee is broken up by the first frost of autumn, and reconstitute at the arrival of spring by the impregnated females who alone survive the winter. The female bumble bee buries itself in the earth, when the males and neuters are destroyed by the frost. The large yellowtailed bumble-bee, the most common sort here in Cheshire, which builds its nests in mossy pastures, is that which I should advise your correspondent to select for New Zealand." (p.7)

"he was never without a plurality of dogs", 1881

Several cameos of Cotton in his later years were provided in William Beament's (1881) *An Account of the Ancient Town of Frodsham in Cheshire*. "Except when prevented by sickness or the return of his New Zealand malady, the vicar, who had always one or more curates, never spared himself, but always took his share of the duty, whether in the desk or in the pulpit. … Self-sacrifice and good feeling were parts of the vicar's character, which made him at all times ready to lend a helping hand to the deserving poor; to the young he was kind and gentle, and while he loved to see them learn, he would at proper times relax and not only promote their games, but play with them himself. But he had other objects besides his flock to share his kindness, and these were the four footed and winged creatures. He was never without a plurality of dogs, and one of these, named Gip, became the pseudo author of a number of clever papers contributed to the *Field* and other journals, descriptive of a tour which the dog and his master had made together; … his fondness for animals and bees left him some love to spare for flowers, a beautiful branch of creation; and every year when his roses and tulips were in full blow, it was announced that they would be 'at home' on the afternoon of a day named, and on these occasions the visitors partook of an *al fresco* tea, in the vicarage garden. …" (pp.256-259)

"I know that bee well", 1886

A whimsical tale of Cotton's innovative handling of an "unjust accusation" may be found in Francis Doyle's 1886 *Reminiscences and Opinions of Sir Francis Hastings Doyle, 1813-1885*: "At Christ Church, not in my time, but a year or two afterwards, Cotton, one of our distinguished Eton men, a Newcastle scholar, thought proper to adapt the rural economy of the Fourth Georgic [79] to Peckwater, [80] the subdivision of Christ Church where he lived. He devoted himself assiduously to bees,

---

[79] From *Wikipedia*: Virgil (Publius Vergilius Maro) 70BC to 19BC, "was a classical Roman poet, better known by the Anglicised form of his name as Virgil or Vergil. His three major works are the *Bucolics* (or *Eclogues*), the *Georgics* and the *Aeneid*"

[80] From *Wikipedia*: "The Peckwater Quadrangle (known as "Peck" to undergraduates) is one of the quadrangles of Christ Church, Oxford, England. … The buildings, including the Library, date from the eighteenth century. They are built in the then-fashionable Classical style. First floor rooms in this quad have traditionally been particularly sought after by undergraduate members of the college due to their size, oak paneling and high ceilings."

and troubled his contemporaries (so they said at least) with continual buzzings and an occasional sting. In these cases he always denied stoutly that his bees were in fault, and once when Dean Gaisford, [81] having sent for him, told him plainly that his bees must be sent away because a gentleman commoner had just been stung in Tom Quad, [82] he replied instantly: 'Mr. Dean, I assure you that you are doing us a great injustice. I know that bee well; he is not mine at all, but belongs to Mr. Bigg of Merton. [83]

There was some humour in the assumption that every member of the 'House' would feel aggrieved by the Dean's frivolous accusation, but the gentlemanly character and inoffensiveness of Cotton's favourites must be made known and vindicated. Could a Christ Church bee with an Eton pedigree, trained within the sacred precincts of the 'House', so far forget his noble origin as to sting a well-affected Tuft? Perish the thought! Whereas the stinging proclivities of Bigg's bees was a matter of common knowledge to Cotton and his friends." (p.155) [84] Merton College was located within Oxford. Cotton's assertion that he "knew that bee well" is pure invention, an imaginative and playful falsehood likely to be believed by those ignorant of bees. It also demonstrates a mischievous but likeable sense of humour.

---

[81] From *Wikipedia*: "Thomas Gaisford (1779-1855) was an English classical scholar …he entered the University of Oxford in 1797, becoming successively student and tutor of Christ Church. … From 1831 until his death, he was dean of Christ Church."
[82] From *Wikipedia*: "The Great Quadrangle more popularly known as Tom Quad, is one of the quadrangles of Christ Church, Oxford. It is the largest college quad in Oxford, measuring 264 by 261 feet."
[83] From *My Bee Book*, p.330, "Mr. Bigge, of Merton College" was listed as one of the founding members of the Oxford Apiarian Society.
[84] also to be found in Arthur Duke Coleridge's *Eton in the Forties*, 1898, p.315, R. Bentley and Son.

Beament (1881) recalled of Cotton "the vicar possessed a vein of innocent humour" (p.258)

Peckwater Quadrangle, Christ Church, Oxford

Thomas Gaisford, Dean of Christ Church, 1831-55

Cotton indeed kept bees in his rooms. In "the summer of 1836 – In my rooms at Christ Church, I had two stocks of Bees, which worked through a sort of cuniculus [85] in the window sill into the open air; one was in a leaf Hive, the other in an observatory Hive (or, rather in an octagon box, with three glass windows in the back, as they never worked up into the observatory leaves)." [86] At an unspecified time and place Cotton invited bees at large

---

[85] *Wiktionary* defines it as a burrow or low underground passage, as in a rabbit's (English: coney, cony, cunny, bunny) burrow.
[86] *My Bee Book*, p.325

to feed within his rooms. "I was living in a town where I knew some few Bees were kept, and I chanced to have some coarse comb, from which the honey had drained; so, instead of being greedy, and squeezing out all I could get, I determined to give a feed all round to such Bees as chose to accept my invitation to dinner. This invitation I gave by opening the window, and setting the honey on the sill. In about half an hour some foragers found it out; they helped themselves, and carried back the good news to their sisters in the Hive. In the course of the morning my room literally swarmed with Bees, and I need not tell you, as they are grateful creatures, that they did not meddle with me, but, as I sat at my books, repaid me for my treat with their sweet music. In the afternoon they were satisfied, at least for the day, and dropped off, one by one, without committing any excess." [87]

Cotton was a talented storyteller. Most of his tales were true but some not so. Possibly belonging to the former, Cotton related in *My Bee Book* "I myself was once blowing into a glass, to drive the bees out when, in drawing my breath in sharply, I swallowed a bee. I prepared myself for a run to the doctor's, had I felt its sting in my throat, or lower down in my 'inside pocket;' [88] but the bee passed so rapidly down that he had not time to sting; when he got to his journey's end, no doubt not a little surprised at the path he had travelled, he resigned himself to his fate, like a good bee, and did not revenge himself by stinging me." (p.97)

---

[87] *My Bee Book*, p.276

[88] From Cotton's 1837 *A Short & Simple Letter to Cottagers – letter the second, on the natural theology of bees* "They have two stomachs, like cows; in the first stomach, the cow and the Bee, when they are feeding, put the one grass, and the other honey: if the Bee wants to make wax, she shifts some honey into her second stomach, which is a regular 'Inside Pocket,' just like that into which men put their breakfasts and their dinners." (p.10)

"a bodyguard of them used to attend him to lecture and chapel", 1886

James Anthony Froude's *Oceana, or England and her colonies* [89] provides what can only be an exaggerated remembrance of Cotton. Froude was a contemporary of Cotton's at Oxford - the latter was there from 1832 until 1838, with Froude attending between 1836 and 1840. The year before the publication of *Oceana*, Froude was engaged upon a tour of Australia and New Zealand. While at Cambridge, NZ, "...We had been directed to the least tumultuous of the Cambridge hotels. We found a *table d'hote* laid out there for forty people at least, some going up and some returning. [90]

The food was tolerable; we found, for one thing, New Zealand honey especially excellent, taken from the nests of wild bees, which are now in millions all over the colony. They are the offspring of two or three hives, which were once kept, when I was at Oxford, [91] in the rooms of Cotton, of Christ Church,

---

[89] Froude, James Anthony (1886) *Oceana, or England and her colonies* (pp.262-262). Quotation also found in Coe, Charles Clement (1895) *Nature Versus Natural Selection: An Essay on Organic Evolution.* Swan Sonnenschein, London. (p.51.); also in *Longman's Magazine*, 1886 (p.661)

[90] The partial quotation I found via Google Book Search. At this point the quote has the words "in London ten years before." The preceding words I acquired from a 1985 reproduction of Froude's book (p.130) which omits the "London" phrase, so there may be more of relevance in the original. The 1985 version is titled *Travellers' Tales of Early Australia & New Zealand, Oceana, the tempestuous voyage of J. A. Froude, 1884 & 1885*, edited by Geoffrey Blainey. Publ. Methuen Haynes, North Ryde.

[91] Re Froude - from *Wikipedia* "Beginning in 1836, he was educated at Oriel College, Oxford, then the centre of the ecclesiastical revival now called the Oxford Movement." Cotton and Froude would have come into contact through their joint interest in the Oxford Movement which

between whom and his bees there was such strong attachment that a bodyguard of them used to attend him to lecture and chapel." A variation on this appeared in *Chambers's Journal of Popular Literature, Science and Arts* in 1893 "It is told that he was accustomed to keep them in his sitting-room, and they had become so attached and familiar with his person, that a squad of them used to attend him at lectures and chapel. Cotton went to New Zealand with Bishop Selwyn, and took his bees with him, and they have multiplied in this marvelous manner." (p.262) Where could the zany addenda of "a squad" and "a bodyguard" have originated? Its fiction is obvious to any skilled beekeeper.

James Anthony Froude

Under the page heading "bees are my bodyguard", the following tale was originally published in Captain John Gabriel Stedman's 1796 [92] *Expedition to Surinam: Being the Narrative of a Five*

---

sought to demonstrate that the Church of England was a direct descendant of the Church established by the Apostles.
[92] From *Wikipedia*: John Gabriel Stedman (1744 –1797) was a distinguished British - Dutch soldier and noted author. He was born in the Netherlands … His years in Surinam (South America) were

Years Expedition Against the Revolted Negroes of Surinam in Guiana, on the Wild Coast of South America, from the Year 1772 to 1777, Elucidating that Country and Describing Its Productions, with an Account of Indians of Guiana and Negroes of Guinea. "On the 16th I was visited by a neighbouring gentleman, whom I conducted up my ladder; but he had no sooner entered my aerial dwelling than he leaped down from the top to the ground, roaring like a madman with agony and pain, after which he instantly plunged his head into the river; but, looking up, I soon discovered the cause of his distress to be an immense nest of wild bees, or *Wassee Wassee,* in the thatch, directly above my head, as I stood within my door, when I immediately took to my heels, as he had done, and ordered them to be destroyed by my slaves without delay. A tar mop was now brought, and the devastation just going to commence, when an old negro stepped up, and offered to receive any punishment I should decree, if even one of these bees should sting me in person. "Massa," said he, "they would have stung you long ere now had you been a stranger to them; but they, being your tenants, that is, gradually allowed to build upon your premises, they assuredly know both you and yours, and will never hurt either you or them.

---

characterized by encounters with African slaves and colonial planters as well as the exotic local flora and fauna.

Stedman in Surinam [93]

I instantly assented to the proposition, and, tying the old man to a tree, ordered my boy Quaco to ascend the ladder quite naked, which he did, and was not stung. I then ventured to follow; and declare, upon my honour, that even after shaking the nest, which made the inhabitants buzz about my ears, not a single one attempted to sting me. I next released the old negro, and rewarded him with a gallon of rum and four shillings for the discovery. The swarm of bees I since kept unhurt, as my body guard, and they have made many overseers take a desperate leap for my amusement, as I generally sent them [ie., the overseere] up my ladder on some frivolous message, when I wished to punish them for injustice and cruelty, which was not seldom." (p.205)

---

[93] From Wikipedia: Stedman stands over a slave after the capture of Gado Saby, from the frontispiece of his *Narrative of a Five Years Expedition against the Revolted Negroes of Surinam* (1796)

Cotton reproduced this story in his *My Bee Book* of 1841, correctly attributing it to Captain Stedman. [94] The assertion that bees know their master may have appealed to William. A talented story teller himself he would have appreciated the yarn, at the same time realising the so called bodyguard bees were not consciously protecting their master, but simply stinging anyone that came too close to the hive. Others, in recollection of the contents of *My Bee Book*, may have years later incorrectly interpreted the experience and applied it to William Charles Cotton.

"at daylight he used to crow like a cock", 1903

From James Beresford Atlay's (1903) *Sir Henry Wentworth Acland ... a memoir*, Acland's biograpger stated Cotton was "distinguished among his fellows by overflowing animal spirits and an inexhaustible fund of humour." Atlay notes at this point in a footnote: "Once on a visit to *Holnicote* [Acland's 'much-beloved holiday home on the borders of Exmoor'] his room was near that of the housekeeper, Mrs. Fletcher. About daylight he used to crow like a cock, and this so exasperated the old lady that she declared to Leopold Acland, [95] whose guest he was, that none of his brothers had ever brought such a 'riotous-like' gentleman to Sir Thomas's house before."

---

[94] The popularity of Stedman's adventures persisted as evidenced by the repeated publication of this engaging story over the next 165 years. eg., *The European Magazine, and London Review*, 1797; Rev. John Adams' *The Flowers of Modern Travels: Being Elegant, Entertaining, and Instructive Extracts Selected from the Works of the Most Celebrated Travellers*, 1816; in *The Friend*, 1839; Charles Knight's *Penny Magazine of the Society for the Diffusion of Useful Knowledge*, 1844; James F. Robinson's *British bee-farming, its profits and pleasures*, 1880; and the republication of Stedman's book by the Folio Society in 1963.

[95] Leopold, Henry's younger brother

CRIBB, R. J. *Queensland Bee Book*: being a practical treatise on bees, their management and culture in Australia : together with a description of implements and inventions used in the apiary. 1891, 1/- (one shilling). Worldcat.org produced two hits, one at SLQ, another at Qld. Dept. Primary Industries. Contains his catalogue of bee goods. "Carroll taught R. J. Cribb and his father and eventually in 1889, R.J. Cribb bought out Carroll. Cribb revised *My Little Bee Book* and published it as the *Queensland Bee Book* in 1891, priced at one shilling. … as well as describing beekeeping, has a comprehensive section on equipment" Weatherhead (1986, p.19)

A book review appeared in The West Australian, 29 August 1892 "We have received a copy of a useful publication called the *Queensland Bee Book*, by R.J. Cribb. The little work is a practical treatise on the care and management of bees in Australia. A full account is given of the ways and habits of the little honey-makers, and what is even more valuable, all modern appliances are described, and a list of the latest inventions are given, the modes of treatment being fully gone into. The pamphlet should be in the hands of all bee masters." (p.4) The *Queenslander*, 17 December 1892, advised Root's "A B C of Bee Culture" price 7s. 6d. and Cribb's "Queensland Bee Book" 1s., could be obtained from Messrs. Gordon and Gotch.

Evidence of Cribb's death appeared in the *Brisbane Courier*, 7 June 1916, "Thursday, June 8, at 11 o'clock, on the premises, *Dunmore*, Milton road. Important realisation sale. In the estate of R. J. Cribb, deceased." Among the many items for sale were "VALUABLE BEE-KEEPER'S PLANT, &c, comprising Bee Hives. Frames, Sections, Foundation Mill, Honey Tank, Extractor, large quantity of honey corks and about 100 lb beeswax." (p.12)

DICKINS, Charles. *The Australasian Bee Keepers' Guide Book for Amateurs giving plain and practical instruction on*

the profitable management of bees in moveable comb hives, with numerous illustrations ..., 1887, Adelaide, Scrymgour & Sons, 1887. adv, s/c, illus, price one shilling, 21cm., pp.38 + pp.18, NLNZ, ML, SLSA (catlg: 638.10994 D552). At rear of book is priced catalogue of bee goods (pp.18) available from C. Dickins & Son, beehive appliance manufacturers, Wakefield Street, Adelaide. This book, unfortunately, lacks an Australian character. <u>Chapters</u>: Natural History, Apiary, Comb Foundation, Comb-honey, Diseases, Extracted Honey, Foods & Feeding, Handling Bees, Hives, Introducing, Moving Bees, Queen Rearing, Races, Robbing, Swarming, Transferring, Uniting, Wax Extracting.

One of his advertisements for "Italian bees and queens and all modern beekeeping appliances" can be found in *The West Australian*, 22 March 1888 (p.1) The last page of the book contains an interesting poem, author unknown:

> A SWARM OF BEES WORTH HAVING
>
> **B** patient, B prayerful, B modest, B mild,
>
> **B** wise as a Solon, B meek as a Child,
>
> **B** studious, B thoughtful, B loving, B kind.
>
> **B** sure to make matters subservient to mind,
>
> **B** cautious, B prudent, B trustful, B true,
>
> **B** courteous to all men, B friendly with few,
>
> **B** temperate in argument, pleasure and wine,
>
> **B** careful of conduct, of money, of time,
>
> **B** cheerful, B grateful, B hopeful, B firm,
>
> **B** peaceful, benelovent, willing to learn,
>
> **B** courageous, B gentle, B liberal, B just,
>
> **B** aspiring, B humble because thou art dust,
>
> **B** patient, circumspect, sound in the faith,

> **B** active, devoted, B faithful till death,
> **B** honest, B holy, transparent and pure,
> **B** dependent, B Christ-like, and you'll be secure.

At the monthly meeting of the South Australian Beekeepers' Association in March 1887 "A promise was obtained from Mr. Dickens, jun., an English beekeeper, of a paper for the text meeting. ... Mr. Dickens, sen., was elected a member. Mr. Dickens, jun., advocated a standard frame for South Australia, and a discussion followed, the members present quite agreeing with the idea. ..." from the *South Australian Register*, 11 March 1887 (p.5)

A book review appeared in *Castner's Monthly and Rural Australian* for January 1888, Australia's centennial year. "We have received from Messrs. Turner & Henderson, of Hunter-street, Sydney, a bee book all amateur bee keepers should see. It is by Charles Dickens [sic.] of Adelaide ... and, as far as we can judge, it will be of the greatest possible value to all amateurs who keep or contemplate keeping bees, and can be obtained at a small cost. After looking through this book carefully, we venture to say that even experienced bee keepers may consult it with advantage; while to the thousands of bee keepers whose experience is limited it will be invaluable. The book is so arranged that the information it contains on any given topic can be got at once. ... Of course in a small book each subject has to be treated briefly, but in this case each is intelligently treated and well illustrated. So well, indeed, that with no other guide any amateur bee keeper may safely get rid of the old gin case hives and enter into the use of the bar-framed hives with much success. We feel sure it only needs to be known that this bee book can be obtained for a small sum from Messrs. Turner &

Henderson to lead many amateur bee keepers who want information to secure it."

The following review appeared in Perth's *Western Mail*, 7 January 1888: "*The Australian Bee Keepers' Guide Book* is the title of a small book received from the author, Mr. Charles Dickins, of Adelaide, by the last mail. The work is specially for the use of amateurs, to whom it gives plain and practical instruction on the profitable management of bees in moveable and comb hives. It is admirably written, and exceedingly interesting. It cannot fail to be of great value to beekeepers in this colony, and has the great advantage of being clear and concise and expressed in the plainest and simplest manner. In lieu of preface, the author addresses his readers by asking the question: 'What are the attractions of bee-keeping?' This he proceeds to answer as follows :- '1. It is an instructive pursuit. It brings its devotee face to face with some of the most remarkable phenomena of insect life, improves his powers of observation, and frequently incites him to a detailed study of that branch of natural science. 2. It is an agreeable recreation, and, its operations being conducted almost entirely in the open air, a healthful one. 3. It yields honey and wax. 4. When its principles are thoroughly understood, and its practice mastered, it is very profitable. To those who are thinking of making a commencement in bee-keeping, the motto may be recommended, 'Make haste slowly.' Begin with one or two colonies only, adding others gradually as experience increases, for it is only by practical work in the apiary, that lasting success can be attained.' The work is published at the price of one shilling, and presumably may be had of any book seller. The information contained in the work is of the most useful kind." (p.32)

Yet another review appeared in the *South Australian Advertiser*, 1 June 1887 "We have received from the author, Mr. Charles

Dickins, a copy of the *Australasian Beekeepers' Guide Book for Amateurs*, which professes to give plain and practical instruction on the profitable management of bees in movable comb hives. This little work, which is profusely illustrated, after giving a sketch of the natural history of the bee, deals briefly but clearly with their management, diseases, foods, feeding, and handling. The descriptions and illustrations of the various kinds of hives, with remarks on introducing, moving, transferring, swarming, uniting, wax extracting, the rearing of queen bees, and useful hints to beginners, make this little production one which cannot fail to be of use to the class for which it was especially written, and it will also no doubt be of value to those who have passed beyond the amateur stage." (p.5)

The following details about Dickins activities have been extracted from Bridget Jolly's *First flights in South Australia's systematic beekeeping and honey harvesting, First part.* [96] "Dickins, a certificated expert of the British Beekeeper's Association, arrived in Adelaide from London in 1887, and with his son operated a Steam Hive Factory as beekeeping appliance providers on the south side of Wakefield Street, city. An importer and manufacturer of mills for making wax comb foundation (a specialty that he also supplied), he offered accurate steam carpentry hive-making, honey and beeswax merchandising, and to import 'Foreign Bees' (Italian, Carniolan, and Cyprian, at 30/- each). Dickins also sold 'guaranteed pure Ligurian queens', as well as bee feeders and smokers. …

… Dickins operated a roller skate factory, [97] repaired roller skates, and sold a patent lubricant for skates and bicycles. [98] He

---

[96] Refer www.sahistorians.org.au/.../first-flights-in-south-australias-systematic- beekeeping-and-honey-harvesting-part-i-2.doc

[97] *Express*, 18 May 1888, p.2c.

[98] *Garden and Field*, vol. 15, June 1889, p.iii.

sold the 'Standard Langstroth Improved Simplicity Hive' (a modification designed by the American Amos Root) for 10/-. His premises included a showroom, a carpentry area (with mortising machines, planers, and steam saws run by an eight horse-power engine), a painting area, a blacksmithery, and a tin shop. [99] Dickins advertised his services mainly to fruit growers, claiming ability to establish apiaries 'in any part of the Colonies', and offered to estimate for the 'complete fitting up of Bee Farms up to 500 Stocks.'

At a SA Beekeepers' Association monthly meeting in 1887 Dickins presented his *Australasian bee keepers' guide book*, that cost 1/- and was hailed as the first manual for beekeepers published in South Australia. [100] (p.25)

Albert Gale

GALE, Albert (1834-1922). **Australian Bee Lore and Bee Culture**, 1912, pp.313, illus, UWSH, deluxe ed., royal blue, additional gilt detail on cover (author name, also William Brooks logo and name), spine title "Australian Bee Lore" in three lines, glossy frontispiece "Advance Australia"; secondary issue in varying cloth colours eg., red, green, light blue, no frontispiece (although still heads list of illustrations), spine title in full. William Brooks & Co., over 60 illus, 15.5x25cm, Illustrated by E. M. Grosse. 8 shillings & sixpence. "Print on Demand" copies available on internet, some with no illustrations; original copies rare, $70 to $215, depending on edition. Several copies found on the net early 2010, $210; another in early 2011 of the secondary issue $110. Subtitled: *Including the Influence of Bees on Crops and the Colour of*

---

[99] 'A Beehive Manufactory', *Advertiser*, 15 December 1887, p.6d.
[100] 'Beehive', *Garden and Field*, vol. 13, no. 146, July 1887, p.16c.

Flowers and its Influence on Bee Life. Articles reproduced from *The N.S.W. Agricultural Gazette*.

Author described within as: Late Bee Expert and Lecturer on Apiculture to N.S.W. Government. Gale had a strong association with Hawkesbury Agricultural College, pictures of which appear in this book. Some illustrations are of a wistful and humorous nature where use of a magnifying glass can sometimes reveal a surprise. Valuable historical detail, fascinating illustrations, the "Alice in Wonderland" of Australian bee books. It was this book that inspired me to commence researching the introduction of honey bees into Australasia. A special moment for me was its discovery in an antiquarian book shop in Paddington, Sydney, December 1994.

By the term "Late Bee Expert" I initially took to mean Gale had deceased before publication. However, via web site http://members.optusnet.com.au/aquaticlife/Mogurnda.htm in 2007 I find Albert Gale was a fish breeder in 1915. "Many of the fishes that we maintain and breed today were maintained and bred many years ago, often under aquarium conditions that today, we would consider very primitive. *Mogurnda adspersa* were bred as early as 1912 by Albert Gale of The Royal Zoological Society of New South Wales. ... The *Mogurnda* genus ... are found around the world in tropical and temperate waters. They are commonly known as gudgeons in Australia. ..." The bibliography lists "Gale, A. (1915). Aquarian Nature Studies and Economic Fish Farming. W. A. Gullick, Government Printer, 86pp."

from Gale, p.221, hive components. The engraver's sense of humour is revealed to the sharp-eyed.

From members.optushome.com.au/chelmon/Rainbowfish.htm "…Albert Gale in his book *Aquarian Nature Studies & Economic Fish Farming* [101] made known the hobby of keeping Australian freshwater fishes. This book covered many subjects on the captive maintenance and care of a number of species. A section of the book also explored the possibilities of commercially breeding Australian freshwater fishes for the aquarium hobby. … Albert Gale was a member of the Royal Zoological Society of New South Wales and regularly wrote articles about Australian freshwater fishes for *Aquatic Life*, an international monthly magazine devoted to the study, care and breeding of native, exotic, gold and domesticated fishes, other animals and plants in the home aquarium and terrarium. This magazine was edited by W. A. Poyser and published by Joseph E. Bausman in the USA during the early part of the last century." Web site www.aquatic-gardeners.org/jare.html states *Aquatic Life* was first published in (Sept.) 1915.

Chapters: Introduction of Bees, Introduction of the Italian Bee, Bees Position in the Animal Kingdom, Species & Varieties, Bees' Home, Bee-keeping, Queen bee, The drone, Mysteries of Drone Production, The Working Bee, Fertile Workers, Selection for Stock, Educating Bees, Why Do Bees Swarm?, Swarm Catching - Hiving & Transferring, Taking bush Swarms, Handling, Division of Swarms, Re Queening, Transferring, The Historical Bee-Hive - Its Evolution, Movable Bottom Boards for the Langstroth Simplicity Hive, Concrete Floors, Hawkesbury Agricultural College Apiary, Advance of Bee-Life Under Domestication, Appliances & How to Use Them, Characteristics Sites for an Apiary, Hive Arrangements, Evolution of the Bee-Hive, Bee-keeping in Bar-Frame Hives, Bee-Wintering, Notes on Honey, The Value of Beeswax, The Influence of bees on

---

[101] Two copies found on the net early 2010, 1st ed. 1915, 2nd ed. 1916, $55

Crops, Artificial Fertilisation, Colour of Flowers and its Influence on Bee-Life, Bee calendar.

Background centre left, Gale, p.221
Two box hive photographers in trouble

The illustration previous to Gale's portrait is titled "Langstroth's Hive and its Fittings" which appears on page 221 of Gale's 1912 *Australian Bee Culture*. On careful study you may detect the illustrator's sense of humour at work. Inspect it a while then check the background scene, centre left. Only hinted at to the observant eye is a comical episode being played out - see further on for a magnified image.

Book Review: The following review appeared in The *Sydney Morning Herald*, 6 December 1912. "It cannot be said that the production of first-class honey and beeswax as a commercial product has attained the dimensions that it ought to have done when the suitability of many parts of this State for tho bee-farming industry is taken into consideration. Besides the influence of bees in the fertilising of crops and the inter-pollination of fruit trees a few bee-hives are a valuable adjunct to the farm. It is not so long ago since it was prophesied that this State would become, in the Mosaic sense of the term, "a land flowing with milk and honey'." That prophecy does not appear to be drawing near to its fulfilment as far as the honey is concerned. As time goes on, and the woodman's axe is plied to the roots of the trees, it seems that the prophet did not look sufficiently far ahead, otherwise he would have pictured a land flowing with milk, but the honey flow would be spasmodic, or even cease where the ironbark and eucalypts have gone up in smoke to make way for the settler. This aspect of the case was vividly portrayed some years ago by Mr. Albert Gale, the well known bee expert and lecturer on apiculture.

A timely publication on "*Bee Lore and Bee Culture*," by Mr. Gale, comes to us from William Brooks and Co., Ltd., and it may be at once said that it is one of the most interesting and comprehensive volumes on apiculture which have yet been issued. Mr. Gale has collected and revised some of his published articles, chiefly those that have appeared from time to time in the *Agricultural Gazette*. One of his reasons for so doing is to make known the history of the introduction into this State of so valuable an insect as the honey bee. A large part of the work was uttered from public platforms, and it is only fair to say that what was then voiced was obtained by research and lifelong observation; "not as wisdom learned, but as knowledge gained from the book of nature." The work is very comprehensive in its character. The author discourses in an entertaining way on the etiology [102] of beekeeping in all its varied aspects, and settles some apparently disputed points in regard to the introduction of bees into Australia.

The ancient writings, sacred and profane, are frequently interspersed with references to bees and their habits. In the earliest Jewish sacred writings both bees and honey are often referred to. Honey is first mentioned when Joseph was in Egypt. Aristotle and other ancient philosophers did not deem the subject of too trivial a nature for investigation. Virgil and the early historians and scientists patiently pursued the same track with a zeal worthy of the men and their times. It was not, however, until tho close of the seventeenth century that any practical means and appliances were constructed for looking into and observing the bees actually engaged in their domestic duties.

Bee farmers will be well repaid by careful study of *Bee Lore and Bee Culture*. Some of the more important chapters may be indicated. They include an interesting outline of the bee's position in the animal kingdom, the introduction of the Italian bee, the various species and varieties, beekeeping methods, the drone, which is often maligned and looked upon as an interloper rather than a factor practically equal in importance to the queen bee; the working bee, the selection for stock, why bees swarm, handling, swarm catching, hiving and transferring, taking bush swarms, requeening, appliances, and how to use them, and the

---

[102] The study or causes or origins

characteristic sites for an apiary. The influence of bees on crops is also treated, and in all these chapters there is an inexhaustible fund of information and practical advice for the bee farmer. A knowledge of the queen bee is the axis around which revolves successful beekeeping, and its failure is generally more or less caused by a want of that knowledge. A knowledge of a queen bee is not the survival of the fittest, as Mr. Gale intuitively remarks, but the selection of the fittest. As in the selection and rearing of the best breeds of livestock, the necessity for eliminating the worthless and raising the type is necessary to success. "Swarm from your best colonies" is a golden rule. "Breed your queens from the same is still more golden," says Mr. Gale. "The queen of every swarm that is thrown off from a colony whose work is centred in self should be at once destroyed, and one that is a direct descendant from your best colonies introduced. If this substitution he impracticable, unite the workers with some others, the weakest you have, which has a queen from a pet colony. In no way be a party to perpetuate a physical or industrial deformity." In these words the author indicates the surest method of obtaining a pure hive. "Go in for queen-rearing," he adds, "or purchase from a dealer of good repute for healthy bees, for all useless and degenerating queens should be superseded. Remember, like produces like, and good, healthy queens produced good healthy progeny." " (p.6)

In found the following interesting item in the *Sydney Mail*, 3 December 1892: "Mr. Albert Gale, technical lecturer, Department of Public Instruction, brought to us this week for inspection an excellent sample of honey, which is of a bright ruby colour, and as clear and attractive in glass as ordinary port wine. This was taken from hives at Mr. Gale's residence, Stanmore, and was extracted in the presence of Mr. Allport, a well-known apiarian. Mr. Gale informs us that throughout all his experience with bees he has never seen a similar colour in honey. Some of our readers may have had a similar surprise; if so, we shall be glad to publish their views on the subject." (p.4) I recall an article about a beekeeper who harvested red honey – the bees were subsequently observed stealing syrup from a cordial factory.

In the early 1990s I came across an abandoned apiary at Bilpin, west of Richmond, NSW. One hive survived despite its harsh situation. The bees were fierce – they needed to be to fight off the termites that threatened their home; and to thrive regardless of their damp and overly shaded location, compounded by their abandonment by an absentee beekeeper. Acres of aged apple trees surrounded the long forgotten apiary. The honey tasted as good as it looked, delivering a rich apple flavour. Most surprisingly it was of a consistent green colour – the same rich hue as the skin of Granny Smith apples.

The *American Bee Journal*, 21 Sept. 1893, carried an article on the office bearers of the NSW Bee-Keepers' Union. "Mr. Albert Gale, Vice-President, is another old bee-keeper, having kept bees in the old straw-skep in Monmouthshire, in 1858. About 25 years ago he kept bees on the Clarence River in gin-cases and boxes ... he moved to the Monaro district some 18 years ago, taking his bees with him, and eight years later he located at Gordon, near Sydney, where he kept some 18 colonies in Berlepsch hives ... appointed apicultural lecturer by the Government in 1889."

An obituary for Gale appeared in *The Sydney Morning Herald*, 28 March 1922, following his death on 9 March at his Stanmore residence: [103] "The death occurred recently of Mr Albert Gale, of *Tredegar*, Sebastopol-street, Stanmore, at the age of 87. Educated for the teaching profession, Mr. Gale for many years a Public school teacher. Twenty-eight years ago he was transferred to the Department of Agriculture, and up to his

---

[103] *The Sydney Morning Herald*, 10 March 1922, p.8

retirement about eight years ago acted as a lecturer on natural history. Mr. Gale was a keen student of natural history, and contributed many papers on the subject to the scientific journals and the *Agricultural Gazette*. He has written books on bees and fish life, and corresponded with some of the foremost naturalists of England and the United States. Mr. Gale is survived by Mrs. Gale and three sons and two daughters." (p.11)

Albert Gale, as pictured in the *American Bee Journal*, 21 Sept. 1893

GURR, Caleb George (1856-1929) **Beekeeping and honey production in South Australia**, 1909, Adelaide, pp.12, SLSA (catlg. 638.14 Mortlock Pamphlets) An item of mention in the South Australian Parliament appeared in The Adelaide *Advertiser*, 27 August 1909: "OMISSION OF IMPRINT. Mr. JACKSON asked whether the Government will prosecute the printer of the brochure on "*Beekeeping and Honey Production in South Australia*," by C. G. Gurr, Inspector of Apiaries, owing to absence of name of printer." (p.9) From slsa.sa.gov.au/manning/pn/u/unley.htm "Biographical details of C.G. Gurr are in the *Register*, 20 December 1899, page 7c." NLA has digitized this newspaper only for the years 1839-1846 as at Sept 2010, so I haven't as yet been able to view it. Another obituary (SLSA catalogue) appeared in the *Chronicle*, 10 October 1929 (p. 21, col. a) It's possible there's an image of him in the *Pictorial Australian*, September 1892 (p. 141).

Gurr commenced beekeeping in October 1885. The catalogue of the State Library of South Australia states he was an auctioneer, and the Mayor of Unley in 1892 and 1900. He purchased his first hive from Mr. F. A. Joyner, a member of the South Australian Beekeepers' Association and a beekeeper, at that time, with three years experience. As part of his paper "My Experiences in Beekeeping" read before the Association, Joyner wrote of having sold a hive to Mr. Gurr, of Fullarton, in October 1885.

Caleb Gurr was an auditor, later councilor, then mayor (1891-1892 and 1899-1900) of the City of Unley (Courtesy of the Unley Museum). [104]

---

[104] Details and photo sourced by Bridget Jolly

From the *South Australian Advertiser*, Friday 7 May 1886 "… yesterday I received the following memo, from him [Gurr] concern them; — "The hybrid bees I bought from you in October last have not been idle. I have taken from them 171 1-lb. sections fully completed, five frames of honeycomb weighing at least 6 lb. each, and they now have 10 frames full and 28 sections in various stages. This swarm has therefore during seven months gathered and stored about 270 lb. of comb honey. I have fully decided to my own satisfaction that black bees are nowhere alongside of Ligurians or first-cross hybrids. Soon after finding out the value of Italian bees I got two gentlemen to join me in sending for queens from Italy.

The steamer *John Elder* [105]

---

[105] *John Elder* - 3,832 gross tons, length 382ft x beam 41.7ft, one funnel, three masts, clipper bows, iron hull, single screw, speed 12.5 knots, accommodation for 70-1st, 100-2nd and 273-3rd class passengers. Crew of 104. Launched on 29th Aug. 1869 by John Elder & Co., Glasgow and named for her builder, she was owned by Pacific Steam Navigation Co. In 1877, her third mast was removed and she was placed on the joint PSNCo. - Orient Line Australian service and

We sent for twelve, and were advised that they were shipped by the *John Elder*. That wretched steamship, not content with being delayed behind a sunken barge in the Suez Canal for nearly two weeks, must needs add to our misfortune by breaking her machinery, and having to put up at Port Said for repairs. When news of these disaster reached me my ardor sank to freezing point, and my expectations as to the buzzing capacities those bees would exhibit when landed here were very meagre - extremely meagre. However, the *John Elder* arrived one boisterous Saturday night, and, thanks to Mr. Dollman, I had no difficulty in getting the bees off. I got safely home with them at 10 o'clock at night, and began opening them. In all but five boxes every bee was dead and dry; in one of the five I picked out the queen apparently dead, but while examining her found signs of life, and handed her to my mother to carefully warmed, fed, &c; in another box the queen alone lived, and in the three others the bees were fairly well. Of these five queens three only prospered. I lost one by carelessness in introducing, one died whilst caged, and the remaining three were safely introduced.

Just after getting these queens I discovered foul brood in one of my hives, which I burnt, bees, comb, and all; but finding several others affected I made a clean sweep of the thing and seized this opportunity to change all my old hives for those of the Langstroth size. I destroyed every comb and frame I possessed, putting the bees into clean hives with frames of clean foundation, and feeding them with syrup containing salicylic acid according to Mr. Muth's method. I am thankful to say I have not seen a sign of foul brood since, and I need hardly add I

---

started her first voyage from Adelaide via Suez to Liverpool on 19th April. On 27th Jan. 1879 she started her first London - Melbourne - Sydney voyage and commenced her last on this route on 27th May 1886 before reverting to the Liverpool - Valparaiso service.

do not want to. Notwithstanding this serious drawback my bees have done well this season.

I cannot give you any actual results from the whole of my hives, as I have been continually reducing their number by sale. From four of them I have had about a quarter of a ton of comb and extracted honey. Latterly I have turned my attention to queen rearing, and it has been to me a source of constant pleasure and interest. I use Mr. Alley's method, as advocated by Mr. Bonney, and I have been fairly successful. My apiary, if I may be allowed so to term my collection of hives, is now reduced to three Langstroth hives, two Alley's queen rearing hives, and nine queen fertilising hives, and I have no black bees. I have sent to Mr. Benton, of Germany, for a specially selected Italian queen, and I trust she will arrive safely. I hope at some future time to give you next season's report in a concise and reliable form." (p.7)

Gurr was still a member of the SA Beekeepers' Association in 1906. [106] See also Jolly, Bridget. *First flights in South Australia's systematic beekeeping and honey harvesting, Second part.* pp.4-7. Copy available on the web.

HAWKINS, H.J. & HAY, David. (1865) **Handy-Book on the Honey-Bee. How to manage the Honey Bee in New Zealand**, *Compiled by an Old Beekeeper.* revised by H. J. Hawkins, Belvidere Fruit Nursery, and. David Hay, Montpellier Nursery. price 2s. 6d. pp.67, 19 cm. The revised edition has 88 pages. Though not an Australian work it deserves entry here as it may well have been used by Australian beekeepers. Held by NLNZ and three other NZ libraries. At head of title: Chapman's handy-book on the honey bee. The *Turnbull Library Record*, Issue 9 (p.8), states "In 1868 Chapman, the enterprising Auckland publisher, issued a little book - *How to Manage the Honey Bee*

---

[106] The Adelaide *Advertiser*, 8 December 1906, p.12

in New Zealand, and in 1881 Isaac Hopkins published at Thames his *New Zealand Bee Manual*. ..." An advertisement for the book found in the *Daily Southern Cross*, 29 October 1867 (p.1) At web site localhistoryonline.shorelibraries.govt.nz I found: "An 1868 (?) copy of this book is held at Auckland City Library. Henry Hawkins learned beekeeping methods from Maori. Refer - *The Story of Birkenhead* . Margaret McClure, 1987, p. 28." Univ. Otago Library gives its publication year as 1867.

I found this book description in *Trubner's American and Oriental Literary Record* (1865), also in the 15 May 1869 issue, p.461: "... by H.J. Hawkins, Belvidere Fruit Nursery, and David Hay, Montpellier Nursery. This little work contains the information required in keeping and managing the Honey Bee, how to get plenty of pure white honey all the year round without destroying the bees, the easiest methods peculiarly suited to the climate are given, how to manage the Honey Bee, how to make and manage the different hives, bell-glasses, swarming and hiving; how to convey Bees to a distance, uniting stocks, taking honey, and the profits of bee-keeping, and a Sermon on Bees by Dr. Cumming [note: *The Times* Bee Master]; extracts are given from Mr. Cotton's letters, and also from some of the recently published English and Continental works."

A description of Hawkins book first appeared in *New Zealand Publications, a descriptive list of works recently published by Geo. T. Chapman, Bookseller, Auckland*. The description therein was copied almost word for word into Trubner's work. Two newspaper comments were provided: "The experience of such a man as a practical bee-keeper in New Zealand is highly valuable to the colonists." - *New Zealand Herald*. "It is certainly very strange that bee-keeping in New Zealand should be easy to manage, and so profitable, and that honey is so scarce and expensive. ... This little work is just what is required to enable every country settler to make a very large annual profit out of bee-keeping." - *Daily Southern Cross*

HOCKINGS, Harold J. (1883) ***Notes on two Australian species of Trigona***. read August 1st 1883. pp. 149-157, 21 cm. Extracted from an unidentified publication. Notes on two Australian species of Trigona read by Harold J. Hockings. Though not a work on the European honey bee, I thought it worthwhile to include this work because of it displays 19th century interest in Australia's native bees. Written up in an issue of *Aussie Bee*, Issue 2, May 1997. NLA Call number NP 595.7990994 H685

Obituary. "Mr. Harold J. Hockings, aged 82, formerly well known in business circles in Brisbane, where he was a commercial broker for many years, died yesterday at Thursday Island. [He] was ... born in Ipswich [and] educated in Brisbane, in which he spent most of his life. He was a keen naturalist and geologist, and made a special study of native bees, specimens of which he forwarded to many scientific bodies in England and America. For a year he had been living at Thursday Island with his sons Messrs. N. F. and J. Hockings, wM are interested in the pearling industry." (*The Courier-Mail*, 21 January 1939, p.8)

Isaac Hopkins

Isaac Hopkins, as pictured in 1904

HOPKINS, Isaac. (1881) ***The Illustrated New Zealand Bee Manual***, *giving full instructions for the humane and profitable management of the honey bee* .... 1st ed. Thames Goldfield Advertiser Office. pp.vii, 147, ill.; 19 cm. 1st ed. of 1000 copies sold out within 13 months. Holdings: (1) SLNSW, (2) NLNZ, (3) Lincoln Univ., Hopkins books undoubtedly found a market in Australia. Paper cover edition cost 2 shillings, cloth 3 shillings.

This review appeared in the *Otago Witness*, 29 October 1881: A Colonial Manual. "*The Illustrated New Zealand Bee Manual*," published by I. Hopkins, of the Thames, Auckland provincial district, contains a great deal of interesting matter for beekeepers generally, and can be recommended accordingly. Although disagreeing with the writer on some minor points, in the main he confines himself to the most modern methods in bee-keeping, and on the whole there is very little to cavil [107] at in the book. Mr Hopkins acknowledges his indebtedness for a great deal of information to various well-known eminent apiarians, and the plates especially remind one of an old acquaintance, "*The A B C of Bee Culture*," by A. I. Root, of Medina, Ohio, America. This latter alone is a recommendation of the book. The price of the volume (2s) should bring it within reach of everyone who may be interested in bee-keeping; and although the information is given in a rather concise form, it is couched in language plain enough to be readily understood by all who feel inclined to follow the writer's instructions. An alphabetically arranged index would certainly have added to the usefulness of the book."

Seeded by the supply of a copy of Hopkins' book another favourable review appeared in the *Waikato Times*, 6 October 1881. "… Dealing with the subject by the light of practical experience in this colony, the Annual deserves to find its way into the hands of every bee master in New Zealand, to whom its lessons must of necessity be more valuable than those imparted by books written thousands of miles away in places with conditions bearing little or no relation to those of this country. The author in his preface states that he has been induced to publish the book at the request of a number of apiarists who had read his letters on the subject to the local papers. …" (p.2)

---

[107] From wordnetweb.princeton.edu/perl/webwn
"to raise trivial objections"

NOW READY,

To be had of all Booksellers,

THE

NEW ZEALAND BEE MANUAL.

PROFUSELY ILLUSTRATED,

CONTAINING full Instructions for the Humane and Profitable management of the Honey Bee, being a Complete

HANDBOOK TO MODERN BEE CULTURE

BY I. HOPKINS.

PRICE—2s., CLOTH, 3s.

New Price Lists of all Apiarian Supplies may be had on application to the author, the Apiary, Parawai Thames, N.Z. 2810

Thames Star, 21 November 1881, (p.1, col. 6)

The *North Otago Times*, 14 October 1881, reported positively: "This manual, by Mr I. Hopkins, a successful apiarist at the Thames, in the North Island, containing exhaustive instructions for the not only profitable but also humane management of honey bees, is written principally for New Zealand bee-keepers, but its directions are equally applicable to bee culture in Australia. ..." (p.2)

The *Southland Times*, 8 November 1881, "Bee Culture. — We have received what seems to bean admirable little book on beekeeping, styled the *New Zealand Bee Manual*. It is written by Mr I. Hopkins, and bears to have been published, this year, at the Advertiser office, Thames Goldfield. The glance we have given over its contents, and over the woodcuts with which it is largely illustrated, has left the impression that every branch of the subject has been minutely and ably dealt with. The style is pleasant, and evinces the enthusiasm proper to so very engaging a study. We intend to make a closer acquaintance with the contents, and in the meantime recommend the book to all who desire to make bee-keeping an occupation, whether for pleasure or profit. The price is only two shillings." (p.2)

Another copy left at the *Thames Star*, 1 October 1881, solicited the following "Mr I. Hopkins, the author of the "New Zealand Bee Manual," has left a copy of the publication at our office. It is a very neatly got up volume of 149 pages, profusely illustrated, and replete with all the information necessary for bee-keeping. Mr Hopkins says he endeavored to make the work as interesting, plain, and practical as possible, and we believe it will prove a complete guide to modern bee-culture. As Mr Hopkins has made this subject a special study for a number of years, persons interested in the subject cannot do better than accept the advice given by him, and at once purchase a copy of the new publication." (p.2)

In the *Poverty Bay Herald*, 10 October 1881 "We have received from the Thames Advertiser office a copy of a very neat and useful publication entitled "*The Illustrated New Zealand Bee Manual*." The work in question is compiled by Mr. I. Hopkins, who has for the past eight years paid particular attention to the humane and profitable management of bees, and who has for the last three years devoted himself to this business. It is a complete book of reference to the apiarist, embracing as it does all branches of the subject taken in hand. Besides a vast amount of practical information — such as recipes, calendar of operations, &c, there are several pages of very pleasant and interesting reading. We would recommend those of our country settlers and suburban residents who have interested themselves in this industry, to obtain a copy of the work. It is published at the very moderate charge of two shillings. The volume comprises 147 pages in a compact form, and is interspersed with many woodcut designs. It is an extremely creditable production of the compiler, and publisher." (p.2) I located other mentions and reviews in the *Grey River Argus*, 13 October 1881 and the *Bruce Herald*, 11 October 1881. There may well have been more.

The *Queenslander*, 9 September 1882, reported to a reader's query: "There is no colonial work on bee culture to be had. [108] Arrangements are making for a supply of *Root's A B C of Bee Culture* from America, one of the best modern works extant; and there is a bee manual published in New Zealand by Mr. Hopkins, which, posted, would cost about 2s. 6d. This latter is largely compiled from the above work - *Root's ABC*. This can be obtained through any colonial bookseller." (p.338)

In the *Queenslander*, 26 November 1881: "*The New Zealand Bee Manual* is the title of a publication forwarded to us. It is illustrated profusely with woodouts, and is without doubt the most complete manual upon the interesting subject of bee-keeping yet issued from the Australasian press. Its moderate price (2s.) should ensure for it an extensire sale. It is published at the Advertiser office, Thames goldfield, N.Z. Although nominally written for New Zealand, the information it contains is equally useful to the apiarist in Australia, and it is up to date as far as modern discoveries go."

HOPKINS, Isaac. (1882) 2nd. ed. **The Illustrated New Zealand Bee Manual**: *Giving Full Instructions For The Humane And Profitable Management Of The Honey Bee*; also bee-keepers'

---

[108] There was a book, relatively unknown it would seem. This was the *Handy-Book on the Honey-Bee. How to manage the Honey Bee in New Zealand*. Refer main entry under Hawkins.

axioms, honey recipes, and bee-keepers' calendar of operations, making a complete handbook to modern bee-culture. 2nd ed. of 1000 copies, Oct. 1882. Champtaloup and Cooper, Auckland. pp.148. The *Queenslander*, 8 December 1883, described Hopkins' book "an excellent work." Copies: (1) NLNZ, (2) Lincoln Univ. , NZ; (3) Otago Univ., (4) Charles C. Miller Memorial Apicultural Library, Univ. of Wisconsin – Madison, has a copy described as "vii, 148 p., xvi, [1] folded leaf of plates : ill. ; 19 cm.".

Books, Stationery, &c.

BEES. BEES. BEES.

The New Zealand Bee Manual, a complete Guide to Colonial Bee Culture. This is the most reliable book published, and has already met with a large sale on account of its suitability to the colony. Price, posted, 2s. 10d.

E. S. WIGG & SON, Rundle-street.

A.B.C. OF BEE CULTURE. — This is the most elaborate work published in America on Bee Culture, and goes thoroughly into detail, and is full of good illustrations. Price, posted, 8s. 3d.

E. S. WIGG & SON, Rundle-street.

QUINBY'S NEW BEE-KEEPING. — A Complete Guide to successful Bee Culture with 100 illustrations. Price, posted, 8s. 3d.

E. S. WIGG & SON, Rundle-street.

Advertisement, *South Australian Advertiser*, 4 February 1885

Given the 3 known copies of the 1st edition and 5 known copies of this 2nd, that makes 8 known surviving copies out of a combines print run of 2,000. Even together, definitely scarce. Copy located in the retail used book market in 2010 for $315.

This is the first time I've ever seen such a copy for sale in 15 years be it the 1st edition or its reprint aka the 2nd edition. Its poor condition is not surprising given its rarity, antiquarian age and likely heavy use in the field by long departed beekeepers. Described as follows by bookseller: "POOR (in wrappers, lacks rear cover, front cover barely attached, rubbed and soiled, chipping and wear to extrems .w[ith]. some losses, newspaper cutting to inside of front cover, author's advert. tipped-in to tiel [?] page, inscr. to head of title page, prelims. and content edges sl. foxed) scarce early apiarist title - Bagnall 2664" The 1882 edition has not yet been discovered by Google Books world wide digitization program.

The Hathi Trust Digital Library has a digitized copy – the original came from the Univ. of Wisconsin. Text searches are permitted but text is not returned, just the number of occurrences and page numbers are provided "to help you decide if the book is worth buying, checking out from a library, or when working with a book that does not have an index." It is "Full View Available - Public domain only when viewed in the US." Another copy located at NZ's Lincoln Library. No other known library holdings but another original copy might exist out there as modern paperback reprints are to be found on the web, eg., by Kessinger. Their internet blurb states "The publisher of this book utilises modern printing technologies as well as photocopying processes for reprinting and preserving rare works of literature that are out-of-print or on the verge of becoming lost. This book is one such reprint.

This scarce antiquarian book is a selection from Kessinger Publishings Legacy Reprint Series. Due to its age, it may contain imperfections such as marks, notations, marginalia and flawed pages. Because we believe this work is culturally important, we have made it available as part of our commitment to protecting, preserving, and promoting the worlds literature. Kessinger Publishing is the place to find hundreds of thousands of rare and hard-to-find books with something of interest for everyone!" When trying to find old original books on the web eg., by such as bookfinder.com, the few that are to be found are often swamped by a plethora of modern reprinted offerings. Some reprints carry caveats such as "There may be numerous typos or missing text. There are no illustrations or indexes" or "Usually dispatched within 1 to 3 weeks," suggesting an ordered is printed on demand. Another qualification I've found states "This book may have imperfections such as missing or blurred pages, poor pictures, errant marks, etc. that were either part of the original artifact, or were introduced by the scanning process." As a book lover, such a facsimile edition is not for me.

Identification of the original owner of this 1882 Hopkins is tenuous, the result of speculation on my part, however there's a small chance I may be correct. I located via the internet at Hard to Find Books of Pokeno, New Zealand in mid September 2000. Bookseller Warwick advised on the background to its acquisition: "No special story, though it came from the collection of the late historian Alison Drummond, [this fact, attested to by the Ex Libris bookplate] who was the great niece of Elsdon Best and other famous NZ pioneers such as Thomas Wayth Gudgeon, so it may have belonged to one of them." Born in 1841, W.E. Gudgeon, son of T.W. Gudgeon, would have been aged 41 on publication of Hopkins' book. My assumption is that it may have passed to Alison upon the death of one of her relatives. Alison died in 1984 so the book's whereabouts since then are a mystery. She was married in 1935 and had two sons, so it's possible the book may have come from one of their estates. Tenuous, again, but such is the grist of a literary detective.

W. E. Gudgeon

Alison appears to have been a lover of old and rare books. She had her own Ex Libris bookplate, and on the web I've found illusive references to her personal library. In early September 2010 one book from her library went to auction, an 1852 copy of Daniel Defoe's *The Life and Adventures of Robinson Crusoe*, a Maori language edition. So, another possibility is that Alison collected Hopkins' book in appreciation of its rarity.

Drummond's entry in the *Dictionary of New Zealand Biography*, [109] describes her as "farmer, writer, historian, editor." Should bibliophile have been added to those tags? On her retirement in 1967 she "retired to Kawakawa Bay, Auckland. … Alison became involved in the local community, helping to start a library and a Red Cross association, and continued with her literary work." Another extract from the *DNZB* "Alison Drummond was an amiable, affectionate woman with a sense of fun and a large number of friends. She was well organised and kept herself to a strict regimen when writing, but

---

[109] Irving, Esther. 'Drummond, Alison Edith Hilda 1903 - 1984'. *Dictionary of New Zealand Biography*

allowed herself many hobbies and interests. She was an exquisite needlewoman and collected antique work boxes, and was an avid gardener and rosarian, specialising in rare roses."

Whatever the book's ancestry I'm pleased it has passed into my hands. I'll enjoy it and at some future time I hope another bee book collector will value its rarity.

HOPKINS, Isaac. (1883) *Scientific Bee Culture*, in Brett's Colonists' Cyclopaedia, 1883, pp.229-240. The PDF file may be downloaded at culturaapicola.com.ar/apuntes/historia/180_Hopkins.pdf

HOPKINS, Isaac. (1886) *The Australasian Bee Manual*. 3rd ed. Subtitled: with which is incorporated the New Zealand bee manual greatly enlarged, revised and mostly re-written by the author assisted by T.J. Mulvany. Published in Auckland, also in Sydney by M'Neil & Coffee. pp.335. 143 illus., 21 chapters. Held by: ML, NLA, SLV, Univ. Sydney, NLNZ + 7 other NZ libraries, Univ. of Wisconsin. The only edition listed in Ferguson. Though this is a New Zealand book, it was surely used extensively in Australia. My Hopkins copy marked 'Fourth Thousand'. I recently come across a second copy in the retail used market in my 15 years of bee book collecting – it being of the same print run.

The Rev. G.F.M. Fielding's delivery of a lecture on bees and bee culture on 25 January 1887 was reported in the Hobart *Mercury*, 26 January 1887. (p.2) Had Fielding delivered his lecture 100 years later his mastery over the topic would not have been missed. As textbooks on the subject Fielding "alluded to ... *The Illustrated Australasian Bee Manual* and *The A.B.C. of Bee Culture*.

Reviews: The *Queenslander*, 24 July 1886, described Hopkins bee manual as "that capital book of his". The *Queenslander*, 12 January 1889 (p.58) stated it "is the best work on beekeeping as conducted in these colonies." A longer review appeared in the Hobart *Mercury*, 8 July 1886 (p.2) "Bees. - Mr. T. L. Hood, himself au authentic and successful apiarist, announces that he has on sale *The Australasian Bee Manual*, a complete guide to bee culture in the Southern Hemisphere, written by Mr. Isaac Hopkins, of Matamata, N.Z. The work has reached its third edition of 4,000, and in its present form, well printed, well compiled, and profusely illustrated, it presents one of the most useful technical guides to rational bee-keeping yet published. The author, in giving an epitome of present knowledge upon all apicultural names, scientific and theoretical, has availed himself of the able co-operation of several leading bee-keepers in New Zealand, Sydney, Queensland, Victoria, Adelaide, and Hobart, and has also made free use of all the standard works and technical journals already published in Ireland, America, and Germany, and, like [a] bee soaring from flower to flower, he has culled many golden morsels of sterling value. He appears also to have spared no trouble or expense in procuring illustrations necessary for the completeness of the work, and the result of his labours is a compact and most reliable volume of instruction."

Another glowing review appeared in "The Honey Bee" column of the *Queenslander*, 20 March 1886: "*The Illustrated Australasian Bee Manual*, by Isaac Hopkins, Matamata Apiary, Auckland, N.Z., and published by him, is certainly the most complete guide to modern bee-culture yet published in the Southern Hemisphere. It is octavo size, with 143 illustrations, and consists of 336 pages. It is the outgrowth of that useful little book called *The New Zealand Bee Manual*, published in 1881. This having passed through two editions, and the demand still continuing, the author determined upon issuing instead a complete guide. A careful perusal of it shows that it is what it professes to be. It is equally applicable to bee-culture in any of the Australian colonies as in New Zealand, and no bee-keeper, whether amateur or professional, can afford to be with out it.

The chapter on the history of the honey bee, and of its introduction into the Australasian colonies, is interesting even to the general reader; the lover of natural history, if not already acquainted with the subject, will be delighted with the chapter descriptive of the queen bee, her marvelous reproductive powers from only one impregnation, the parthenogenesis of the drones, the power the queen possesses of controlling the sex of the egg as laid, and the power the worker-bees have of producing a queen from the egg of what ordinarily would become only a worker-bee.

The construction of hives and all mechanical appliances is fully treated of, and all measurements and details are given so plainly that they can be easily followed. Bar-frames, section boxes, comb foundation, smokers, reversible frames, honey extractors, and the arrangements of the extracting house are not only plainly described but also fully illustrated. Natural and artificial swarming are explained, and the best manner of working is taught. The chapter on queen-rearing is particularly instructive, and likely to be useful to all apiarists who would keep in the front rank.

The latest investigations of that distinguished English scientist, Mr. Frank Cheshire, in the treatment of that dreaded disease of the apiary commonly called foul brood, but which now is known as bacillus alvei, are given with microscopical illustrations of the bacillus in all its stages of development. For the information given in this chapter alone the book should be possessed by every bee-keeper, because this disease is so fearfully contagions that it means the entire destruction of the apiary in which it may appear unless checked immediately it is discovered. There is much useful information in the book other than what we have hinted at, and we are pleased to see such a practical work issuing from the Australasian Press. From time to time we shall give useful extracts from it ie our columns." (p. 472)

Gleanings in Bee Culture for May 1886 carried a review of the misnamed *Australian Bee Manual* "We are just in receipt of a new book on bees, bearing the above caption, by Isaac Hopkins, Matamata, Auckland, New Zealand. It is a large work, of 330 pages, and illustrated with 143 engravings. The author seems to take up very thoroughly the scientific and physiological structure of the bee, at the same time setting forth a full elucidation of the practical management and care of an apiary. We presume it is written for and adapted to the climate of Australia, and we are glad to note that the friends of that far-off land have made such progress. We have not had time to examine into the soundness of the author's views on the various subjects, but may give a more extended review of the same soon." (p.372)

The following article presents an 1888 view on the role of women in the home. In the *Sydney Morning Herald*, 24 November 1888 (p.9), in the WOMAN'S COLUMN. BEE-KEEPING. A SIMPLE WOMAN'S INDUSTRY, an article inspired by Hopkins' *"Australian Bee Manual"*. 'Pleasant words are as an honeycomb, sweet to the soul and health to the bones.' - Prov. xvi., 24. "In my mind's eye I see homes where responsibilities are increasing quite out of proportion to decreasing fortune. The brave breadwinner grows daily more bowed and despondent; he reflects when too late upon the questionable wisdom of many acts, self-dissatisfaction breeds irritability that vents itself unreasonably on the noisy boys and girls whose appetites are surely phenomenal and as to their clothes, why no children ever wore out boots and hats as quickly, no others ever wanted so many things! The mother believes she is conscientiously fulfilling her duty by making a domestic drudge of herself that the severest economy may be practised, yet with all her good intentions ends do not meet. She looks about for means to help her husband by bringing to the mill grist of a substantial sort, and adds to her already overburdened shoulders the strain of morning pupils or boarders.

She is totally unfitted for the worry and additional work, and in the end is obliged to acknowledge that it was a mistake to undertake so much.

Poor thing, her mistake is a very natural one. The well-intentioned self-effacement that forgot in the accumulation of petty matters that each human atom holds within its grasp great possibilities for good, overlooked in its zeal the fact that we are not placed here to be miserable, but to add our mite to the sum of the general happiness by the balance of demand and concession. So long as men must work, women must weep, I suppose. Nothing will change our natures to the extent of drying up the fountains of salt tears; but it is quite possible to turn winter storms to April showers by means of light remunerative occupations that do not tax the attention too much, and yet afford a healthy outlet for otherwise brooding thought.

One such occupation is bee-keeping. Not bee-keeping in the colonial acceptation of the term, when a few tea chests or gin-cases are smeared with syrup, provided with a roost, and become the unhealthy shelter of a swarm of unwary bees, doomed to live or die without further thought of their welfare on the part of their captors, who consider that they do more than their duty by making the process of robbing as merciless as possible; that is, as they know how, by the use of sulphur fumes. I mean the proper cultivation of bees for the sake of their honey, conducted with a certain amount of knowledge and intelligence.
…

Bee farming, per se, is not to be recommended to a man as a means of livelihood unless he is disabled from more active or lucrative pursuits, for it can scarcely be regarded as a profitable investment for large capital, or as a large employer of labour; but as a fair field, and certainly as a fairly remunerative one for the industry, skill, and perseverance laid out upon it. The labour and capital required to start it are small, but the skill, tact, patience, and perseverance necessary to the acquirement of a successful apiary are considerable. For these reasons it is an industry peculiarly adapted to women, and is being largely | adopted by them in parts of the world suitable for it.

Hopkins, in his pleasantly practical *Australian Bee Manual*, tells us that in both England and America at the present time some of the most successful apiarists are ladies, and several of the most extensive beekeepers in America are assisted by their wives and daughters. Professor Cook, who states that Mrs. L. R. Baker, of Landsing, Michigan, who has kept bees very successfully for four years, read an admirable paper before the Michigan convention of beekeepers, in which she said: 'But I can say, having tried both (referring to boardinghouse-keeping) I give beekeeping the preference as more profitable, healthful, independent, and enjoyable, I find the labours of the apiary more endurable than working over a stove, and more pleasant and conducive to health. I believe that many of our delicate and invalid ladies would find renewed vigor in body and mind in the labours and recreation of the apiary. My own experience of the apiary is that it is a source of interest and enjoyment far exceeding my anticipations.'

This is strong and encouraging testimony, but it is not all; there are many instances of people of both sexes who have regained health and strength under the pleasantly stimulative effect of this employment. One notable instance in this respect may be quoted in the person of Mrs. L. Harrison, of Illinois, now one of the most successful lady apiarists and writers on bee matters known. This lady was at one time told by her physician that she could not live; but, as she states herself, 'apiculture did for her what the physicians could not do - restored her to health, and gave her such vigour that she has been able to work a large apiary for years.' What English and American women can do on one side

[of] the world the Australian women can certainly do on the other. ...

Undoubtedly one of the strongest causes of domestic jars and foolish marriages is the lack of some fixed interest to occupy the idle thoughts of many women. It is against nature that they should be content to be employed in petty domestic concerns that need only mechanical attention and provide no food for thought. Occupations that carry them into a different atmosphere, both mentally and physically, will do much to silence the futile questions of the day – 'Is life worth living?' 'Is marriage a failure ?' Let each woman find a healthy outlet for her energies in some such pleasant hobby - as this, and we shall hear of fewer tragedies in domestic life. This special industry may seem too simple a matter to influence such important results, but, remember, it was the mouse that released the lion. It is trifles that make the sum of life."

HOPKINS, Isaac. (1904) 4th ed. *The Illustrated Australasian Bee Manual:* And Complete Guide to Modern Bee Culture in the Southern Hemisphere. Gordon and Gotch. pp.162, 78 illus. 18 chapters. Holdings: Hocken Collection, Univ. Otago; Univ. Sydney. Contains updated information on the introduction of bees into Australia and New Zealand. In the mid 1990s I came across a battered 4th edition copy owned by a very aged beekeeper at Springwood in the Blue Mountains, New South Wales. I still have it.

HOPKINS, Isaac. (1905). *Bee-culture*. I. II. III. IV. V. The use of comb-foundation. Ripening extracted honey. Foul brood. The large bee-moth. Apiculture in relation to agriculture. Wellington, By authority: John Mackay, govt. printer. 2 editions. 3rd ed 1909.

HOPKINS, Isaac. (1907, 1909). *Bee-culture*. Dept. of Agriculture. Division of Biology., Wellington, New Zealand, J.

MacKay. 1909 3rd. ed. is 79 pages. Bu lletin (NZ Dept. of Agriculture. Divisions of Biology and Horticulture), no. 18. 79 p., [16] p. of plates : ill. ; 25 cm.

HOPKINS, Isaac. (1911) *The Illustrated Australasian Bee Manual* 5th ed., pp.173, 82 illus., 19 chapters. Two copies located in early 2010: $55 and $85. The Brisbane *Courier*, 29 July 1911, provided this review: "I have received a copy of the *Australasian Bee Manual*, written by Mr Isaac Hopkins, late Chief Apiarist to the New Zealand Government. It is published by Messrs Gordon and Gotch, and contains 173 pages, well printed, and profusely illustrated, it is a fifth revision of a previous publication. The author, recognising the rapid progress which is being made in the beekeeping industry, decided to revise the text matter of the last edition, and bring it right up to date. His recent position as Chief Government Apiarist has served him in good stead, and given him many opportunities of determining the best methods to be adopted in carrying out the work of the apiary. He takes you step by step in the manipulation and working of an apiary which, if followed literally, means success. All his writing and suggestions are aptly substantiated by excellent illustrations of a most up to date character. Being of Australasian origin and applicable to our climatic conditions, the book should be in the hands of every beekeeper who wishes to keep abreast of the times." (p.15) In the Adelaide *Advertiser*, 12 March 1913 (p.4) "Correspondents … cannot do better than consult the *Australasian Bee Manual* by I. Hopkins, formerly chief Government apiarist in New Zealand. Knowledge and system are indispensable."

The Brisbane *Courier*, 2 October 1915, provided the following in its column On the Land - The Apiary. "There are two very good works published in Australia, and many beekeepers would prefer them on account of being more adapted to climatic conditions. One is called *Australian Bee Culture,* and is written by A. Gale, a beekeeper who has been much heard of in Australian bee-dom. The other is by I. Hopkins, and is called *The Australasian Bee Manual*. The information contained in this volume is both sound and practical. The work, however, which is most in favour among beekeepers is the *ABC of Bee Culture*. The information required is always so easily obtained on account of the subjects being treated in alphabetical order. ..." (p.13) The following reader was in agreement - from *Gleanings in Bee Culture*, 1 December 1886 "A kind word for the ABC from one of our Australian friends. Please send to me by post, 2 copies of *A B C*, cloth; the ones I have had are all sold, and also the one to arrive next mall. It's the best on bees published. I would not be without a copy on any account. Fred'k A. Hudson. New South Wales, Australia." (p.953)

HOPKINS, Isaac. (1916) **Forty-two Years of Bee-keeping in New Zealand**, *1874-1916; Some Reminiscences*. pp.38. Held NLNZ and 5 other NZ libraries.

Isaac Hopkins, ca 1916

HOPKINS, Isaac. (1926) ***Practical beekeeping, being the sixth edition of the Australasian Bee Manual***. 6th ed. Whitcombe & Tombs. pp.288. 26 chapters, 147 illus. Copies: NLA, SLNSW, NLNZ and other NZ libraries (see Google Book Search)

HOWARD, A. W. ***Bees as connected with horticulture***, a paper read before the South Australian Gardeners' Society, on Saturday evening, May 3, 1884. pp.2,, 21cm. Mortlock Pamphlets call# 638.1 H848 Mortlock Pamphlets

Angus Mackay

MACKAY, Angus (1834-1910). ***The Semi-Tropical Agriculturist and Colonists Guide***, 1875, Geo Slater & Co., Brisbane. Published in late March 1875. Eight pages on bees and beekeeping, eight illustrations, adv, h/c, 145x225mm, price originally ten shillings and sixpence. Can claim to be the second book produced in Australia to have content on bees – Carroll's 1875 *My Little Bee Book* being the first and exclusively dedicated to bees and beekeeping. A copy of Mackay came up for sale in 2006 at $450 and another two in 2010, $150 and $500. Library Holdings: ML, NLA, OML, SLQ (John Oxley Lib.), UQ Lib., Matheson Lib - Rare Books at Monash Univ., Univ. Melbourne Lib., Historic Houses Trust of NSW, Fisher Rare Books (Univ. Sydney) Ferguson #12017, list copies at M.L., N.L., O.M.L.

Includes chapter on *The Honey Bee in Australia,* 8 pages, pp.153-160, remainder contains various agricultural entries & illustrations. [110] Essentially the basis for an updated version which appeared in his 1885 *Elements of Australian Agriculture*. This work duplicated the contents of James Carroll's 1875 *My Little Bee Book*. Of the Italian bee, Mackay simply says: "The

---

[110] Refer the story on Carroll's 1875 *My Little Bee Book* and Mackay's role in adopting much of Carroll's work in his texts.

foregoing refers to the black or English bee. The Italian bee has the reputation of being a still better honey-gatherer; it is a quieter insect, and has beauty to recommend it, being beautifully striped. I [111] am in the hope of introducing them soon." One retail copy located April 2010 on the internet, $500. One book store stated Very scarce item - only 2 or 3 sightings in the last 30 years." A second edition appeared in 1890 and a third in 1897, neither having any content on bees.

In April 2010 several booksellers had one copy each of Mackay's "Agriculturist" books for sale, these being an 1875 *The Semi-Tropical Agriculturist and Colonists Guide*; a re-titled 1890 *The Australian Agriculturist and Colonists' Guide* subtitled *... With Calendar of Field and Garden Work, from January to December. ...*); and an 1897 edition, also re-titled *The Australian Agriculturist and Guide for Land Occupation* (subtitled *Plain Experiences in Station, Farm, Orchard and Garden Work, Dairying, Cattle, Sheep, Pigs, Ensilage Making, Poultry Farming, Fruit Preserving, Pests of the Agriculturist, and how to Check Them, Home Helps, Directions for Treating Wounds, Snake-bite, Drowning & c.,*)

An advertisement appeared in *The Queenslander*, 5 September 1874, declaring "In the press: will shortly be published, a new work; by Angus Mackay ... is the result of Ten Years of active experience amongst Australian Colonists." [112] Working back gives the year 1865 for the commencement of Mackay's agricultural experience.

I wanted to know how much content there was in his book on bees so I emailed several book sellers and asked if their edition contained anything on bees and/or beekeeping. Their

---

[111] "I" refers to Carroll, not Mackay, for Carroll was the original author.

[112] Thanks to Sim (1999) for discovering this advertisement

motivation, by inference, was that if their copy had a section on bees, then I could well be a genuine purchaser. The 1897 response was negative, the National Library of Australia replied to my query on the 1890 edition and one bookseller response on the 1875 edition was positive: 7 ½ pages including 6 illustrations. Regrettably, the $500 price tag was a bit too high for me.

Around 1880 Mackay was editor of the *Town and Country Journal*. [113] Many issues contain contributions on beekeeping. At this time he imported Italian bees from America. They were worth from ₤2 to ₤5 each. The paragraphs contain details on: the native bee, the common bee, queen, drones, workers, breeding, eggs and larva, swarming, hiving bees (sheet method and moveable comb hives), second and other swarms, loss of queen, uniting weak swarms, handling bees, artificial swarming (including instructions for those still using common box hives), bee stings, honey gathering, honey plants, bee food (including how to use and make an inverted jar feeder), wax and comb building, propolis, pollen, honey extractor, hives (specifically the Woodbury), making bee hives, super boxes and bell glasses, transferring to moveable comb hives, bee quilt, the bee moth, protection (veils), useful hints for beginners.

On the honey extractor "This machine has been used by American bee-keepers for some time. I imported one in 1873, and found it to be a rather rough affair, the maker not having hit upon what he was aiming at – the application of centrifugal force. He made the body of his machine revolve around a centre-shaft. Mr Mackay, [114] of the *Queenslander*, promptly remedied the defect, and supplied plans for the machines I am now

---

[113] An extensive biographical entry appears in *The Immigrant Bees, Vol. V*.
[114] See the section on James Carroll who was the original author of the text in Mackay's book.

making – the best, probably, that have been invented for extracting honey from the comb. The principle is similar to that of the centrifugal machines used for expelling the moisture from sugar; but in the case of the extractor, two tiers of arms – four in each – spring from a central shaft; four faces, of any desired size, are thus obtained at the ends of the arms.

The planes between are fitted with wood, for the reception of bar-frames filled with comb and honey. Outside of each frame is wire netting, size 4 to the inch. There is an outside stationery casing of tin, against which the honey is thrown as the machine revolves." The paragraph goes on to explain how the four combs are uncapped and the frames reversed after the honey is expelled from the first side.

Review: In the *Northern Territory Times*, 14 August 1875 "The work is by Mr. Angus Mackay, and was recently published in Brisbane. The articles of which it consists have appeared from time to time in the columns of the *Queenslander*, and republished in a collected form they constitute an unassuming handbook of agriculture, which will not only be of service to persons who contemplate entering upon farming in Queensland, but will repay perusal by experienced settlers. The author explains in his preface that the work "is simply an arrangement of every day colonial experience in bush life, stock farming, gardening, dairying, housekeeping, and kindred subjects," and adds that his "leading effort has been "to connect the system of agriculture, including stock-farming as followed in the old land, with what is gradually proving to be the best practice in the warmer sections of Australia." While these sentences give a fair description of the general character of the book, they convey but a slight idea of the amount and variety of the information upon rural topics which the writer has brought together.

Now Published,
To be obtained from all Booksellers.

THE SEMI-TROPICAL AGRICULTURIST and COLONISTS' GUIDE: A New Work; by ANGUS MACKAY.

This volume is now published, and has been will received. The contents embrace the keeping of Horses, Cattle, Sheep, Pigs, Poultry, Bees, Farming in all its details, Implements. How to cure Meat of all kinds; to make Bread, Butter, Cheese, Soap, Candles; to cure Skins, preserve Birds, &c.

Gardening.—Budding, Grafting, and General Principles. Insects injurious to vegetation, &c.

Methods of treating Snake Bite, Accidents in the Bush, apparent Drowning, &c.

Also, a mass of PRACTICAL INFORMATION valuable to Colonists in Warm Climates, and especially to Australian Colonists.

The whole is the result of Ten Years of active experience amongst Australian Colonists. *With numerous Engravings.*

Brisbane: Geo. Slater & Co.; Sydney, J. J. Moore; Melbourne, Geo. Robertson; Adelaide, E. S. Wigg & Son; and all booksellers. 10s. 6d.; postage, 1s.

From the Brisbane *Courier*, 12 January 1876, p.6

The "Guide" is a sort of "Enquire Within" upon almost every subject of farm management, and although it has reference more particularly to the soil, climate, and general circumstances under which the Queensland farmer has to deal, few persons in this colony who gain their living from the soil could fail to find something in it of service to them. The volume opens with an article in which some practical directions are given upon land selecting, and essays follow upon draining, ploughing, manuring, and every kind of field work. The various crops suitable to a semi-tropical climate, such as the sugarcane, tea, coffee, chicory, cotton, tobacco, and arrowroot, are described, and full instructions are given as to the most improved method of growing them. Brief treatises are also incorporated upon the cultivation of wheat, barley, rye, oats, maize, and similar grain crops. Fruits and vegetable gardening affords matter for a series of papers, which are supplemented by others upon fruit drying and preserving. Farm implements come in for a large share of attention, and numerous engravings are furnished of appliances for saving labor and reducing the cost of production. In connection with stock-keeping the different breeds of sheep, cattle, and horses that are found to answer in Australia, the most profitable system of managing them, and the usual remedies for diseases to which they are liable, are all carefully described. There are also papers upon the rearing of poultry, bee keeping, silkworm culture, and many similar adjuncts to remunerative farming. In addition to the more pretentious essays which fill the greater part of the work, paragraphs are interspersed throughout it containing recipes, and hints for making the most of little things which in the house and on the farm are often wasted. In order to render the "Guide" as useful a book of reference as possible to persons in the bush, one section of it supplies "medical help in time of need" by dictating the course of treatment to be pursued in cases of accident, snakebite, and sickness.

The faulty arrangement of the work is a decided blemish, but this the author explains was unavoidable in consequence of the circumstances under which it was sent to press. As compensation a very complete index of contents has been added. Upon the whole the "Semitroptcal Agriculturists' and Colonists' Guide" is a book which most farmers in Australia will find handy to have by them. The Adelaide publishers are E. S. Wigg and Son. - *Register*." (p.2)

Review: The Brisbane *Courier*, 24 April 1875 "Mr. Angus Mackay is known from one end of Queensland to the other, and wherever he is known he is accepted as one of the best authorities on matters connected with country pursuits. It was once our good fortune to be present when Mr. Mackay introduced himself in person to one of those hard working, intelligent bushmen-farmers who know not what it is to rest from Monday morning to Saturday evening, and who devote a portion at least of every Sunday to the attentive study of the *Queenslander*; especially to those columns in it which are allocated to information on farming in all its branches. To him the editor was probably the most important personage in Queensland. We question very much whether the Governor himself would have exercised anything like the same fascination over his imagination that had long been wielded by the indefatigable presiding genius of the *Queenslander*.

Mr. Mackay was to him his constant guide, his ultimate appeal, the highest authority to whom it was possible to refer; and he had pictured to himself that the possessor of this intelligence must be, like Saul, at least a head and shoulders taller than any ordinary mortal. It is, perhaps, needless to say that Mr. Mackay does not in stature exceed the limit of ordinary humanity; and when the son of Anak, forester, backwoodsman, and reader of the *Queenslander*, came to measure himself alongside of the man whom in imagination he had pictured as at least six inches taller than any one else in the colony, it was not a little amusing to observe the change which came over his features when he discovered the illusion of his expectations. Was it possible that the gentleman before him did not stand quite six feet in his "stocking feet!" The incident referred to really happened, and serves to illustrate the hold which Mr. Mackay has secured in the esteem of the intelligent and hard-working colonists whom he addresses in the *Queenslander*.

The book now before us is the concentrated essence of the good fare which Mr. Mackay has provided for his readers during the last year, and it requires no foresight to predict for it the success which it will undoubtedly attain. It is a summary of colonial experience such as has been lately presented to the readers of the *Queenslander* in those portions of it devoted to bush-life, stock raising, farming, gardening, dairying, housekeeping, and so forth. ... We predict for Mr. mackay's Colonists' Guide a wide circulation, and deserved popularity. It is one of the most practical and useful books ever published in Australia, and being specially applicable to semi-tropical Australia, it will find here a large and appreciative number of readers." (p.6) [115]

An insight into Mackay's nature is provided by an advertisement for the sale of his property in the *Brisbane Courier*, 12 April 1884 "It would be simply impossible for the auctioneer to overrate this charming property, around which there is an historical "ring" from the fact that it was from this spot Mr. A. Mackay made his raids wholly mounted upon his horse with his blanket strapped before the saddle upon the farmers in every direction for many miles, gathering information for and soliciting interest in a certain newspaper then about to be started under the title of the *Queenslander*. It is doubtful if Mackay or

---

[115] A pointer to other reviews appeared in The *Queenslander*, 1 May 1875, page 6. "we believe ... the Colonists' Guide [to be] one of the most valuable works published in Australia. The *Courier* of Saturday last gives a lengthy review of the work; The *Telegraph* follows on Satur day evening; our Ipswich contemporaries and several other journals have reviews also."

any of those associated with him at that time dreamt of such success attending the efforts they then put forth in launching their literary infant. The *Queenslander* has proved one of the most successful weeklies in Australia, and I believe the success in a great measure was owing to the untiring exertions of Mr. Mackay, and there is no doubt he was enabled to endure a good deal, both of the mental and physical labour he underwent and with comparative ease by the aid of the pure air and bracing climate of his happy home at LIZZY LEE, which, although so near to the centre of Brisbane, is perfectly free from the disagreeable smells and the racket of city life." (p.8)

MACKAY, Angus. ***The Honey Bee in Australia***, c1884, 2/-. Published by John Sands, printers. An advertisement for this 32 page pamphlet appeared at the rear of *The Elements of Australian Agriculture* (1885). The only copy known to

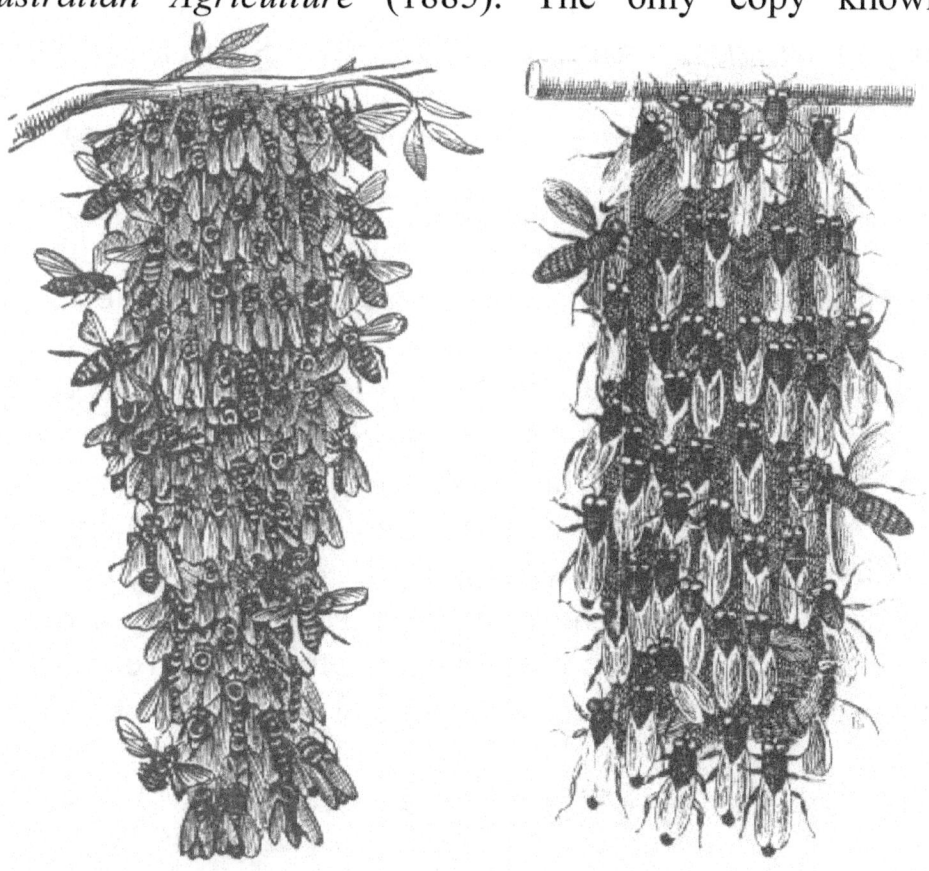

Above, at left, engraving from Mackay's Semi-Tropical Agriculturist and Colonists Guide, 1875. At right, from Thomas Wildman's A Treatise on the Management of Bees, 1770.

me resides within the Mitchell Library, SLNSW. The introduction to this latter work states, in part "Bee-keeping in Australia is a separate paper, and was not at first intended for this work, but is added because of the wide field which this industry is offering in connection with Australian agriculture." Two non-beekeeping titles by Mackay, *The Sugar Cane in Australia* and *Helpful Science for Agriculturists,* together with the other titles described herein, as well as several more held in various libraries, rate Mackay as a prolific agricultural and beekeeping author.

MACKAY, Angus, 1885. **Elements of Australian Agriculture**, illus., pp.175, Library Holdings: ML, NLA, SLTAS, SLQ. Ferguson #12020, lists copies at M.L., N.L., S.L. Tas. *Worldcat* states it is held by 14 libraries worldwide. Refer http://www.worldcat.org/search?q=no:%22026243411%22

Copies can be found between $40 and $100. Beekeeping is covered in the chapter titled "The Honey Bee in Australia" on the 28 pages, pp.148-175. This is an update on the same chapter which appeared in *The Semi-tropical Agriculturist and Colonists' Guide* (1875). Of the twenty-seven (or 29, depending on how they're counted) beekeeping related illustrations, seven lend a touch of magic to this book, though, unfortunately, they are not Australian scenes as they were copied from an April 1873 edition of New York's *Harper's Weekly*. The first of these "A Modern Bee Farm" shows an apiarist walking by a row of eight, wide bodied, single box hives; another ten hives take the middle ground with three more beyond. The engraver's name of

"Winston" [116] is clearly marked. The second scene shows in fine detail a swarm hanging from a branch; the third, a beekeeper ladling bees with his bare hands into a bar-frame hive. Some of the accompanying text is as follows "Re swarming, the bees fill themselves with honey, and at such times they are not at all disposed to sting. They can then be handled with ease, and when put into the hive, as shown in the illustration, they take to the combs at once, evincing their pleasure at the discovery of the new residence, by the joyful humming of bees ... All the other

---

[116] Web site printsandprintmaking.gov.au identifies Charles Edward Winston, born London England, 27 March 1825, died Sydney, 5 January 1893. He worked in Australia (SA, VIC, NSW) from 16 January 1851 *(Harpley)*; and New Zealand 1863-64. He was a woodcut engraver, the technique also known as xylography, artists sometimes nicknamed "woodpeckers". A longer entry by Thomas A. Darragh appears in the *Dictionary of Australian Artists Online.*
http://www.daao.org.au/main/read/6692 "Winston trained as a wood-engraver under C. Whymper, presumably a connection of the eminent engraver Charles Whymper. Arriving at Adelaide from London in the ship *Harpley* on 16 January 1851, Winston seems to have worked in South Australia with Samuel Calvert. ... By late 1852, however, Winston had set up business as a wood-engraver in Geelong. ... by 1859 Winston had established a business in Neave's Buildings, 42 Collins Street, East Melbourne. ... Winston moved to Dunedin, New Zealand, in about 1863 and set up as a wood-engraver in Princes Street South. ... He was back at Melbourne by 1868 and in business as a designer and engraver on wood at 41 Swanston Street. ... Many of his engravings, mostly of buildings after drawings by Albert Cooke, appeared in the *Illustrated Australian News* between 1868 and 1873. In 1876 Winston was in Sydney, his engraving rooms being on the upper floor of the Town Hall Hotel. In March 1886, described as 'the well-known wood engraver, whose productions in all classes of work, including the best book illustration, have been circulating through various colonies for many years past' ... He was buried in Balmain Cemetery"

bees of the swarm, to the very last one, on such a sound being heard, join in the melody, and march in regular order after their fellows, into the new hive." (p.155). Another engraving shows a veiled beekeeper searching for a nest in a bee tree, the beekeeper holding a smoking roll of calico. Instructions are provided for transferring combs from common box hives, gin cases or a tree, to the moveable-comb frame hive, but no text supports the ladling technique.

The sixth engraving is of "Mr. Jas. Carroll, of *Lizzielea* apiary, Queensland, and amongst the first practical bee masters in the colonies." (a facsimile appears in *The Immigrant Bees, Volume II*) The last of this impressive and endearing set of engravings is titled "Don't Fight with Bees". "Work quietly, and avoid sudden jars. Never fight your bees; always keep cool. If you get stung and don't like it, if the bees look angry, retire quietly and remove the sting at once; apply the barrel of a large-sized key to the wound. (note: *The Semi-Tropical Agriculturist* explains that the (hollow) barrel, once pressed against the wound firmly for a few seconds, causes a drop of clear liquid (ie., poison) to issue from the wound. "The key should be applied until no more poison will issue.") Use plenty of smoke. If you are timid, use a bee-dress or veil over the face and head. ... Always work among the hives during the middle of the day when the bees are busy, and crowds of the workers are out. ... Bees do not intend to sting when they come prospecting about you. They are curious to see what you are. Stand very still and they will go. Should they seem irritable, leave them for that time; or you can pacify them with smoke as recommended; but do not run away, fighting as you go. The bees will beat you at that, sure." (p.175)

On the last page there is an advertisement for Australian agricultural works by Mackay. *The Honey Bee in Australia* is priced at two shillings, while *The Semi-Tropical Agriculturist, and Colonist's Guide* is priced at ten shillings and sixpence. [117] The price difference is reflective of their relative number of pages. The former work is identical to the bee chapter in *The Elements of Australian Agriculture*.

I like this book, particularly its gilt stamped cover illustration: an outline map of Australia and its six named States; book title in large lettering with author's name below the map. The South Australian State looks overly large today for it runs the full length of the continent, from the Great Australian Bight north to the Gulf of Carpentaria. Its Northern Territory had to wait until 1911 for it to be proclaimed as a Commonwealth administered.

Four illustrations in this book were "lifted" from an April 1881 issue of the New York publication *Harper's Weekly*. The joke was on me for I'd reproduced them in my works, thinking they were original Australian woodcuts.

Review: From the Brisbane *Courier*, 1 October 1885 "The author of this work is so well known as a writer upon all topics connected with agriculture in these colonies that the reader may feel satisfied as to the reliability of the teaching inculcated. The purpose of the work is mainly introductory to the more thorough study of the many branches of agricultural science, but there is much practical information in it that would be useful to the selector himself. The subjects treated of embrace climate, rainfall, winds, soils and their analysis, chemistry of agriculture, plant life, crops of Australia, drainage, irrigation, manures, sheep and wheat farming, dairying, &c. The different subjects are concisely yet plainly treated, and illustrations are freely made use of to assist the letter-press. The paragraphs are numbered, and at the end of each chapter are a series of questions useful to assist the learner, to a recollection of the teachings. Queensland crops, soils, and agriculture are freely

---

[117] Two copies found on the net early 2010 priced at $150 and $500.

referred to, as might be expected from the author of the *Semi-Tropical Agriculturist*; therefore much of the information is directly applicable to cultivators in this colony. The work is decidedly educational, and could with advantage be introduced into our State schools. We understand that it has already been taken up by the Board of Technical Education, Sydney, for their classes. The subjects treated of are so clearly explained that any of our State school teachers, even if ignorant of agricultural science, yet would find no difficulty in imparting the knowledge to his class. Certainly in all our rural schools this work should find a place among the class-books, The chapter on climate excepted - which treats more particularly upon the climate of New South Wales - the whole of the teachings are equally applicable to Queensland as they are to New South Wales or Victoria." (p.3)

title page illustration to *The Honey Bee in Australia,* 1885, as "borrowed" from New York's *Harper's Weekly*, 13 April 1881

MACKAY, Angus **Bees and Honey in Australia**, c1885, Sydney, pp.32, illus, adv, s/c, illus, 12.5x19cm, Ferguson 12021, lists one copy at M.L. (this copy inscribed on title page by author "His Honour Judge Windeyer, with respects of the Author, Sydney, Dec. 19/85."

Don't Fight with Bees

The next page carries a pencil notation that this copy was donated to the Mitchell Library 14 April 1914 by Miss Windeyer. A selection of biographical notes on her father, Sir William Charles Windeyer (1834-1897): he was one of the first graduates of the University of Sydney in 1856; admitted to the New South Wales bar in 1857, a law reporter to the *Empire* newspaper, then country Crown prosecutor; in 1859 elected to the Legislative Assembly thereby gaining a seat in Parliament before he was 25 years of age; from 1862 taught Latin and Greek one evening a week at the School of Arts; he also followed a political career on and off for the next 20 years; in 1870 made Solicitor-General; a judge of the Supreme Court 1879 to 1896; he advocated the preservation of open spaces for the people, and was responsible for securing several small reserves in Sydney. With his wife Mary (Bolton)[118] they had three sons and six daughters. From *The Cyclopedia of New South Wales* (1907) "His one great indulgence was to get away to his country home and to work in his garden." (p.298) This would have been his mother's house and garden, the remnant of her husband's property at Tomago, Hunter Valley. There is a chance that Mackay's gift of his book targets Windeyer as a fellow beekeeper. Windeyer's fifth daughter, Margaret (1866-1939) completed a library course in 1897 in America under Melvil Dewey; returned to Australia in 1901 and worked at the Public Library of New South Wales. In 1910 she transferred to the Mitchell Library, Sydney, where she worked for 16 years.)

The same page carries a beekeeper's monthly calendar eg., "January. – Honey coming in freely from the gums and other forest trees, where they abound. Drones may be too plentiful, and their increase should be stopped by taking out drone comb." Following an advertisement for *the Town and Country Journal* "Special illustrated articles appear in the Journal upon Bee Keeping and Honey making, with diagrams and descriptions of all new developments in the art from all parts of the world." The contents are identical to the chapter "The Honey Bee in Australia" as contained in *The Elements of Australian Agriculture.* The title page illustration shows a veiled beekeeper, bare hands, waist length long sleeved work coat, inspecting a frame of bees at arms length.

---

[118] From *Mary of Maranoa*, p.245

SIR WM. WINDEYER.

MACKAY, Angus *Bee Keeping as a Business in Australia*, (1882, 1895), Batson & Co., Sydney, pp.65, illus, adv, h/c, 13x19cm, posted, 2/-, 2nd ed. written after encouragement from the publishers of *The Rural Australian* as the first edition had gone out of print, as stated in the foreword to the first edition. No known library holdings of the 1st ed., maybe some exist in a private library, either treasured or forgotten. Ferguson 12028 lists only the 1895 copy held at ML; copy at Melbourne Univ., another known in a private collection. Original price two shillings. An advertisement for the 2nd edition appeared in the *Australian Bee Bulletin*, July 1895, declaring the book "now ready". Inside the cover appears an advertisement for *The Rural Australian*

For Information Concerning Bees!
For Progressive Bee Keeping!
For How to Make Bees Profitable!
READ
The Rural Australian.

Chasing a swarm of bees? [119]

"A Special Department is given to Bee Keeping, to which the author of this Work, Angus Mackay, F.C.S., Instructor in Agriculture of New South Wales, is a frequent contributor, as are many of the leading bee Keepers in Australia."

Subtitle: "Containing details of various Families of Bees, and how to work them for profit." Mackay was an instructor in agriculture, Technical College, N.S.W. The Introduction is dated "Technical College, Sydney, June, 1895". "I have a hope that

---

[119] No, this image presented just for fun – from Mackay's 1897 *The Australian Agriculturist and Guide for Land Occupation*. These two are racing to see the ensilage feed silo opened!

there is enough in the little book to enable intelligent persons to make a start – and none others are likely to succeed in bee-keeping on a profitable basis. But I would be sorry indeed were anyone to suppose that even the rudiments of bee knowledge are exhausted. The business is very progressive: so are successful bee-keepers. Not a year has passed during the twenty-five years in which I have been attending to bees in Australia, without something useful coming to light. The bee-keeper has to study his flocks of captious but willing little workers all the time, and read, and think, as opportunity occurs. Bee literature is an immense help; and successful bee-keepers are keen readers, as the journals which attend to bees give evidence. ... the experimenting stage has been gone through in Australia; that bees of the best known qualities and the most suitable working appliances are all available here; that it does not cost much to provide all that is required for a start; and that, provided the locality is suitable, there are many inducements for extending Australian bee-keeping." Several illustrations are borrowed from his previous works, as are some from *The ABC of Bee Keeping*. Mackay's portrait (shown above) is the frontispiece. He commenced beekeeping c1870.

"A Real Australian Bee Book at last !" began a pre-publication book review on the same page of *The Rural Australian* as the advertisement depicted below. "HOORAH ! The proprietors of the RURAL AUSTRALIAN have every pleasure in announcing that they have arranged with the Instructor in Agriculture in New South Wales, Angus Mackay, F.C.S., for the production of a new and thoroughly Australian work on bee-keeping. They have got portions of the manuscript: the printers are at work upon it. They have enough in hand already to show that "Australian Bee-keeping as a business" – the title the author has chosen – will be thoroughly practical, as might be expected from Mr. Mackay's long experiences as a bee-keeper and teacher of bee-keeping. It will be a small work only, for the author does nor use two words when one gives the necessary information; but it will be ample for the instruction of beginners, and also as the much wanted connecting link between the many useful works, British and American, and bee-keeping in Australia. The price will be 2s. ; by post, 2s. 2d. ; and orders may be sent at once to the office of the RURAL AUSTRALIAN, Sydney."

Angus Mackay, 1895

"Our Bee Book" headed the review in the September 1895 issue of *The Rural Australian* "This is what the *Clarence and Richmond Examiner* says about it, and the criticism is fairly representative of press opinions all over the country:– "BEES AND BEE-KEEPING. - We have before us, under the title of 'Bee-keeping as a business in Australia,' a very well got up and instructive little book by our old friend, Mr. Angus Mackay, F.C.S., Instructor in Agriculture, Technical College of N. S. Wales, author of '*Helpful Science for Agriculturists,*' '*The Sugar Cane in Australia,*' '*Australian Agriculture,*' and numerous other works on the industries connected with the land and the Australian colonies. The work before us is a valuable one, as may be gathered from the brief remark on the title page – 'containing details of the various families of bees and how to work them for profit.'

The book is well illustrated, showing at a glance examples of all connected with bees and bee-keeping, as described at greater length in the letterpress. As a frontispiece to the work there is a striking likeness of the author. The work is printed and published at the moderate price of 2s., by Batson and Co., Limited, Clarence-street, Sydney, and does that firm credit in every respect. Did our space admit, we should have been pleased to quote from the pages of this little book. But the price is so small that we hope it will find its way into the hands, not only of those who have already entered into the increasing army of bee-keepers, but also into those of many who are seeking a profitable as well as interesting pursuit. The field is large, and Mr. Mackay's work will be found a valuable aid to those who enter it in pursuit of profit."

Another review appeared in The *Sydney Mail*, 20 July 1895 "A little book entitled *Beekeeping as a Business in Australia*, first published in 1882, has been reprinted by Messrs. Batson and Co., Limited. The author, Angus Mackay, F.C.S., has brought his subject up to date, and presented a topic, most interesting in itself, in simple language. The text is, moreover, illustrated with many woodcuts of bees and comb, hives and appliances. Beekeeping should be a fascinating pursuit with young persons, and this little work is calculated to arrest their attention and lead to the enlargement of one of the minor industries of agriculture." (p.29)

The July 1895 issue of *The Australian Bee Bulletin* acknowledged receipt of a copy of Mackay's new beekeeping work. 'It contains a concise and well-written epitome of matters relating to beekeeping from an Australian standpoint. No beekeeper can read it through without feeling interested, or seeing some well-known idea dressed in different language, making it more impressive than it had seemed before. Every beekeeper who wishes to succeed cannot do without a good library of bee literature, and this little work of Mr Mackay's should undoubtedly find a place among such." (pp.75b-76a)

During my fifteen years of collecting beekeeping books, with an emphasis on Australasian works, I've come across only one copy of this work outside the ML holding. I've never located an 1882 edition.

Will be Ready in May.

Bee Keeping

AS A BUSINESS

In Australia.

BY

AGNUS MACKAY, F.C.S,

Instructor in Agriculture, Technical College,
New South Wales,

Author of "Helpful Science for Agriculturists," "The Sugar Cane in Australia," "Australian Agriculture," &c., &c.

Containing Details of Various Families of Bees, and how to work them for profit.

WITH NUMEROUS ILLUSTRATIONS.

Price, 2s.; by post, 2s. 2d.

BATSON & CO., Limited,
PRINTERS AND PUBLISHERS,
146 CLARENCE ST., SYDNEY.
And all Booksellers.

advertisement, *The Rural Australian*, May 1895

MOLINEUX, Albert (1884) *A Few Words about Bees and Bee-Hives*. A Paper read before the South Australian Gardeners' Society on Saturday Evening, March 1st, 1884. Small quarto, drop-title, 4 pages (two conjugate leaves printed in two columns); one copy located on the retail market late 1990s for $250, not found in 2010.

Albert Molineux (1832 - 1909), by unknown photographer, State Library of South Australia.

A short extract from the *Australian Dictionary of Biography*: "Molineux, Albert (1832-1909), farmer, editor and promoter of agriculture, was born on 11 July 1832 in Brighton, Sussex, England ... With free passages the family sailed for South Australia in the *Resource* and arrived on 23 January 1839. ... Albert went to school and then worked on a farm at Klemzig but left to become a printer's apprentice. In 1851 he joined the gold rush to Victoria and returned in 1855 with modest success. He worked with his father on a farm at Gilbert River and then became a compositor ... In 1875 Molineux decided to produce an agricultural journal and with a fellow compositor ... and on 10 August produced the first edition of the *Garden and Field*. ...

He also wrote for the *Observer* in 1875 and was later its agricultural editor. With these positions and his own journal he exerted great influence on South Australian agriculture. ... In private enterprise Molineux was managing director of the South Australian Fishing Co. until it failed ... Through the *Garden and Field* he published material from the Chamber of Manufactures, the Royal Agricultural and Horticultural Society as well as various specialist groups. As a committee member of the Field Naturalists Society he was indefatigable in seeking specimens, made the first trawling nets and obtained many specimens of fish hitherto unknown. ... he was nominated to the Linnean Society by Ferdinand Mueller and Charles French and elected a fellow. He also wrote pamphlets on bees, forest culture and *Handbook for Farmers and Gardeners in Australia* (Adelaide, 1893). ..." [120]

MURPHY, Michael. (1885) **Handbook of New Zealand gardening: with a chapter on bee-keeping**. Whitcombe & Tombs, Christchurch - vii, 188 p.: illus., plates; 19 cm. Copies: University of Otago Libraries; SLNSW; Univ. Melbourne. 2nd ed. 1888, rev. and enl. Publ. Christchurch, Whitcombe & Tombs, 224 p., [3] folded leaves of plates: ill.; 18 cm. other eds 1885 and 1895. Murphy was born 1833, died 1914. Though a NZ book it was surely used by Australian beekeepers, hence its inclusion here. I located one copy at a second-hand bookshop in Maleny, a hinterland town above the Sunshine Coast, south-east Queensland.

---

[120] Marie Mune, 'Molineux, Albert (1832 - 1909)', *Australian Dictionary of Biography*, Volume 5, Melbourne University Press, 1974, pp 265-266.
adbonline.anu.edu.au/biogs/A050305b.htm

Tarlton Rayment

RAYMENT, Tarlton *Money in Bees in Australia*, c1917. 1st ed., Whitcombe & Tombs, pp.280, illus cloth colour h/c with d/w, over 100 illlus, index, UWSH, SLVic, SLSA, NLNZ and others. Price 8/6 (8 shillings & sixpence), 7/6 & 7/10 posted 1918. In 2010 I located various copies on the net from $50 to $90 as well as "print on demand" new paperbacks. Subtitled: *A Practical Treatise on the Profitable Management of the Honey Bee in Australia*. Notes: intro by W. S. Pender, editor *Australasian Beekeeper,* numerous illustrations hand drawn by author, Historical notes, Reviewed *ABK* Dec. 1915, comments *ABK* Sept. 1916, pp.44-45 by W.C. Humphrey of Hazeleigh Apiary, Kincumber. Chapters: Part. 1. Spring: Australian Bees, Locations & Buildings, Working Equipment, Preliminary Work, Manipulating Frames, Extracted Honey, Working to Increase, Out-Yards & Italianising. Part. 2. Summer: Swarms & Swarming, Comb Honey, Working for Comb-Honey, Queens, Queen-Rearing, Queen-Mating, Pollen & Pollen Substitutes, General Summer Work, Robber Bees, Feeding Bees, Enemies of Honey-Bees. Part. 3. Autumn: Bee Diseases, Nectar & Honey-Dew, Superseding Queens, Spare Combs, General Autumn Work, Preparation for Wintering. Part. 4. Winter: Heating Honey, Preparing Honey for Sale, A Winter Flow of Honey, General Work in Winter, Exhibiting, Beeswax, Foundation, Travelling Bees. Part 5. Australian Honey Plants. Honey Flows & Their Sources, List and Particulars in Alphabetical Order. over 100 illus. ₤4/10 in 1967, $150 to $160 depending on edition.

Biographical The contribution to follow titled "Tarlton Rayment - Naturalist And Taxonomist, A Biographical Note" appeared in

Sphecos for December 1984, [121] a newsletter describing itself as "a forum for Aculeate wasp researchers". The biographer, Norman Rodd, is a fascinating character now in his late eighties, an "amateur" entomologist of note himself. I purposely visited Norman in 1995 at his leafy retreat, Mt. Tomah, Blue Mountains, NSW, for Norman had known Rayment over a period of many years. Before I discovered Lynette Young's biography *The Melody Lingers On*, I had hopes of producing a one myself, hence my visit to a man who knew my intended subject well.

But first, an interlude prior to Norman's reminiscences, a short story of my own. In researching Rayment's life and works I came across an article in *The Sydney Morning Herald* for 23 March 1992. (p.3) a rare native bee *Leioproctus filamentosa* with a particularly long tongue had been supplied to Rayment by an anonymous amateur entomologist. "The little bee was found, near its small burrow in the ground, in 1946 at Lane Cove and given to a noted amateur naturalist, Mr Tarlton Rayment." Rayment, in disecting the bee and drawing it, had misplaced the bee's head, the thorax and abdomen only remained. Then a visiting American entomologist had rediscovered a new specimen, hence the newspaper article. This I took with me to my Norman Rodd interview. Having shown Norman the article he expressed detailed knowledge of the incident. Innocently I asked "Who was the anonymous entomologist". My jaw dropped in amazement as Norman blandly replied "That was me".

---

[121] see also *Sphecos*, No. 12, June 1986: a note by Roger Morse on the safe repository of Rayment's drawings in the E. F. Phillip's collection at Cornell University.
http://entomology.si.edu/Hymenoptera/Sphecos/Sphecos_12_June-1986.pdf

"It being now within a few weeks of twenty years since Tarlton Rayment's death it is now possible to look back on the man and his achievements with some degree of perspective. Knowing of my past (now somewhat distant) association with Rayment, Arnold Menke (note: the then editor, based at the National Museum of natural History, Washington DC) has asked me to prepare this biographical note for the benefit of *Sphecos* readers. Having willingly agreed to do so and having begun to assemble some background material I almost immediately came up against a small puzzle regarding Rayment's life span. In Anthony Musgrave's *Bibliography of Australian Entomology 1775-1930*, Rayment's year of birth is stated as 1886 which would have made him in either his seventy-eighth or seventy-ninth year when he died on June 6, 1964. On the other hand, a, memorial notice in *Victorian Naturalist* of August, 1964 states that he died in his eighty-second year. I have not yet been able to discover the reason for this discrepancy so it must suffice to say that he lived to a reasonably ripe age despite quite severe health problems which he experienced in this latter years.

For a clear appreciation of Rayment's position in the history of Australian entomology it is necessary to realise that his considerable success as a natural historian and a taxonomist were apparently achieved entirely without the advantages of any formal education in the natural sciences and also with only minimal financial rewards for his efforts. At which stage of his life he may have become interested in natural history it has not been possible to determine and in fact practically nothing has been recorded of his youthful days. What we do know is that he originally set out to study art and that his main early interests were in music, drawing and painting. It appears that he soon became disenchanted with the formal aspects of art instruction and at about the same time became acquainted with the writings of J. H. Fabre which were to have a profound influence on his future involvements with the insect world and on his philosophical attitudes as expressed in his own writings.

Unfortunately again for his biographer no substantial information is available regarding a large slice of Rayment's life between the end of his discontinued art studies (presumably in his early twenties) and the next important step towards his involvement with things entomological. It is known that he took up residence in the Gippsland hills in the south-east of Victoria sometime prior to 1912 and that he subsequently proceeded to build up a business as a commercial apiarist. This eventually developed into a quite large and successful enterprise of some hundreds of hives producing both honey and queen bees. For an enquiring mind such as his and under the influence of his already developed interests in the broad field of natural history it is inevitable that he should then become aware of the existence of the many species of native bees in the surrounding countryside. Thus began his studies in this field which steadily expanded and became his consuming interest for the remainder of his active life. He did retain some connection with apiculture at least until 1929 when he contributed a number of articles to the *Australian Beekeeper* under the title of "The Wild Bees of Australia". [122] I know also that he was in demand as a guest speaker to apiarists meetings for a number of years after that.

Prior to 1929 his first papers on native bees appeared in *Victorian Naturalist*, the journal of the Field Naturalists Club of Victoria of which he was a prominent member for many years and at one time its president. His contributions to *Victorian Naturalist* spanned the years between 1927 and 1954, a total of 90 papers and notes being recorded over this period. Notable among these was a series of 25 papers entitled *New Bees and Wasps*.

---

[122] see also *The Brisbane Courier*, 30 January 1909, p.15

In his early ventures into taxonomy Rayment had the benefit of encouragement, advice and close friendship of T. D. A. Cockerell who had already written many papers on Australian native bees, commencing as early as 1904 and subsequently culminating in his monumental catalogue and keys to *The Bees of Australia* published in *The Australian Zoologist* between 1930 and 1934. In the introductory part of this work Cockerell referred to the paucity of studies on the habits of Australian native bees and in this connection paid a tribute to Rayment as follows: "Some worthwhile work has been done by Mr. Tarlton Rayment at Sandringham, Victoria. With the utmost enthusiasm he has watched and recorded the nesting habits of the species in his neighbourhood, discovering many hitherto unrecorded facts." Rayment for his part, certainly valued his association with Cockerell very highly and spoke of him often as his guide and mentor. In a letter to me dated March, 1948, he wrote: "I regret to say that my loved friend and collaborator and sometime master, Prof. Cockerell, has died at San Diego, Calif., U.S.A. We had a long and beautiful association, such as is enjoyed by few humans. A fair and lovely light has gone out of my life."

Believed to be a rare image of Tarlton Rayment,
From Hobart's *Mercury*, 26 May 1923

My own association with Rayment did not begin until 1944 and in looking back to that time I have been reminded that this actually began through the appearance of an article of his in the then popular Australian geographical magazine *Walkabout*. The subject of the article was an account of his observations on a colony of Bembex wasps nesting in a river bank in central Queensland. Illustrated as it was by a number of fine pen and wash sketches of the wasps in flight and at their nest sites together with his identification of *Trigona* bees as the wasps' larval food, this all served to re-awaken my lifelong interest in natural history and to quite rapidly lead me into active collaboration with Tarlton. Our association continued with only minor interruptions for the following ten years, after which the increasing pressures of earning a living in my own profession largely put an end to my entomological activities and caused them to lie dormant for almost another twenty years. That my interest did not die altogether was undoubtedly due in large part to the lingering effects of stimulation, encouragement and real kindness earlier accorded me by Tarlton.

Money in Bees in Australia
Tarlton Rayment's self portrait, 2nd. Ed. 1925

He had the ability in high degree to transmit his own enthusiasms to others by his never failing generous recognition of their efforts. That he had this generosity of spirit in himself I know sometimes made it difficult for him to accept ungenerous criticism of his findings. In 1949, referring to one of his current major research interests he wrote: "Had some disappointments in research of *Halictus* owing to lack of perception in other people; hard enough to take when Nature defeats one but when ones fellows do it ..." Nevertheless, he appears to have rarely been sufficiently affected by criticism to cause him to discontinue his endeavours nor, on the other hand, to be less ready in his praise of others. As an example I well remember him advising me to "look out for a young man named Charles Michener who is doing some excellent work" - or words to that effect! For a worker who continued to expand his interests well beyond his original field and who had a tirelessly enquiring mind for the natural history of his country, it is not surprising that he sometimes got slightly out of his depth and made mistakes of interpretation. But then who even among the trained professionals do not fall into similar traps from time to time in their careers. Indeed how dull life would be for our taxonomists if their predecessors had not made mistakes for them to uncover and correct! What is certain is that Rayment's successes and achievements far outweigh his failures. His contributions to the taxonomy and natural history of Australian *Hymenoptera* were considerable by any standards and, if he has to be judged against others, it must be taken into account that he was essentially a self-motivated amateur with all the limitations that this implied in access to literature and other back-up resources enjoyed by professional workers. True, he did have a connection with the Victorian Museum as an honorary research associate and with the C.S.I.R.O. (note: Commonwealth Scientific and Industrial Research Organisation) as a recipient for some years of a small research grant but otherwise he was very much a worker in isolation. Add to this that his financial circumstances were obviously meager and perhaps even precarious at times and his achievements can be better appreciated.

In a brief note such as this it is not appropriate to provide a complete bibliography of Rayment's publications. Mention has already been made of his numerous papers in *Victorian Naturalist* and in addition to these he made notable contributions to *The Australian Zoologist, Proceedings of the Royal Society of New South Wales*, and *Journal of the Royal Society of Western Australia*. (note: an extensive bibliography of Rayment's works will be found in Lynette Young's biography *The Melody Lingers On.*)

Finally this note although compiled primarily for the interest of *Sphecos* readers, would not be complete without a mention of Tarlton Rayment's achievements quite outside the fields already dealt with. He was in fact a man of many parts including poet, song writer and novelist. In the latter category his best known work was *Valley of the Sky* first published in 1937 and based on the life and times of one of the pioneer settlers in the Gippsland district. Up to 1951 this had already run to eleven editions and for all I know more may have been added since then. I've read it and highly recommend it to all.

Of a more technical nature were his publications on commercial bee farming, viz. *Money in Bees in Australasia*; *Profitable Honey Plants in Australasia*; *The Commercial Bee Farm* and *Bread of the Bee Hive*. [123] Royalties from the sale of these works would have made some contribution to Rayment's income and together with a small government grant mentioned earlier would have given him some security during the years he devoted to his taxonomic and other entomological writings none of which would have been incoming producing.

---

[123] Of these three I'm sure that the last was never published. The prospective publishers, Angus and Robertson, when queried in 1995, had no record of its publication. It survives in manuscript at the Mitchell Library, a victim apparently of wartime paper shortages. Additionally, Rayment's surviving papers give evidence of publisher procrastination. Of the numerous illustrations referred to I could find no trace.)

William Morton Wheeler, another contemporary who had a strong influence on Rayment's life and philosophies, once wrote, "It is difficult to say whether Rayment is an artist or a scientist, for he has an avowed conviction that Taxonomy is an art. This after all is not so very remarkable as it seems because the objective in each case is the pursuit of Truth." This would seem to be as good a note as any on which to end these recollections of Tarlton Rayment as an individual and as a worker in what may be regarded as a transition period of Australian entomology. He was a man very much in tune with nature, quite deeply religious but with a strong aversion of "churchianity" and above all he possessed the ability to communicate with and inspire others. So, perhaps not one of the real giants but one surely above average stature in the history of natural science in this country.

Footnote: After his death his large collection of bees and other groups was acquired by the C.S.I.R.O. and is now lodged in the Australian National Insect Collection in Canberra, A.C.T. It is also of interest to note that a large number of his original drawings had already been acquired by the library of Cornell University as early as 1951. I do not know how this came about and would be grateful if any reader could enlighten me. Are those drawings still at Cornell?"

Roger Morse, Professor of Apiculture at Cornell University, Ithaca, New York, was kind enough to respond in April 1995 to my query regarding the holdings of Rayment's works at Cornell. He wrote in part "We have Rayment's drawings. ... they are in a safe place as the 'Mann Library Balcony' is locked away from everything else. I looked at Rayment's plates yesterday ... they are bound in a book about three inches thick. The book is in a wooden box about two by two and a half feet in size. They are in mint condition. I was once told that we have the plates because Rayment did not get along well with his colleagues in Australia, a thought about which I have no data." Readers of *The Melody Lingers On* can better understand the background to this last statement.

The Oxford Companion to Australian Literature (2nd ed., 1994) gives Rayment's birth year as 1882 "born Reading, England, came to Australia in 1902 and worked as a professional beekeeper and commercial artist." The *Australian Dictionary of Biography* "... apiarist, biologist and writer ... educated at an Anglican school, Tarlton was a brilliant scholar with a gift for painting. He trained for a time as an artist and architect but, fascinated by bees since childhood and influenced by the work of Jean Henri Fabre and Professor D. A. Cockerell, turned to natural history. After a brief stay in India he arrived in Melbourne in 1902 and moved to Ballarat, then Leongatha, where he took up bee-keeping. ... After severe bush fires near Leongatha, Rayment moved about 1908 to Briagolong, where he set up his three hundred hives. ... His best known work was *A Cluster of Bees* for which he received world acclaim."

Book Review: In the *Sydney Morning Herald*, 6 September 1916 (p.9) "As an attempt is being made in this State to encourage agriculture, both by the provision of new laws governing the industry and by providing instruction through the Department of Agriculture, reliable literature on the subject is to be welcomed. Therefore, Money in Bees, a practical treatise on the profitable management of the honey bee in Australasia, by Mr Tarlton Rayment, should find many readers, and be the means of promoting interest in the industry. The author is a successful Victorian beekeeper, consequently his book is full of helpful instruction. Written by one acquainted with local conditions, and to suit same, it is of far more practical service than any outside publication. No doubt the most experienced apiarist will find a benefit from a perusal of this book, but certainly the beginner will find it fills a great want. The subject is handled in an attractive and most comprehensive manner, and the text is assisted by a large number of illustrations. The four seasons of the year are covered consecutively. A description of the honey bee is followed by a chapter on locations and buildings, then the reader student is given a description of the working equipment required |n beekeeping, and from that on every phase of the industry is explained clearly and concisely. Not the least interesting section of the book is that devoted to Australian honey plants. The author claims that this is the first of its kind. He writes - 'The inquirer will search in vain the book-shelves of the leading city libraries for information regarding the honey-producing capabilities of the indigenous flora. This deficiency is not due to any laxity on the part of library authorities, because up to the issue of this little chapter no information dealing with the subject has been published. It is admitted at the outset that this tabulation is not complete, for it is not possible in a small compass to enumerate all plants of value to the apiculturist. Again, in many of the remote portions of this continent, there are areas of country many miles in extent literally covered with blossoms. No honey flowers have been recorded from these sources because no bee-farmer has tried them, and that is the only way to test the country.' The chapter contains a long descriptive list of local plants. In an introduction to *Money in Bees* Mr. W.S. Pender, of West Maitland, editor of the *Australasian Beekeeper*, writes: - 'In this volume an attempt has been made - I think very successfully - to provide a concise, explicit, and eminently practical guide-book, covering the elementary as well as the more advanced phases of practical apiculture. It is extremely practical from beginning to end, while every operation is lucidly described.' Our copy comes from the publishers Messrs. Whitcombe and Tombs, Ltd, Melbourne."

Another book review titled "A Book That Was Wanted" by W. C. Grasby appeared in Perth's *Western Mail*, 18 August 1916: "Mr. Tarlton Rayment, of Bow-Worrung Forest, Victoria, has written and Whitcombe and Tombs, of Melbourne, have published, a book entitled *Money in Bees, A Practical Treatise on the Profitable Management of the Honey Bee in Australasia.* The price is 7s. 6d. In a brief introduction, Mr. W. S. Pender, Editor of the "Australasian Beekeeper," says :-"No apology nor elaborate explanation need be made for the publication of a practical guide to beekeeping in Australasia; so far the industry has been but little catered for." One may endorse Mr. Pender's remarks and welcome this new book as being one certain to prove of very great value to amateur beekeepers, while it will also be useful to those who have had a great deal of experience; in fact the more one knows the more information be can usually obtain from the work of others. The book is well written, and deals in a simple way with the varied information which the beginner in beekeeping desires and has such difficulty in securing at present. This is not because there is any lack of literature on bees, but because Australian conditions differ a very great deal from those of other parts of the world where the books are written.

The book is both well illustrated and well printed, and the illustrations will assist the beginner very greatly. It is not necessary to attempt to outline the contents of the book further than to say that the chapters include articles on Australian bees, locations and buildings suited for an apiary, working equipment, the preliminary work, in establishing an apiary, the method of manipulating the swarms, extracting honey ... The author has broken new ground in his attempt to deal with the Australian honey flows and then sources, and his work in this connection will not only be of direct use, but will form the foundation for further observations and records. Australian plants provide a rich honey harvest, and it is surprising how little attention has been devoted to the study of the plants which produce the honey.

One is not unfriendly in suggesting that this portion of the book will be considerably revised in the second edition, and there are various little points which might be a little more clear; such for example, as the wording of the paragraph relating to ventilation when closing a hive for removal. The information in regard to Western Australian honey plants is somewhat meagre, and does not appear to be quite accurate. From the author's remarks one would conclude that the yate tree is the chief honey producer in this State, whereas the area of yate-gum forest is small compared with that of other trees. Then, the mention of sandalwood as a honey producer would lead an outsider to imagine that this tree was still very plentiful, while it is an unfortunate fact that this interesting shrubby tree has been nearly exterminated from all of the settled districts. These, however, are small matters. …" (p.4)

WHITELAW, T. E. *Foul Brood: its symptoms and treatment*, 1912, Department of Agriculture. R.E.E. Rogers, Government Printer, Adelaide. SLSA Mortlock Pamphlets, Call #638.15 W594. pp.8, illus, 25cm

Books 1919 - 1945

AUSTRALIAN ARMY EDUCATION SERVICE. *Bee-keeping (A.I.F. Land Book No. 13)*, 1919, London Department of Agriculture, Victoria. pp.27, s/c, 14.5x22cm. ML, SLV, The University of Melbourne Library. Catlg: b24891654; possible copy at University of New England. Dixson Library, catlg: 8536-25060. Notes: to be used as basis for lectures by instructors, in conjunction with *ABC & XYZ of Beekeeping*. Possible author RAYMENT, Tarlton. Contains list of other land pursuits text books. Gives cost of 'black' hive at 30/-, 'Italian' 45/- (shillings).

Glass original whole plate negative held by Australian War Memorial. "Demonstration in beekeeping at Crabstone Experimental Farm, Aberdeen, Scotland, to Australian and American students, May 1919"

Some illustrations would have added character to this work, obviously intended for the occupational training of Australian soldiers about to return home. Chapters: Introducing, The Beginner, New Swarms, Composition of a Colony, Brood, Material Collected by Bees, Araratus & Hives, Extracting, Feeding, Varieties, Queen Rearing, Preparation of Wax, Pests & Diseases.

BEUHNE, F. R. *Honey Flora of Victoria*, (see also previous chapter) 1922 (pp.148) 70 illus; 1923; 1925 pp.170, hardbound, 82 illus, 28 chapters; 1935, 1942 (pp.168) brown cover, Beuhne not attributed as author (deceased 1933) but essentially his work, 28 chapters; 1945 (pp. 168), green cover. 80 illus, paperback, one & sixpence. $10 to $50, one copy located in black full calf $60. Price varies according to edition.

BLACKET, PENDRILL C. *Talks to Beginners in Beekeeping*, 1934, Dimmock, Maitland. pp.149, illus, s/c, index, 14x21.5cm. Notes: author formerly editor *Australasian Beekeeper*. Except for one article, illus and text (49 articles) appeared in *ABK*. $50. Copy at NLA.

DEPARTMENT of AGRICULTURE, Vic. *Bee-Keeping in Victoria*, 1941, 1942 pp.168, illus. Notes: interesting period photographs, portrait of F. R. Beuhne. 1st ed ca. 1915, others in 1925, 1934, 1942, c1945. SLSA has various copies. Foreword: originally prepared by F. R. Behune, a former bee expert of the Dept of Agriculture. Material first printed in the Journal of Agriculture, commencing Jan. 1912. 1923. $35. Chapters: Biology of the Honey bee, Hive and its Components, Handling of Bees, Establishing an Apiary, Spring Management, Summer Operations, Wintering of Bees, Diseases of Bees, Pests and Enemies of Bees, Queen raising and Re-Queening, Honey and Beeswax, Miscellaneous Operations, Honey bees in Agriculture and Horticulture

GOODACRE, W. A. *The Beginner in Bee Culture*, 1934, illus., Sydney, Farmers' Bulletin No.129 (NSW Dept. Agric.), illus, s/c, adv, pp.91. $30. Copy located 2010 for $33. 2nd ed. 1921, originally cost nine pence (SLSA) pp.56; 3rd ed. 1929 (SLSA) pp.82. another ed. 1935, this the second impression of the 4th ed., making 12,000 copies printed. Essentially the precursor to *Bees and Honey*, also by Goodacre, and carries the same cover photo. In the *Agricultural Gazette of N.S.W.*, 1 Nov. 1933 "*The Beginner in Bee Culture* by W. A. Goodacre, is a booklet on beekeeping that can be recommended both to the commercial apiarist and to the man with only a few hives. It is published by the Department, and is priced at Is. 2d., posted. It has sold widely not only in New South Wales but also in the other States."

GOODACRE, W. A. ***The Honey and Pollen Flora of New South Wales***, 1938, pp.195, numerous b&w photos & illus, 11 colour plates, folding map, colour frontis., h/c, index, gilt title on cover, 16x24cm. 5 shillings. <u>Notes</u>: photos of giant trees dwarfing axemen, fine drawings. Reprinted 3rd imp. 1951, again in 1958. $75 to $95. One edition sighted signed by author, as owned by "Bumble" H. Graham Smith of Hawkesbury Agricultural College.

GOODACRE, W. A. ***Bees and Honey***, 1941, pp.139, illus, p/c, 15x24cm. 2 shillings & sixpence. $20. 3rd ed. 1950, pp.150. other eds. Located 1945, 1954.

<u>Book Review</u>. From *The Sydney Morning Herald*, 29 December 1941 "The war-time demand for honey has stimulated interest in beekeeping in many districts. In view of the fact that there are scores of newcomers to the industry and that others are likely to take it up in the post war years, a completely revised edition of *Bees and Honey*, by W. A. Goodacre, senior apiary instructor, of the Department of Agriculture, should be welcome. It is a complete handbook on apiary practice, based on extensive scientific research into breeding, management, and equipment; is written in a popular style, and is profusely illustrated."

Henry Hacker

HACKER, Henry *An Introduction to Beekeeping*, Dept of Agriculture and Stock, Queensland, Division of Entomology and Plant Pathology, Bulletin No. 11, May 1935, pp.46, illus, s/c (blue), index. Notes: Considered rare. Copy at Dept. of Employment, Qld. Contains staff list of Division, first published in two parts in *Queensland Agricultural Journal,* Vol. XLIII., Pts. 4 & 5, April - May, 1935, photo of a period apiary, historical notes on introduction of bees to Australia (Gregory Blaxland 1805, Samuel Marsden 1810, Wallace 1822, Italian bees 1874-1878). Foreword: Provide the prospective beekeeper with a concise account on phases of the industry the subject of most inquiries. Chapters: The Honey Bee, Products of the Hive, Apiary Equipment, Commencing Beekeeping, General Management of Bees, Insect Enemies and Diseases of the Hive Bee.

An absorbing tale of Hacker's insect collection work with the Queensland Museum appears in *A Time for a Museum, The History of the Queensland Museum, 1862-1986.* Quoted is this extract from Marks, E.N., 1973. Henry Hacker (1876-1973) *Ent. Soc. Qld News Bull.* 100:13-16 "not only did Henry Hacker have great observational and practical skills in dealing with insects, enthusiasm for collecting them, and an 'eye for a species', but he was also physically tough, resourceful and self-reliant, with a capacity for meeting awkward situations, and mentally tough too, for when he had determined on a course he pursued it despite hazards and discomforts." Hacker employed a bicycle in his collection expeditions, and in 1907 made a 500 mile ride from Charters Towers to Cloncurry. "He traveled widely, later graduating to a motor cycle on which he earned a reputation equal to his earlier one on the bicycle, and made prodigious collections." (p.184) Though seconded to the Dept. of Agriculture in 1929, he "remained in charge of the museum's insect collection, working one or two days a week there until his retirement in 1943. ... Hacker gave up entomology and all connection with it after his retirement ... although he lived for 30 more years, dying in 1973 at the age of 97."

Henry Hacker, self portrait, in his room at the Queensland Museum, September 1940. [124]

From the *flyaqis* [125] web site: "Hacker was an entomologist at the Queensland Museum between 1911 and 1929, then Queensland Dept of Agriculture & Stock 1929-1943. Born Leyton, England. Collected Coen district 1904, Cloncurry 1907. Excellent collector with great knowledge of Queensland insects. Mainly published on Hymenoptera and hemiptera. Foundation

---

[124] From *flyaqis* web site
[125] flyaqis.mov.vic.gov.au/chaec/hacker.html

member of Ent. Soc. Qld, frequent exhibitor at meetings. President 1934."

Refer also (1) Hacker, H., 1907. "An entomologist's cycling trip to Cloncurry (Queensland)." *Tasmanian Nat. 1:12-13;* (2) Marks, E.N., 1974 Obituary – Henry Hacker 1876-1973. *Mem. Qld. Mus. 17:191-194;* (3) Marks, E.N., 1973. Henry Hacker 1876-1973. *Ent. Soc. Qld. News Bull. 100:13-16;* (4) Hacker, H. 1921. Catalogue of Australian Bees. *Mem. Qld. Mus. 7:88-163.*

Found on the *Trove* web site: "Henry Hacker, who was in charge of the Queensland Museum's entomological collection from 1911 to 1943, was born in Essex, England on 31 January 1876. He began his study of entomology at the British Museum but soon embarked on a wandering life, travelling to Australia for the gold rushes and taking out a Miner's Right at Charters Towers. About 1897-8 he began collecting Australian insects. He served as a Trooper in the Boer War and was discharged at Durban in 1901, giving his trade as miner and his intended place of residence as Johannesburg. In 1902 he made the first of three collecting trips to parts of Australia which were entomologically unknown.

From *Trove*: "Possibly Henry Hacker with his equipment for gathering specimens and samples, Cairns, ca. 1907"

In August 1904 he took out a Miner's Right at Cairns and made Coen his base. In 1909 he married Constance Callaghan and they settled in the Upper Mulgrave Valley, south of Cairns. However their rubber farm was unsuccessful and they moved to Brisbane. On 7 March 1911 he was appointed to the staff at the Queensland Museum where he worked until his retirement in 1943. He died in Brisbane on 21 September 1973. (Information taken from: Obituary, Henry Hacker 1876-1973 in Memoirs of the Queensland Museum, Vol. 17, no.1, 1974, p.191.)"

See also: *The life and experiences of Henry Hacker in times gone by*, edited by D. Hallam, Bowen Hill, Qld. Queensland Women's Historical Association, 35 Jordan Terrace, Bowen Hills QLD 4006], c1994. [31] p. ill., ports.; 21 cm. "produced in conjunction with Hacker Family on the occasion of a display of Henry Hacker's photography at Miegunyah September - October 1994"

HACKER, Henry. (1932) *The honey bee*, Beekeeping leaflet no. 2. Dept. of Agriculture and Stock, Division of *Entomology* and Plant Pathology. Brisbane, 6p. 24 cm. Copy at NLA.

HACKER, Henry (1933) *Hints to beginners in beekeeping*, Beekeeping leaflet no.3, Brisbane, Division of Entomology and Plant Pathology. Copy at NLA.

HACKER, Henry. (1934) *Products of the Hive*, Beekeeping leaflet no. 4, (Brisbane, Government Printer, Division of Entomology and Plant Pathology. 7 p; 25 cm. Copy at NLA.

KEEN, G. H. *Introducing Queen Bees*, 1936, *Australasian Beekeeper*, Maitland, pp.14, 11.5x15cm. sixpence. Notes: Author contributed to *ABK* under pseudonym 'South Island' in 'New Zealand News'. Being a keen observer and realising the difficulties of others by his own experiences, he set out to give beekeepers of all ranks or status something really worth while. Reviewed in *ABK* Dec. 1936, pp.173-4. Another edition (nd.) small booklet, 20pp.

PENDER, W. S. (revised by JAMES, George. of Satur Hill, Scone) *Australasian Queen Rearing*, 1926, Pender Bros, . West Maitland N.S.W., pp.59, 2nd ed., illus, s/c (green or brown). $25 to $95. Another, 2nd ed., 1963 reprint of 1926 ed., also a 1976 reprint. Copy (1926) at NLA. Notes: Pender was Editor *Australasian Beekeeper*, printed by E. Tipper, photo of J. E. Wing of San Jose, California. Foreword: Gives the beekeeper any of those associated with him at that time dreamt of such success attending the efforts they then put forth in launching their literary infant. The *Queenslander* has proved one of the most successful weeklies in Australia, and I believe the success in a great measure was owing to the untiring exertions of Mr. Mackay, and there is no doubt he was enabled to endure a good deal, both of the mental and physical labour he underwent and with comparative ease by the aid of the pure air and bracing climate of his happy home at LIZZY LEE, which, although so near to the centre of Brisbane, is perfectly free from the disagreeable smells and the racket of city life." (p.8)

MACKAY, Angus. ***The Honey Bee in Australia***, c1884, 2/-. Published by John Sands, printers. An advertisement for this 32 page pamphlet appeared at the rear of *The Elements of Australian Agriculture* (1885). The only copy known to

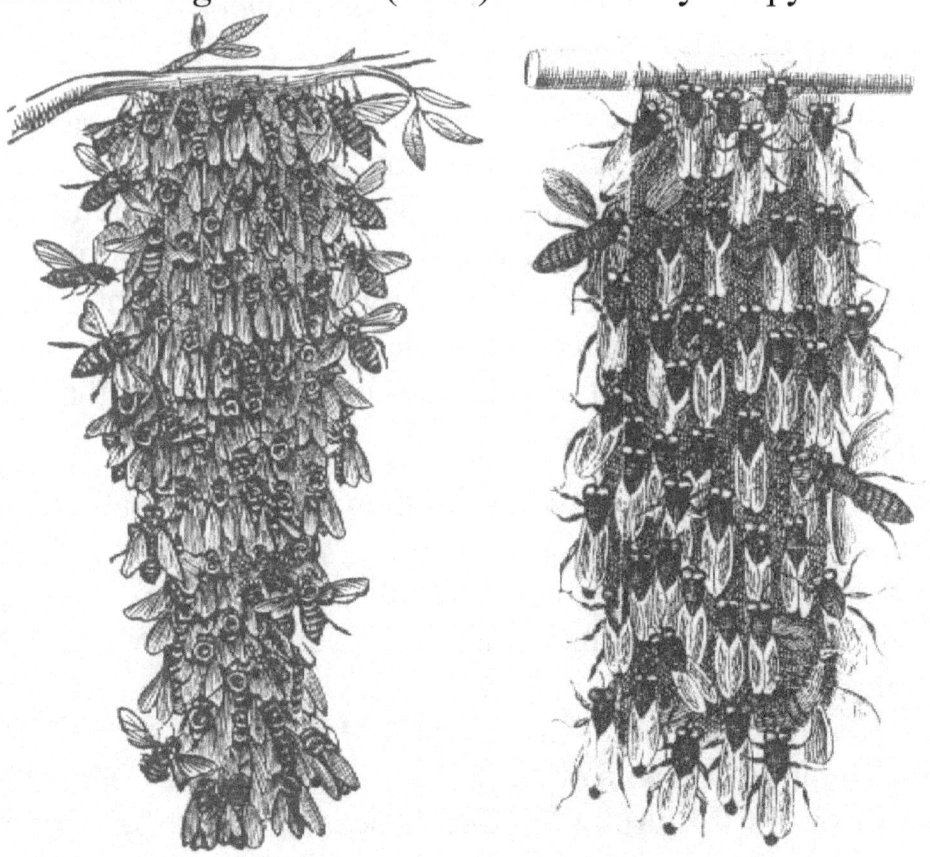

18x11.5cm. Another edition Wilkie & Co., Melbourne, 1930. "For children aged 8 to 9 years", written as a school reader. Whitcombe's story books ; no. 312. SLV (823A/RAY 192-A, Grnd Fl, Children's Literature, Rare). NLA. alternate title *Goldwing, the story of the honey bees palace*. Considered rare. Cover title: Goldwing, the story of the honey bees palace.

RAYMENT, Tarlton, c1921. **Golden City of the Bees**, 1st ed., Whitcombe & Tombs. School reader, possibly same as *Goldwing* above

RAYMENT, Tarlton, **Money in Bees in Australia**, 1925. 2nd ed., Whitcombe & Tombs. pp.280, over 104 illus, illlus boards, deluxe edition illustrated cloth & matching d/w, index, 14x21.5cm, also green illustrated cloth h/c ed. Some seen rebound in plain green cloth. 2 shillings & sixpence. Subtitled: *A Practical Treatise on the Profitable Management of the Honey Bee in Australia.*

Notes: intro by W. S. Pender, editor *Australasian Beekeeper,* numerous illustrations hand drawn by author. Work possibly commissioned by Commonwealth Department of Defence for their Soldiers' Educational Classes. Laurie Braybrook confirmed in a personal communication (July 1995) that Rayment's book was written for repatriated soldiers. This edition has more historical (ie. Early beekeepers & intro of bees) content than 1st, lacks section on honey flora.

Chapters: Part 1. Spring: Australian Bees, Locations & Buildings, Working Equipment, Preliminary Work, Manipulating Frames, Extracted Honey, Working to Increase, Out-Yards & Italianising. Part 2. Summer: Swarms & Swarming, Comb Honey, Working for Comb Honey, Queens, Queen Rearing, Queen Mating, Pollen & Pollen Substitutes, General Summer Work, Robber Bees, Feeding Bees, Enemies of Honey-Bees. Part 3. Autumn: Bee Diseases, Nectar & Honey-

Dew, Superseding Queens, Spare Combs, General Autumn Work, Preparation for Wintering. Par. 4. Winter: Heating Honey, Preparing Honey for Sale, A Winter Flow of Honey, General Work in Winter, Exhibiting, Beeswax, Foundation, Travelling Bees, Honey Flows & Their Sources. Part 5: Special Subjects. Evolution of Modern Hive, To Cope with Weeds, Metal Combs, The Economic Aspect, Weight of Swarms, Remedial Treatment of Stings, Hopkins method, Physiology of Queen, Minute Parasites, Bees of the Old World, Wild Bees, Portable Honey-house, A New Melter, A New Wax Press, To Unsolder Tin Caps, Centenary, How Bees Were Spread, The Bees' House, Wheels to Go Faster, The Printed Word, $35 to $160

RAYMENT, Tarlton *Profitable Honey Plants of Australasia*, 1925. Whitcombe and Tombs, Melbourne. Subtitled *A Handbook, the first of its kind, on Australasian plants that fill the treasury of the bee-hive, and render possible the financial success of the modern Bee-farm. A complementary volume to 'Money in Bees in Australasia'.* An addition note on the title page *With numerous illustrations expressly drawn by the Author to illustrate the remarkably rich honey-resources of Australasia, with an annotated list, and two appendices containing a census of the Acacias and Eucalypts.* 1st ed., illus, frontis, h/c illustrated green cloth, matching d/w (bee, eucalypt flower and seed pods), pp.132, SCL. Chapters: Honey-flows and their Sources (Dearth of Information; Botany for Bee-keepers; Classification; Wind-loving Flowers; Insect-loving Flowers); Flowers and Bees Mutually Dependent (Moth and Fly flowers; Why Plants Yield Nectar; Fertilization; The Bee and the Apple; An Exception to the Rule); Pollen (How Pollen is Gathered and Stored; Floral Nectar; Chemistry of Honey; Extra-floral Nectar; Plant Honey-dew; Insect Honey-dew; Manna; Nectar Secreting Conditions; Honey; How the Honey Flora of a District may be Changed; Propolis); Annotated List of Honey Plants; Census of the Genus Acacia; Census of the Genus Eucalyptus; Notes: probably the first book of its kind in Aust. The 1st ed of *Money in Bees* contained some of this material, now larger and published in a separate volume. This book contains surprises, particularly beautiful prose, equal to that in *A Cluster of Bees*. A sample "... let us away to some great field where the White Clover covers the earth like snow, where under a clear sky, in the warm, bright sun, we too shall stand enthralled by that ineffable fragrance wafted from a million miniature distilleries. The bee alights, and no fruitless searching is possible with that ethereal odour as a guide. Yea, and even more, there are gaily coloured lines that invariably point the road to where the exquisite drops glisten as crystal gems. There are many who seek to explain away the honey guides and to rob them of the poetry of nature, but there they are pointing the path to the overflowing treasury of the nectaries. But the way is seldom 'broad and straight' - anthers, ripe and ready to burst with their riches, oft bar the way. They are pushed aside. Lo, a shower of golden dust descends upon the little labourer as it drinks the warm sweet offering. Such untiring industry makes the thirst of the bee insatiable; it wings away to another flower ... and a quiescent stigma awaits the living pollen-granule." Parts of this book will one day be rightfully recognised as a great literary contribution. One illustration caught my eye, that of a diagrammatic view of the tongues of *Prosopis, Halictus, Apis* and *Bombus*. $40 to $120, rare. £5 in 1967, $130 in 2010.

Tarlton Rayment in 1937, from *The Melody Lingers On*

RAYMENT, Tarlton 1935. ***A Cluster of Bees***, 1st & limited ed., Endeavour Press. pp.752, over 165 illus comprising 1,721 diagrams, colour plate, h/c, typically in dark green cloth, one sighted in dark blue, index, 15x22cm. Notes: Rare, limited edition, lists 33 subscribers, intro by Prof. E. F. Phillips of Cornell University, colour plate of carpenter bees, all illustrations hand drawn by author. The original drawings are held at Cornell. A masterpiece, pleasant reading and detailed bee drawings, sections of beautiful prose, describes finding of *Apis aenigmatica* - Australia's true honeybee, Gippsland, Victoria. Introduction: "Somehow Fabre and Rayment seem to fit the same mould. They are alike in a never-ending ability to work and to observe." Chapters: 60 essays on the life histories of Australian bees, with specific descriptions of over 100 new species. $250 to $600, rare.

RAYMENT, Tarlton, (1953) ***Bees of the Portland District***, Portland Field Naturalists' Club. pp.39, s/c. Rayment's biography by Young lists 33 pages of his published works between 1914 and 1956. Many of his articles appeared in newspapers and journals such as *Farmer & Settler*, *Australasian Beekeeper*, *Victorian Naturalist* and *Walkabout*. Extant copies of Rayment's independently published works are exceedingly rare today.

The Field Naturalists' Club was a non-profit-making society organised to foster an appreciation of the unique Flora and Fauna of this historic district. Introduction: extract "Historic Portland, on the extreme south-west coast of Victoria, saw the first furrow ploughed in the State for agriculture. ... The insects of the district have been assiduously collected during the seasons 1950-51-52-53 by Clifford Beauglehole, of Gorae West. He has added very considerably to our knowledge of the rich insect fauna of Portland, as his collections amply demonstrate, for they include many species new to science." Contains specific descriptions of 28 new species, 15 allotypes, 3 sub-species. This book concentrates on Australian native bees, however it's last paragraphs state "The social bee is too well known to need description here. *Mellifera* was introduced to Australia in 1822, when ten colonies of English black bees were landed in Sydney from the convict ship *Isabella*, commanded by Captain Wallace. The Italian golden bee arrived later in 1862 ... and cross-breeds of these two bees are now distributed over the entire Commonwealth. ... The Italian bee is probably derived from a crossing of the blacks of Europe and the yellows of Egypt, and it is significant, that as one goes north, the bees become blacker; as one goes south, the bees become yellower; the two races meeting on the Mediterranean shores. The Grampians (Mt. William, alt. 3,825 ft.), immediately to the north of Portland, are the home of many large commercial apiaries, and many tons of high-grade honey are harvested each year from such rich sources as Yellow-box, Yellow-gum, etc."

portrait of Tarlton Rayment, 1949,
by his biographer, Lynette Young,

VICTORIAN APIARISTS' ASSOCIATION *The Honey Book*, s/c booklet, cover in dark blue with a bee alighting on a blossom. SLNSW. No details available as cover only held by the library, contents lost, could be a recipe book or information on honey. date of publication unknown, but likely pre 1939.

Writer Dorothy Wall
Image from National Archives of Australia

WALL, Dorothy, (1934) 1894-1942 *The Tale of Bridget and the Bees* written and illustrated by Dorothy Wall. London, Methuen, pp.56, ill. (some col.); 22 cm. Another ed, Poughkeepsie, Artists & Writers Guild (1935), up to US$200. SLV. ML copy (823.912/W187.1/13) inscribed by author. Juvenile fiction, synopsis: With the help of a little man named Ginger-Pop and a little magic, Bridget visits the beehive. The illustrations are enchanting, some in colour. Some mix accurate depictions of bees and comb with fanciful images of drones, workers (house bees armed with brooms!) and the Queen. *The Australian Dictionary of Biography* supplies "(1894-1942) born

12 January 1894 at Kilburnie, Wellington, New Zealand, migrated to Sydney in 1914 … An ardent defender of Australian flora and fauna, Wall drew to educate as well as entertain." Dorothy produced two of her Blinky Bill books at the Blue Mountains village of Warrimoo where I lived for seven years before moving locally to Springwood. The village sign beside the Great Western Highway at Warrimoo declares it to be "Blinky Bill Country". Thought to be absent from this region, a Koala colony was recently discovered in the lower Blue Mountains."

An obituary appeared in *The Sydney Morning Herald*, 27 January 1942 "The death occurred recently at a Neutral Bay private hospital of Mrs. Dorothy Badgery, well known as Dorothy Wall, author of children's i books. Miss Wall's books, which she illustrated, included the "Blinky Bill" series and "Bridget and the Bees." Before she became ill, she was working on a book about the "Rats of Tobruk," and had completed a set of illustrations. She was a New Zealander, and had lived in Australia for more than 20 years. Her son, Peter, now 16 years of age, was the origin of some of "Blinky Bill's" remarks and observations." (p.9)

Books - Post 1945

ADAMS, S. G. *The Truth About Royal Jelly*, nd, 27th ed., pp.16, s/c, 14x21.5cm, issued free. Notes: A passionate treatise on the benefits of RJ. Authored by Manager of Mudgee Honey Co., product promoted is 'Goldvita' RJ Capsules. Foreword: The health and all round efficiency of our people would be greatly enhanced if everyone took intermittent courses of RJ and ate Honey every day of their lives. Chapters: How Royal jelly is Produced, Uses, RJ Production an Art, Clinical tests, Great Results from France, Excellent Results in Geriatrics, Spectacular results in Neuro-Psychoses, Work of Dr. Decourt, Splendid Results in Pediatrics, More on geriatrics, Contribution by Dr. Ardry, Work of Dr. Jacoli, RJ in Pediatrics, RJ a Wonderful Investment, Summer Fatigue, More on Malnutrition in Babies, Duodenal Ulcer, More on Neuro-Psychoses, Storing & Keeping Qualities, Conclusion, Finding from Mexico, Warning About RJ Mixtures & Cheap Imitations, testimonials, Vigorous at 85 Years of Age, Testimonial from Spectacular Recovery from serious Blood Disorder, Other Interesting Findings, Conference Findings, TJ for Athletes, Misc., Bronchial Asthma, For Renewed Energy & improved Mental Ability, Blood Disorders, Report from Europe, Experiments on Animals & Insects, Special Recommendation, testimonials Picked at Random, High Standard of Clinical Tests.

APIMONDIA. *First Australian Bee Congress*, Oct. 13-16, 1972, Queensland,. Apimondia Publishing House, Romania, ed., Smith, Dr. Francis. pp.239, s/c, illus, colour plates. Notes: Consists of papers presented at the conference. UWSH. $50

APIMONDIA *The XXVI International Congress of Apiculture*, Adelaide, Oct. 13-19, 1977, Apimondia Publishing House, Romania, pp.615, h/c, illus, colour plates. Consists of Congress proceedings. Photograph of Dr. Keith Doull. .UWSH. $100

AUGHTERSON, W. H. *The Diseases of Bees, Symptoms - Treatment and Control*, 1957, Pender Bros, Maitland, pp.48, illus, s/c (brown). 6/9, 7/3 posted (*ABK*, Feb. 1959). NLA. Illustrations by A. J. Giblett. <u>Foreword</u>: Written to give apiarists a more thorough insight into bee diseases than can usually be given in books which cover the complete subject of beekeeping. <u>Chapters</u>: American Foulbrood, European Foulbrood, Parafoulbrood, Sacbrood, Fungous Diseases of Brood, Miscellaneous Diseases of Brood, Nosema, Acarine, Amoeba, Septicemia, Paralysis, Fungeous Diseases of Adult Bees, Dysentery, Regulations re the Importation of Queen bees into Australia. $10 to $20

AUSTRALIAN HONEY BOARD, *The Australian Honey Cookbook*, 1983, 1st ed., pp.37, illus, gloss colour s/c, 16.5x23.5cm. $10

AUSTRALIAN HONEY INSTITUTE, *Secrets from the Honey Pot,* 42 Tested Recipes with Honey. Ca. 1950-54, Melbourne. pp.32, numerous illus, $12. <u>Chapters</u>: Recipes: for thye cake tin; fancy breads; children's favourites; cold weather desserts; afternoon tea ideas; for a sweet tooth; thirst quenchers; tasty supper dishes. Opening article on migratory beekeepers, with 3 supporting photos – I like the one depicting a bush bee camp with family members enjoying lunch.

The cocktail recipes look good, will definitely try the gingerade. ½ cup honey, 4 teaspoons lemon juice, 1 cup water, 1 teaspoon ground ginger, 1 tablespoon sugar. Put water, ginger, honey and sugar into a saucepan, boil till it syrups, stir in the lemon juice and leave till cold. Strain. Serve with iced water; or maybe with soda water.

AUSTRALIAN HONEY BOARD, (197?) *The wonderful story of Australian Honey*. Crows Nest, N.S.W., pp.7, (2 fold.): ill., 28 cm. Bees --Juvenile literature

Abram's bee house, Parramatta, 1883
From *The Immigrant Bees, 1788 to 1898*

<< caricature of Wilhelm Abram of Parramatta, from the *Town and Country Journal,* 24 Nov. 1883, as reproduced in *The Immigrant Bees, 1788 to 1898*

AYLING, Robert I. (1999) **Rev. John Ayling, Australian Pioneer: The Life of Rev. John Ayling, Clergyman, Educator, Beekeeper, 1825-1897**. (1999) pp.242, list of illustrations, index. Limited edition of 100 copies, signed by author. pp.171-183 cover Ayling's contribution to Australian beekeeping. Copies on internet $120 to $195.

BARRETT, Peter J. *The Immigrant Bees 1788 - 1898, A Cyclopaedia on the Introduction of European Honeybees into Australia and New Zealand* 1995, ISBN 0 646 25812 5. Dewey 638.10994, published by the author - 1 Banjo Place Springwood, 2777, N.S.W., Australia. pp.201, illus, s/c (yellow), index, biblio, out of print mid 1998. A limited number were produced in hardcover. Now out of print. Notes: Reviewed *ABK* April 1996, *NZBK* June 1996, *Apicultural Abstracts* 1996, Vol. 47, No. 2. "A seminal work", "of value to those interested in beekeeping history". 1st edition limited to 100 copies signed by author, 4 subsequent printings.

Chapters: The Native Bees, The dark European Honeybee (N.S.W., Tas., W.A., N.Z.), The Italian Honeybee (N.S.W., Tas., Vic., Qld., S.A., N.Z), Bees Afloat, The Bees Spread Over the Land, Exports.

BARRETT, Peter J. *William Charles Cotton, Grand Bee Master of New Zealand, 1842 - 1847*, 1997, ISBN 0 646 29300 1. Dewey 638 1092, published by the author - 1 Banjo Place Springwood, 2777, N.S.W., Australia. Notes: Based on Cotton's journals written between 1841 and 1848 held within the Dixson Colledtion, SLNSW. A5, s/c, pp.160, 40,000 words, 34 illus (15 from his journals, 10 from *My Bee Book* and 9 supporting) table of contents, detailed index, bibliography. Included is a translation of his Maori beekeeping work *Nga Pi (The Bees)* and 14,000 words taken from his N.Z. journals and letters.

Cotton's house and attached apiary, Auckland, 1845

Covers the story of Cotton's (Te Ketene) beekeeping activities in New Zealand. There is an Australian connection through his contacts with early New South Wales beekeepers including Gregory Blaxland and Elizabeth Macarthur. His bee stocks were sourced from Sydney and possibly Parramatta by his friend James Busby.

Acclaimed for his 1842 work *My Bee Book,* Cotton added to his contributions to British beekeeping throughout his residence of six years in the North Island of New Zealand. His colonial beekeeping activities, shared with settler and Maori alike, are revealed in all their fascination. Through his written word while in New Zealand, Cotton provided the key to the mystery of whether or not he achieved his aim to ship bees from England in 1842.

Chapters: Some Biographical Background; His Plan to Bring Honeybees to New Zealand; Plymouth to Sydney; A beekeeper without bees, 1842; Culture Shock; James Busby and three hives of bees, 1843; The Bishop and the Baron; A Beekeeper with Bees, 1844; Unanswered Questions & Other Peoples' Bees; Auckland, 1844; A Love and a Disability; 'The Great Cotton' octagonal hive; Bee Matters amidst the Maori Wars, 1845; The Maoris, New Zealand's first commercial beekeepers; The Comonwelthe of Bees; Auckland and Wellington, 1846;

Farewells and a Legacy; Obituaries; Nga Pi (The Bees). Out of print. A review may be found at lvnydd.sheldonhost.com

BARRETT, Peter J. *The Immigrant Bees 1788 - 1898, Volume II, An Update on the Introduction of European Honeybees into Australia and New Zealand*, August 1999, ISBN 0 9586146 0 1, published by the author at 1 Banjo Place Springwood, 2777, N.S.W., Australia. pp.1650, illus, h/c (burgundy cloth), index, biblio, planned publication June 1999. Limited edition of 25 numbered & signed h/c copies. AUD$75, overseas AUD$80 posted airmail. A softcover edition of 25 copies is also planned at AUD$50, overseas AUD$65 posted airmail. Notes: This update is arranged in the same manner as its predecessor ie., chronological sequence within each state or territory and country. This work is not a novel. It consists of the additional material the author has collected and analysed since the publication of what can now be referred to as Volume I in 1995. Those interested in the solution to the mystery of whether or not William Charles Cotton managed to bring bees with him from England should refer to *William Charles Cotton, Grand Bee Master of New Zealand, 1842 - 1847.*

This second volume was warranted not only because of the additional volume of material presented, but particularly because of:

- the first person, 1834 contribution of Thomas Braidwood Wilson, which, among other gems of detail, tells how he shipped his bees to Van Diemen's Land in 1831
- Mary Bussell's records of bee hives aboard the *James Pattison*, 1834
- T. J. Lempriere and Charles O'Hara Booth, the 'Honey Jar', Port Arthur, Van Diemen's Land, 1836
- Captain Maconochie and Lieutenant-Colonel Hulme, introducer of bees into Norfolk Island, 1840

- Lieutenant Helpman R.N., Swan River colony, 1841
- St Matthew's Windsor, N.S.W., & Fr. Petitjean, Bay of Islands, N.Z., 1842
- Elizabeth Macarthur, pioneer beekeeper, Parramatta, 1842
- Gregory Blaxland, explorer/pastoralist, confirmed as a beekeeper, 1842

SWARMING BAG, A GREAT IMPROVEMENT

(from an article in *The Town and Country Journal* for 24 November 1883 which covered Abram's bee farm, Parramatta)

- Thomas Alison Scott, detailed letter on the management of bees at Brisbane Water, N.S.W., 1842-1845
- James Kidd, superintendent of the Botanic Gardens, absconding bees from six hives, Sydney, 1847
- Introduction of the *Ligurian* bee
    - Edward Wilson, Victoria, 1862
    - S. C. Farr, Canterbury, South Island, New Zealand, 1880

- Charles Rake, Adelaibe, South Australia, 1883
- A.E. Bonney, Kangaroo Island, South Australia, 1884

BARRETT, Peter J. *An Australian Beekeeping Bibliography (Volume I)* 1997, ISBN 0 646 29190 4, pp.38, illus, index, A5, in print, limited to 20 copies, hard covers by arrangement. $16.50 posted within Australia, Chapters: Books to 1918, Books 1919-1945, Books Post 1945, Journals, Other Publications & Ephemera. Includes list of chapters, notes on peculiarities or special features of particular books.

BARRETT, Peter J. *An Australian Beekeeping Bibliography, 2nd ed.* (1997), incorporates Volume I with selected author biographies and significant illustrations from selected works. pp.60, illus, index, A5, in print, $20.50 posted within Australia, overseas airmail $25. Library holdings: SLV, Univ NSW, Deakin Univ. Chapters: Books to 1918, Books 1919-1945, Books Post 1945, Journals, Other Publications & Ephemera. Includes list of chapters, notes on peculiarities or special features of particular books. 3rd. ed., greatly enlarged to 230+ pages, publ. 2011.

BARRETT, Peter J. *The Immigrant Bees 1788 - 1898, Volume III, A Further Update on the Introduction of European Honeybees into Australia and New Zealand,* From January 2001 this working manuscript of some 100 pages grew to over 300 pages by December 2006; it was printed and distributed in May 2007. Concentrates on Australian beekeepers of the 19th century, eg., Frances Maria and Alexander Brodie Spark of *Tempe* on the Cook's River, donors of a hive to William Charles Cotton in August 1843; William Hessel Hall of Lapstone Apiary, Blue Mountains, 1895; Margaret Innes of Port Macquarie, 1843; Edward Wilson who championed introduction of Italian honeybees into Victoria; a first time, accurate recognition of the introduction of Italian honeybees into

Kangaroo Island, championed by Bonney with Buick and Turner the first recipients. Also the story of the introduction of honeybees into the Sandwich Islands, with passing NZ and Van Diemen's Land associations. pp.334, detailed Table of Contents and Index, some colour illustrations.

BARRETT, Peter J. *The Immigrant Bees 1788 - 1898, Volume IV, A Final Insight on the Introduction of European Honeybees into Australia and New Zealand* (2010) 600+ pages

BARRETT, Peter J. *An Australian Beekeeping Bibliography,* **3rd ed.** (2010). New and extended author biographies, book reviews, highlights peculiarities and the magic of some publications. pp.148, illus, index, A5, in print, $55 posted.

BARRETT, Peter J. *The Immigrant Bees 1788 - 1898, Volume V, A Postscript on the Introduction of European Honeybees into Australia and New Zealand* (scheduled for 2012) 400+ pages

BAILEY, Fred, *Beekeeping in Australia, For pleasure and profit*, 1982, William Heinemann Australia. ISBN 0 85859 281 9. pp.139, colour illus h/c (yellow), index, 14.5x21.5cm. Notes: The book I relied upon at the hive to learn beekeeping. Foreword: by Claude ILTON, Mr. Bailey has passed on much of his vast knowledge to beginner and hobbyist beekeepers, to whom I commend this book as a valuable guide.

Chapters: Introducing bees, Natural History of Bees, The Beehive and its Components, Handling Bees, Spring Operations, Swarm Control, The Queen, Artificial Queen Breeding, Summer Operations, Autumn Operations, Plants for Nectar & pollen, Anatomy, Diseases, Enemies & pests, Honey, Honey & Beeswax Recipes, Beekeeping Associations & Clubs.

BENECKE, Fred (2007) *Honey Business: A short history of beekeeping in NSW in the second half of the 20th Century.* Klimpston Press, Nowra, NSW

BENECKE, Fred, and Clemson, Alan (1970) *Showing Honey and Beeswax.* N.S.W. Department of Agriculture

BLAKE, Stanley Thatcher, & ROFF, Charles. *The Honey Flora of South-Eastern Queensland*, 1958. Department of Agriculture & Stock, Qld. . pp.199, illus, h/c, index, 15.5x25cm. 15/- Qld, £1 elsewhere. Notes: revised from author's articles in the *Queensland Agricultural Journal*, new series, Vol. 76-82, May 1953 - Nov. 1956. Sketch map of the region containing the principal honey-producing areas. Reviewed *ABK* April 1959, p.251, Copies at NLA, UWSH. Chapters: Eucalyptus, Tristanias, Angophoras, Tea-trees, Banksias, Callistemons, Wattles, Mangroves, She-oaks, Crop Plants, Weeds, Miscellaneous Plants, Flowering Calendar. Other Eds: 3rd., 1988, 218p., s/c, Department of Primary Industries, Qld., UWS, ISBN 0 7242 2371 1, Reprints in 1959, 1972, 1987, 1988. $30 to $70.

BLAKE, Stanley Thatcher, & ROFF, C. (1972) *The Honey Flora of Queensland*, Department of Primary Industries Queensland, Brisbane, QLD, Australia, 234 pages, b/w illus, h/c. 2nd ed. 1972, 3rd ed. 1988. Copies at SLQ, CSIRO, NLA. Check books.google.com for more locations.

BOLTON, Prof. H. C. *Thomas Bolton, A Pioneer Beekeeper of Victoria*, 1976. *Victorian Historical Journal*. pp.295-305, s/c, reprinted from *VHJ*, Vol. 47, No. 4, Nov. 1976. Notes: biography of Thomas Bolton, 1863-1928. Author was Professor of Theoretical Physics, Monash University, Clayton, Victoria. Not related to Thomas. Well worth reading, researched in depth. My paraphrasing of Prof. Bolton's discussion on some of Thomas' writings "One substantial connected piece of work which though published as a series of articles in *the*

Australasian Beekeeper 1917 to 1919, with the title *Commercial Agriculture*, was arranged in chapters as for a book. More than a manual on beekeeping, a strong personal flavour comes through which allows one to see Thomas Bolton's life and character very clearly. The first books published in Victoria on various technical aspects of beekeeping appeared about the same time and all were appropriately times for soldiers returning to Victoria after the war of 1914-18. It is appropriate to compare Bolton's writing in Commercial Apiculture with F. R. Beuhne's two books, and those of T. Rayment. Both Beuhne and Rayment were more scientific in their outlook. Beuhne was interested in bee diseases and Rayment developed into an entomologist. Beuhne was the Victorian Government Apiarist when he wrote his two books and they are informative in a definitive way. But in neither Beuhne's nor Rayment's writings does the smell of the bush come through as it does in Bolton's where the interaction of man and nature is seen at its most human." In Prof. Bolton's extensive bibliography, there is mention of a book *Samson and the Bees*. It's actual subject matter remains unknown.

BORD, Janet **Honey, Natural Food and Healer**, 1972, Science of Life Books, Victoria. illus, stiffened bds, pp.64, 12x19cm, ISBN 0 909911 50 9. Notes: A quaint little book full of hand drawn illustrations and packed with basic information. Chapters: Honey and Sugar, Honey for Health, The History of Honey, Honey Cookery. $2

BRAYBROOK, Laurie, GOODMAN, R. D.. [1980?] ***Swarming***. pp.9, ill, 30 cm. Melbourne, Apiary Branch, Department of Agriculture Vic. SLV

CHAPMAN-TAYLOR, Ray & DAVEY, Ivo **Practical Beekeeping, Handbook for Australia and New Zealand**, 1988, Inkata Press, ISBN 0 909605 46 7. Dewey 638.1099, 2nd ed., (1981 edition targeted NZ amateurs) 17.5x25cm, pp.164, colour illus s/c (yellow), index, glossary. Copy located on Ebay March 2011 for $35. Notes: chapters are numbered allowing ready reference from other paragraphs, includes most of the content of *Beekeeping in Auckland.* Chapters: Some Problems & Rewards of Beekeeping, Background Information About Bees, The Hive & its Equipment, Siting the Apiary, How to Handle bees, The First Year: How to Begin Beekeeping, The Second Year, The Double Brood Chamber: The 'Leave Alone' Hive, Half-box Systems, Two-queen Hives, Comb Honey, Space in the Hive, Feeding the Bees, Uniting Colonies of Bees, Swarms, Nucleus Colonies, Home-grown Queens, Requeening, Harvesting the Honey, Winter Management of the Colony, Good Combs for the Brood Chamber, How to Move Bees, Natural Enemies, Plants & Bees, Tropical Beekeeping. Copy found 2010 $30.

CHAUNCY, Nan. ***A Fortune for the Brave***, 1954, London, Melbourne, Oxford University Press. pp.198, illus. A novel: Orphan Huon Trivett inherits a remote island off the east coast of Tasmania which holds 'a fortune for the brave' wherein this young boy embarks on an unusual hunt for treasure. SLSA (catlg. Children's Lit. Coll. Aust. 20th c CHA). includes Tasmanian bee culture. Also a reprint 1964, h/c, d/w, pp.198 Oxford Univ. Press, Melbourne. Illustrated by Margaret Holder.

CHAUNCY, Nan. ***Beekeeping***, 1967, Melbourne, Oxford University Press. pp.32. Simply told history of beekeeping in Australia and modern business honey farming. (entry from *Children's Books on Bees and Beekeeping*, Natalie B Hodgson, IBRA, London, 1973) N.L.A. 67-547, ML. Illus by Jane Walker. Written through the eyes of Jimmy, young son of a South Australian beekeeper. Mentions 1822 date for introduction of bees to Australia and existence of a sanctuary for Ligurians on Kangaroo Island.

Nan Chauncy

CLEMSON, Alan. ***Honey and Pollen Flora***, 1985, Dept. Agriculture N.S.W. & Inkata Press, ISBN 0 909605 33 5, 1st ed., 21x28cm. Originally $45, pp.263, numerous colour illus, yellow d/w, green h/c, index, glossary, out of print. $75 to $90. Copies found in 2010 $60 and $160. <u>Notes</u>: A magnificent production on gloss paper, a multitude of colour illustrations. <u>Chapters</u>: Regional map of N.S.W., Nectar & Pollen, Hive Management & Migration, Difficulties Associated with Certain Honey Flows, Trees & Shrubs: Eucalypts, Native Trees & Shrubs, Introduced Trees & Shrubs; Crops: Fruit & Nut Trees, Field Crops; Weeds; Ornamental Trees, Shrubs & Garden Plants,; Distribution Guide; Flowering Calendar.

The Dept. Agriculture flyer announcing the book says, in part "Alan Clemson, a bee specialist (with the Dept.) for 37 years and now retired, has spent hundreds of hours over the past eight years researching and writing ... Well respected for his knowledge of bees and plants, Alan is also an expert with a camera. He took all but two of the 658 colour photographs which illustrate this book. Other plant identification books usually show only one photograph per species. ... (this book) includes three to four photographs showing the various details such as leaves, flowers and bark to help make identification easier. More on the author "... Agriculture asked him to write Honey & Pollen Flora in 1967. Alan had been a keen gardener and beekeeper for as long as he cared to remember. Taking on photography as a more recent hobby, he owned three Nikon camera bodies and 10 lenses. (this book) needed all three talents. For Alan it was a chance to devote time to three of his main loves. Alan began his career with Dept. Agriculture in 1945 after completing firstly a diploma in agriculture at Hawkesbury Agricultural College, and then a stint with the AIF during the Second World War. His first Agriculture postings were as district apiary officer at Bathurst and then at Wagga. In 1952 Alan was appointed principal apiary officer with the Dept; a position he held for 30 years until he retired. In the course of his work, Alan travelled extensively throughout Australia and overseas. Honey & Pollen Flora has been one of Alan's major achievements, taking about eight years to research and write. He finished the book after his retirement in 1983. Alan is married with three children and plans to spend the rest of his retirement continuing to enjoy his garden, his bees, his photography, and travelling."

COOK, S. C. (Sam C.) (1989) *My life with the bees*. Perth, W.A., self published, pp.42, ill., 30 cm. SLV, also LISWA catlg Q638.1 COO, 3rd Fl, Battye Stack. Also sound recording, 3 cassettes, catlg OH2792 A/m.

DEPARTMENT of AGRICULTURE, Vic. *Honey Flora of Victoria*, c1946, pp.136, over 130 b&w illus, 4th ed., paper covers, 15x24cm., index. one & sixpence. Notes: illustrations finely drawn. Chapters: Eucalypts, Banksias, Tea-trees, Myrtles,

Bottlebrushes, Grass Trees, Miscellaneous Flora. 1922-1935 $10 to $45

DOULL, Keith M. (1974). ***Biological and Technical Factors Affecting Profitability in Beekeeping***; Doull worked at the Waite Agricultural Research Institute, University of Adelaide, South Australia. pp.15. biblio, <u>Chapters</u>: Relationship between colony population and honey production; Biological factors affecting production per bee; Practical aspects; Development of colony populations; Rates of development of colony populations; Brood area requirements and hive dimensions; Behaviour aspects of oviposition and foraging; Exploitation of food sources by honeybees; Foraging areas and bee densities; Factors affecting distribution of honeybees; Effects of distance flown on honey production; Importance of pollen; Amounts of pollen required; Quality of pollen;

DURBRIDGE, C J. ***Holding on Beekeeping in Selected Melbourne Libraries***. Brunswick, Victoria : The Author, 1976. pp. vi, 24, 38cm. SLV. What better than listing a bibliography within a bibliography. I've not been able to sight this work as yet.

FIRTH, John William (1954). ***My life as a Bee-keeper***; Biography of a man who commenced beekeeping in N.S.W. in the 1880s, before moving to W.A. in 1902 and settling at Balingup. pp.54. Copy at State Library of Western Australia (LISWA), catlg. ACC 1224A, held at 4th Fl, Priv Arch Stack.

FOOTE, Tom (1997). ***Honey-bees***; translated by Allen Hall. Toowong, Qld., Jollen. pp.12, ill., 21 cm. Subject area: Aborigines, Australian, Queensland, Edward River. Text in Thaayorre dialect with free English translation. "Pormpuraaw, Edward River, Cape York"

GOODMAN, R. D., Department of Agriculture, Vic. ***Honey Flora of Victoria***, 1973, pp.175, s/c, b&w illus, gloss. <u>Notes</u>:

illustrations include trees, bark, leaves, nuts & buds. Chapters: Eucalypts, Pests of the Eucalypts, Miscellaneous Flora, Honey & Pollen in Agricultural Crops, Street Trees, Availability of Forage Plants, Further Reading

Nan Chauncy, *Beekeeping*, 1967

DEPARTMENT of AGRICULTURE, N.S.W., Division of Animal Industry. ***Bees and Honey***, 1959, pp.202, illus, 4th ed. 1966, red cloth h/c, coloured d/w, 14x21cm. Reprinted 1963, 1964. $1.25. Foreword: Designed to meet the needs of commercial beekeepers, of immense value to hobbyists and people who keep bees for pollinating certain crops. Update of the original work by W. A. Goodacre, for many years the Departments Principal Apicultural Officer. Chapters: Hints on Adopting Beekeeping as an Occupation, The Queen and her Subjects, Hives and Materials, Inside the Working Hive, Spring Management in the Apiary, Migratory Beekeeping, Increase of the Colony, Handling the Honey Crop, Producing Section Comb Honey, Production of Beeswax, Food Supplies & substitutes, Diseases of the Brood, Diseases of the Adult Bee, Pests and Enemies, Wintering bees, Useful Tips. $10 to $30. Copies surface regularly, especially on Ebay.

DEPARTMENT of AGRICULTURE, Vic.. ***Bee-Keeping in Victoria***, 1949, 3rd ed., pp.166, illus, chart, s/c, index, UWSH. Notes: interesting period photographs: foundation press, wax press, cappings reducer, uncapping knives & heater, hives made from petrol cases & specifications on how to convert them (pp.20-21). $20. 2011 copy located on Ebay $10.

DEPARTMENT of AGRICULTURE, Vic. LANGRIDGE, D. F., ILTON, C. D ***Bee-Keeping in Victoria***, 1958, 4th ed. pp.167, illus, adv, s/c, index. 2011 copy located on Ebay $10.

Notes: interesting period photographs, portrait of F. R. Beuhne, reviewed *ABK* Feb. 1959, p.204. 5 shillings, 5/10 posted. 1964 ed., 193p. Foreword: originally prepared by F. R. Behune, a former bee expert of the Dept of Agriculture. Material first printed in the Journal of Agriculture, commencing Jan. 1912. Chapters: Biology of the Honey bee, Hive and its Components, Handling of Bees, Establishing an Apiary, Spring Management, Summer Operations, Wintering of Bees, Diseases of Bees, Pests and Enemies of Bees, Queen raising and Re-Queening, Honey and Beeswax, Miscellaneous Operations, Honey bees in Agriculture and Horticulture. $10 to $20

DEPARTMENT of AGRICULTURE, Vic. ***Bee-Keeping in Victoria***, 1981, 6th ed., pp.139, b&w illus, gloss, s/c, 18x25cm, ISBN 0 7241 7866 X, dewey 638.109945, UWSH, 5th ed. 1964. Chapters: Biology of the Honey bee, Hive and its Components, Handling of Bees, Establishing an Apiary, Management of Bees in Spring, Summer Operations, Wintering of Bees, Diseases of Bees, Pests and Enemies of Bees, Queen Raising and Re-Queening, Honey and Beeswax, Miscellaneous Operations, Honey Bees in Agriculture and Horticulture, The Amateur Beekeeper. $22 to $25

DEPARTMENT of PRIMARY INDUSTRIES, Queensland. ***Beekeeping*** Collated articles compiled by officers of the beekeeping section of the Entomology Branch, Dept. primary Industries. 1979, stapled foolscap sheets, pp.53, some historical references on introduction of bees (Brisbane 1854, James Carroll 1866), SLNSW

FIMMELL, Norm S. (1992) *Our Friends the Honey Bees, written especially for children*. Bentley W.A., pp.16, NLA catlg. N595.799/F489. This work apparently not located in collection, catalogue record is marked "with catalogueing", inquiries upon the library staff did not succeed in locating a copy. A future check W.A. State library is necessary.

GOODACRE, W. A. (Special Livestock Officer, Apiculture) Department of Agriculture, N.S.W. *Bees and Honey*, 1954, pp.140, illus, adv, s/c. 2 shillings & sixpence. Notes: interesting period photographs - R. Whiting's Honey House - Molong, G. Roots' apiary plant & truck, A. Yeo - Ashfield, apiary kiosk - Hawkesbury Agricultural College c1915, concrete hive stands - some of which still on site, H. Graham Smith at work, old transport vehicles, bee beard, period dress. Chapters: The Queen and Her Subjects, Hives and Materials, The Inside of a Working Hive, Spring Management in the Apiary, Migratory Beekeeping, The Increase of the Colony, Handling the Honey Crop, Production of Comb Honey, The Production of Beeswax, Food Supplies & Substitutes, Diseases of the Brood, Diseases of the Adult Bee, Pests & Enemies, Wintering of Bees, Handy Hints. $5

GOODMAN, Russell, BRAYBROOK, Laurie; HUNT, Peter; KACZYNSKI, Peter; McMonigle, John *Beekeeping*, 1991, 7th ed., pp.177, gloss stiff covers, illus, index, adv, 17.5x24.5cm, ISBN 0 7241 9839 3, Creative Solutions, Nth Melbourne. Notes: at least 3 impressions, UWSH. $25. Chapters: Biology of the Honey Bee, Hive and its Components, Handling of Bees, Establishing an Apiary, Management of Bees in Spring, Summer Operations, Honey Extracting, Wintering of Bees,

Diseases of Bees, Parasites of Bees, Pests and Enemies of Bees, Queen Raising and Re-Queening, Honey, Beeswax, Miscellaneous Operations, Honeybee Pollination, The Amateur Beekeeper

GUILFOYLE, John L. ***Beekeepers I Have Known***, pp.44, s/c, illus, <u>Chapters</u>: Introduction; Harry; Matsuda; Walter T (Kelley); Sid; Julia; Barney; Alan; Peter; Johnny; Boris; David; Experience; Uncle Peter; Mustapha; Bill; Autobiography. Extract from Intro: "I think beekeepers are a special type of people and I will endeavour in this small book to set out as best I can the characteristics that make up this special type of person. I am sure that you will recognise some of them; but I should warn you that many of the characters in this book are fictional and simply portray some of the characteristics of the beekeepers I have met." Contains stories primarily about overseas beekeepers met during visits to various Bee Congresses. Include some of story about his brother, the wax man

GULLIFORD, Robert (1989) ***Bee keeping for business & pleasure***, Paterson, N.S.W. Home Study Program, NSW Agriculture & Fisheries. 10v. in 6. ill., maps; 30 cm. Contents: 1. Introduction to beekeeping; 2. Hives, equipment and maintenance; Honey and pollen flora. 3. Selecting sites and moving bees; Comb manipulation and hive management. 4. The production enterprises; Swarming. 5. Queen rearing; Diseases. 6. Financial management and decision making.

GULLIFORD, Robert (2001) *A Dictionary of Scientific and Practical Beekeeping*. pp.519, h/c, over 3100 entries. $75 to $90.

GUTH, Steven (1976) *Honeybee*. designed and illustrated by WACKWITZ, Susan. Jacaranda, Milton, Qld. pp.48, ill. (part col.), 22cm. Juvenile literature

JONES, Henry Mervyn *Beekeeping in Queensland*, Goodna, Qld. c1946. Chapters: sets out beekeeping by months of the year. Copies: NLA. pp.16. H. Mervyn.'s father was Henry Lewis Jones. Mervyn was born at Goodna, Qld, on 7 September 1899. He enlisted in the Australian Imperial Force on 6 November 1918 [126] at the age of 19. His declared occupation was "Motor Driver" and his service preference was to be in the Flying Corps. Mervyn's father, Lewis, possessed "a library on bee-keeping, ancient and modern, from the year 1691 to 1897." [127] An article in the Queensland Agricultural Journal for 1976 carried a photograph, annotated as follows: "One of Queensland's early breeders of Italian queen bees was Mr. H. L. Jones of Redbank Plains, via Goodna, who reared queens on this site. This photograph was taken in 1948 when the business was being conducted by his son Mr. H. M. Jones." (p.265) Here follows some biographical details of his father, H. L. Jones.

---

[126] mappingouranzacs.naa.gov.au/file-view.html?b=1818865&s=B2455&c=JONES%20H%20M
http://mappingouranzacs.naa.gov.au/details-permalink.aspx?barcode_no=1818865
[127] The *Queenslander*, 15 May 1897, p.17

Henry Lewis Jones

From the *American Bee Journal*, 28 June 1894, No. 74, in its Biographical series: "Goodna, Queensland, April 13, 1894. Friend York, [128] I send you to-day a photograph of myself, also a description and view of my home apiary of over 200 colonies, and also of my brother's fruit ranch. Perhaps this glimpse of apicultural life in far-off Australia will be interesting to you, at any rate I hope so. I have another apiary about five miles away, stocked with Carniolan bees, which I am endeavoring to breed in their purity. I may also add that I started bee-keeping 13 years ago, aged 15 [in 1881] without a penny capital, and I never borrowed a penny, but sold honey taken from box-hives (bees I obtained from the bush), and strained through mosquito netting, until I got enough to buy a small novice extractor which cost me $20. Frames were made from old cases ripped up with a hand-saw; hives, etc., ditto, and my present establishment (one of the largest in the Southern Hemisphere) is the result. Verily, I have much to be thankful for to the "busy little bee." Yours sincerely, H. L. Jones." (p.809)

York noted: "Mr. H. L. Jones, whose portrait is here shown, lives in far-away Australia. He has kindly sent us his photograph, and with it a picture of his apiary, but the latter was not quite distinct enough for the photo-engraving process which we used in reproducing the portrait of Mr. Jones, hence we omit it. Accompanying the pictures we received the following letter, and also an account of a reporter's visit to Mr. Jones' *Mel Bonum* Apiary, at Redbank Plains, near Goodna, Queensland, New South Wales : [129]

---

[128] George W. York was editor of the *American Bee Journal*

[129] York must have been unaware that Queensland had been proclaimed a State on 10 December 1859.

H.L. Jones, *Mel Bonum* Apiary,
Redbank Plains, Goodna, Qld., 1894 [130]

a reporter's visit to Mr. Jones' *Mel Bonum* Apiary, 1894

The following extract from a long article appeared in the *American Bee Journal*, 28 June 1894 "A Visit to Redbank Plains. Noticing that I was looking a bit 'fagged' a few days ago, the boss told me I might take a run out into the country for a day or so, if I liked. ... I was only too glad of the opportunity of spending a day or two amongst the trees. ... so I gladly availed myself of the offer, and, after some consideration, concluded to pay a long-promised visit to Mr. Dan Jones, of Redbank Plains. ... [I borrowed] a buggy with only one horse. ... [and] secured the services of the owner as driver. ... I had occasionally to hold the reins while my charioteer got down to open gates or slip rails whenever required. There's nothing got in this world without trouble. Well, we set out about 10 o'clock on

---

[130] Image from *American ee Journal*, 28 June 1894, pp.809-811. Lengthy article contains report of a tour of Jones' apiary

a beautifully bracing morning, with just enough chill in the air to make one enjoy life. Nothing occurred on the journey to mar the enjoyment, only the constant and ever-present fear of a breakdown. Such roads! It was like traveling down the bed of a dry creek in many places. My heart went out in pity to the poor farmers, and to their horses for having to travel over such roads, … at length, after a drive of about an hour and a half, we arrived at our destination, and were heartily welcomed by Mr. and Mrs. D. Jones.

"Henry Lewis Jones, Mel Bonum Apiary, with his beehives at *Oakleigh*, Redbank Plains, 1920s." Ipswich City Library holding.

I superintended the work of unharnessing and stabling the horse. … then we were invited to 'come up stairs and have a look round.' Mr. Jones' house is built on a commanding eminence, and a magnificent view of forest, farms, hills and dales is obtainable from the balconies which 'jut' out from each side of the building on the upper story. Here a splendid telescope was brought out, and the eye, by its aid, commanded a scene which it would take a small volume to describe. We were assured by our host that parts of the city of Brisbane can be distinguished on exceptionally clear days. While we were thus feasting our eyes with visions of Nature's loveliness, Mrs. Jones had been preparing a feast of another kind, to which we were summoned, and of which, after our drive, we were nothing loth to partake.

'That's Harry's place over there,' said our host, pointing to a house on another hill something over half a mile away. 'Would you like to take a walk over ?' Then followed a look around the farm and orchard. … and the time was near for our appearance at *Mel Bonum*. Arrived there, we were met by the genial proprietor, who first showed us over his store, in which he keeps supplies of all the latest novelties connected with any incident to successful bee-farming, from all parts of the world, and very interesting I found his explanation of the different devices for carrying on the business.

Pictured above: H.L. Jones' Apiary, Goodna, circa 1898 [131]

'Come along,' says the irrepressible D. J. (What veritable steam-engines for energy those dwellers in the country are, to be sure.) But I was comfortably seated, and not inclined to move for a bit; just walked half a mile, you know, so I said, 'How did you get on at Sydney, Harry?' Mr. H. L. had only returned on the previous evening from the city of 'our beautiful harbour,' whither he had been to attend a conference of bee-masters. 'Oh, pretty well on the whole; there were about 70 representatives present, but I don't think Queensland has much to learn from the other colonies in the way of bee-keeping. They are certainly behind us in the matter of 'strains;' that is, we have here a greater number of different breeds than they have. At the same time, an interchange of ideas and experience such as is to be gained at such meetings must be of benefit to all concerned.

The next thing to which our attention was directed was a honey extractor, constructed so as to hold four large frames of comb at once. It's an extractor all right. In the same room we were shown a high pile of wax, which is used for making foundation and other purposes. While we were examining these things, the proprietor was getting his smoker ready. We came out, and at once proceeded to get my smoker to work. I don't know what he loaded with; mine was 'rough-cut, Queensland leaf only.' A few puffs from the bellows at the mouth of the hive, and off comes the top. 'Would you like to see the queen?' Of course we would, but didn't want to quarrel with the body-guard. Two or three frames were lifted, and at last her majesty was discovered, going in and out amongst her subjects, a real mother to her people. 'That's a pure Italian,' we were informed. We didn't like her any the better for that; we would have preferred an Australian. 'Have

---

[131] http://hdl.handle.net/10462/deriv/130441
Image from State Library of Queensland

you an Australian queen ?' I said. 'Well, you might perhaps call the acclimatized English bees Australian, but the queen is easily distinguished from the others. Of course, there are the native bees, but they are not cultivated.' ....

Labeled "A beekeepers' field day at HL Jones *Oakleigh*, Redbank Plains, Ipswich, 25 Nov. 1933." Given the finery the gathering looks more like a wedding. Image held by Ipswich City Library.

However, we were shown all around, and the qualities of the different kinds of bees were explained in a way that showed our tutor, for the time being, was master of his subject. There was the Carniolan from Austria, the Punic from North Africa, and Italians imported from Italy and America. Mr. Jones is the only bee-master in Queensland who has the Carniolan strain, and the only one in the whole of Australia who has the Punic. He does an extensive business in the different strains, sending queens all over Australia and Tasmania. There are between two and three hundred colonies on the farm, and the quantity of honey turned out must be something enormous. We were shown some very neat and novel cans and jars for packing the honey in, some of which were provided with air-tight caps. The honey is put on the market in a most taking form, and commands a ready sale.

Supplies of all bee-keepers requisites are kept on hand, and sent to any part of the colonies as ordered. Altogether, my day's outing proved most pleasant as well as profitable, and any one in search of information on agriculture, horticulture, or apiculture, can easily find it amongst the Joneses of Redbank Plains. Our journey back was uneventful, but pleasant memories will linger long on the day I spent with genial companions amongst the trees and humming bees." (pp.809-811)

BEEKEEPERS' REQUISITES.

IF you are interested in BEES, and wish to work them to the best advantage, send for my

54-page Catalogue OF BEEKEEPERS' REQUISITES, Italian Queens, &c.

Contains nearly 100 Illustrations, with much Useful Information, and is sent post free.

H. L. JONES, Goodna, Queensland.

Advertisement in the *Queenslander*, 12 November 1898

In 1897 Jones' catalogue listed "a complete beginner's outfit, including a full colony of Italian bees, with two hives, a copy of Root's book, bee smoker, &c, at £2 15s." [132] In The Honey Bee column of the *Queenslander*, 24 September 1898 "We have received a copy of the illustrated "*Catalogue of Beekeepers' Requisites*" for the season 1898-9, issued by Mr. H. L. Jones, of the Melbourne [?] [*Mel Bonum*] Apiaries, Goodna. The catalogue, which has over fifty pages, contains a large amount of general information of use to beekeepers, and this information is rendered all the more intelligible by the numerous

---

[132] The *Queenslander*, 6 November 1897, p.883

illustrations which accompany the letterpress. .An advertisement regarding Mr. Jones's catalogue appears in another column." (p.614s) In Root's *The ABC of Bee Culture* (1899) H.L. Jones was described as "a very extensive and successful queen-breeder"

Remembered in fiction, 1897

H. L. Jones name is perpetuated in *Kirkham's Find* by Mary Gaunt, as follows: "… she had some honey to extract, a good deal too considering she had been working not for honey but for bees, and she had two Italian queens that had arrived by the post that morning all the way from H.L. Jones' apiary at Goodna, Queensland, and if they were to do well they ought to be introduced to their new homes this very night. …" (p.195) [133]

An article on Jones appeared in the 1905 *Transvaal Agricultural Journal*, 1905 "Many people in the several Colonies of South Africa have attempted at different times the importation of pure-bred Italian bees, both from England and from Australia. So far I have not heard of any importation which has been successful. It was our intention, in event of this importation being a success, to distribute these Italian bees amongst our farmers.

Mr. R. T. Stephens of Pretoria, who recently took a vacation in Australia, kindly consented to aid us in importing pure-bred Italian Queen bees from Australia. Through the kindness of Professor French, the Entomologist of Victoria, Mr. Stephens was fortunate in procuring 24 picked and tested Queen bees from the apiary of Mr. H L Jones, Goodna, Queensland. The Queens, accompanied by a number of ..." (p.572) [134]

---

[133] Thanks for this find to Maurice Mishkel in Canada for his fascinating web site
http://www.auspostalhistory.com/articles/188.shtml

[134] This is the extent of text I could extract via Google Book Search.

A visit by Arthur Conan Doyle, 1921

From Arthur Conan Doyle's *The Wanderings of a Naturalist* (1921) "So full was our life in Brisbane that there was hardly a day we had not some memorable experience, even when I had to lecture in the evening. Often we were going fourteen or fifteen hours a day, and a tropical day at that. On January 14th we were taken to see the largest bee-farm in Australia, run by Mr. H. L. Jones.

Ever since I consigned Mr. Sherlock Holmes to a bee farm for his old age, I have been supposed to know something of the subject, but really I am so ignorant that when a woman wrote to me and said she would be a suitable housekeeper to me and said she would be a suitable housekeeper to the retired detective because she could "segregate the queen," I did not know what she meant. [135]

On this occasion I saw the operation and many other wonderful things which make me appreciate Maeterlinck's prose-poem upon the subject. There is very little poetry about Mr. Jones, however, and he is severely practical. He has numbers of little boxes with a store of bee-food compressed into one end of them. Into each he thrusts a queen with eight attendants to look after her. The food is enough to last two months, so he simply puts on

---

[135] From *Wikipedia*: "In "*His Last Bow*", Holmes has retired to a bee farm on the Sussex Downs in 1903–1904, where he takes up the hobby of beekeeping as his primary occupation, eventually producing a "*Practical Handbook of Bee Culture, with some Observations upon the Segregation of the Queen*". The story features Holmes and Watson coming out of retirement one last time to aid the war effort. Only one adventure, "*The Adventure of the Lion's Mane*", which is narrated by Holmes himself as he pursues the case as an amateur, takes place during the detective's retirement."

a postage stamp and sends it off to any one in California of South Africa who is starting an apiary.

Several hives were opened for our inspection with the precaution of blowing in some smoke to pacify the bees. We were told that this sudden inrush of smoke gives the bees the idea that some great cataclysm has occurred, and their first action is to lay in a store of honey, each of them, as a man might seize provisions in an earthquake so as to be ready for whatever the future might bring. He showed us that the queen, fed with some special food by the workers, can lay twice her own weight of eggs in a day, and that if we could find something similar for hens we could hope for an unbroken stream of eggs.

Clever as the bee is it is clearly an instinctive hereditary cleverness, for man has been able to make many improvements in its methods, making artificial comb [136] which is better than the original, in that it has cells for more workers and fewer drones. Altogether it was a wonderful demonstration, which could be viewed with comfort under a veil with one's hands in one's pockets, for though we were assured they would not sting if they knew we would not hurt them, a misunderstanding was possible. One lady spectator seemed to have a sudden ambition to break the standing jump record, and we found that she had received two stings, but Mr. Jones and his assistants covered their hands with the creatures and were quite immune. A half-wild wallaby appeared during our visit, and after some coyness yielded to the fascination which my wife exercises over all animals, and fed out of her hand. We were assured that this had never before occurred in the case of any visitor." (pp.234-235)

---

[136] For "comb" read "foundation"

Arthur Conan Doyle and wife visit
H.L. Jones' bee farm, January 1921.

Previous page: *Mel Bonum* apiary, Goodna, Queensland [137]

"Henry Lewis Jones, Queensland's Queen Bee King" [138] is extracted from the Canadian web site "Australian Postal History" run by Maurice Mishkel. "This printed to private order Queensland postcard with the 1d printed stamp is postmarked Goodna, Queensland, and addressed to Mr. R.S. Kinnear, The Overflow, Nyngan, N.S.W."

---

[137] From: *ABC and XYZ of Bee Culture*, (1903) A.I. and E.R. Root, Medina, Ohio. (p.461) The supporting text states: "We have a very fine view of one of the largest, if not the largest, queen-rearing apiaries in the southern hemisphere. It is operated by Mr. H. L. Jones, of Goodna, Queensland, Aus. This apiary contains about 300 colonies; and while it presents a remarkably neat and orderly appearance, its owner says it was not "got up for the occasion," as the photographer came along unexpectedly." (p.472)

H.L. Jones apiary was again pictured in *The ABC and XYZ of Bee Culture*, this time in the 1908 edition.

[138] http://www.auspostalhistory.com/articles/188.shtml

"The reverse shows an advert for Bee-Keepers' Supplies, Largest Queen-Raiser in Australia, New Catalog, Free, together with a diagram of a 'spinning top', inscribed Always on Top. It is dated 7/10/95, followed by the following handwritten text: Dear Sir, I am forwarding your three nice Carni Italian queens to-day & trust you will receive them in good condition, No. 34. I think you will find an <u>exceptionally</u> fine queen. I am still overwhelmed with orders, but will forward balance of your order shortly. In haste I am, (in print) Yours Respectfully, H.L. JONES."

BEE-KEEPERS' SUPPLIES. GOODNA, QUEENSLAND. 7/10/98

LARGEST QUEEN-RAISERS IN AUSTRALIA.

New Catalog. Free.

Yours of _____ inclosing _____ received.

Dear Sir,

I sent you 6 Queens you first ordered Barnes Italians guaranteeing & truly you will receive them in good condition. No. 3. I think you will pair on Exceptionally fine queens. I am still overstocked with queens but will forward balance of your order shortly.

So trust I am Yours Respectfully. H. L. JONES

JONES, Richard (2005) ***Bibliography of Commonwealth Apiculture: from the databases of the International Bee Research Association***. Commonwealth Secretariat, London. pp.348, wherein pp.1-24 addresses Australian publications, predominately journal articles. Most text available via Google Book Search.

KENEALLY, Thomas. ***Ned Kelly and the City of the Bees***, 1978, Jonathan Cape, London, pp.120, 14.5x22.5cm, h/c, illus d/w, ISBN 0 224 01600 8. £3.50. $5 to $40. Notes: A novel, illus by Stephen Ryan. A delightful children's story enhanced by the full page illustrations. Shows author's good understanding of the workings of a hive.

The jacket blurb as follows: "The summer Ned Kelly lived with the bees was extraordinary, to say the very least. It began as he lay in his hospital bed and looked up to see a lovely dark and gold creature on the window sill gazing at him with pitying eyes. Swallowing the drop of golden liquid Apis the Bee offered, Ned became just the right size to travel on her back if he held on tightly to her armour. Apis was a worker who took things easier than most, claiming the bees didn't know how to relax. She stopped off between chores to listen to the serials on the radio like 'The Search for the Golden Boomerang' (for this was Australia) and she had even taught Selma, the queen of her hive, to speak radio language, so Ned had no trouble understanding either of them.

Thomas Keneally
Image held by National Library of Australia

Ned was filled with wonder on entering the hive, which was like a huge apartment building and factory in one. Nancy Clancy, another human child of insect size, shared her room with Ned and, aside from her habit of speaking in rhyme – which she did to annoy Apis – she made a good companion. They met Romeo the drone, a love-sick male bee who wanted nothing more than to be near Queen Selma and to tell her jokes, and Razzle-Dazzle Basil with his *Power to the Drones* campaign to protect male bees who were generally thrown out of the hive in autumn. They battled against a surprise attack of raiding wasps, rallied to Queen Selma when she was overthrown and, thanks to their tiny size, witnessed plenty of the village dramas – the plotting of a robbery, a proposal of marriage by Ned's doctor and the latest misdemeanours of the school bully.

Ned Kelly and Nancy Clancy astride Apis

Thomas Keneally's thoroughly delightful story, captured in the striking illustrations of Stephen Ryan, will not only bring children hours of entertainment, but probably teach them more that they will never forget about how bees live and work than many a science lesson." $20 to $50

KLUMP, John (2007) *Australian Stingless* **Bees:** *A Guide to Sugarbag Beekeeping*. Blurb: "The 2000 or more species of Australian native bees go largely unrecognized and ignored by most people: this book aims to help change this lack of recognition. The focus of this book is on the social Stingless or sugar bag bees of which Australia has a dozen species. They are important pollinators and producers of honey and wax. Here is a thorough reference covering identification, hive structure, behaviour and much more. Included are instructions for making a hive, finding hives in bushland, keeping stingless bees and extracting wax and honey. Illustrated throughout with full-colour photographs." pp.110

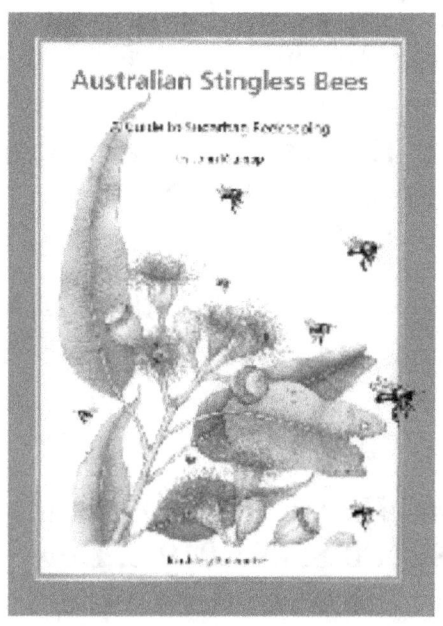

KLUMP, John (2007) *Tips on Stingless Beekeeping by Australian Beekeepers (Volumes 2 and 3)* Vol. 2 contents: Recent tips from 120 Australian beekeepers on: Finding Nests ; Boxing *Austroplebeia* Nests; Siting Hives; Hive Boxes in Current Use; Insulating Hives; New Box Designs; Experimental Heated Hive Designs; Honey Harvesting. Vol. 3 contents: Strengthening Hives; Controlling redators; Dealing with Torelliana Resin; Preventing Fighting Swarms; Causes of Hive Death; Crop Pollination; Preventing Hive Theft; Breeding Queen Bees. For more information refer http://www.aussiebee.com.au/tipsvols2and3.html

LAMBERT, David *Honey Without Stings, Understanding Bees and Sharing the Honey Harvest*, 1983, Western & Co., Kiama. illus stiffened board, pp.24, 14x19cm. Notes: A quaint little book full of hand drawn illustrations and packed with basic information. Chapters: Frames, Foundation, Pollen, Wax, propolis, Workers, Queen, Drones, Life in the Hive, Life Cycle, Expanded Hive, Brood box, Honey super, Clothing, Smokers, Sharing the harvest, Feeding, Flight path, Hive site, treatment of stings, Stings, Robber bees, Uncapping, Extracting, Brood Queen lays upstairs, Re-Queening, Excluder, Hiving swarms, bee trees, Combining colony, Swarming, Winter, Ants, Moths, Spiders, Foulbrood, Bee escape, Wax extractor, Candles. $2. Originally available from Mr. D. Lambert, 30 Merrenburn Avenue, Naremburn, N.S.W. 2065. SLV.

LANGRIDGE, D. F. (Don F.) WIGHTMAN, Bruce D. (1976) *Kill the pests, not the bees*. Department of Agriculture, Melbourne, Victoria. 7 leaves, 26cm. Pollination of seed crops. Effects of pesticides.

LAU, Joy *Bees and Honey*, 1976, Lothian, Melbourne, pp.63, illus, index,, s/c, ISBN 0 85091 019 6, Dewey 595.799, UWSH. Chapters: Bees and Honey, Bees, The Bee Colony, Floral Sources, Beekeeping, Honey, Collecting Honey, Beeswax, Other Products

LEE, John *Beekeeping Thoughts of Springtime*, 1994, the author, Grandview Road, South Wallsend, NSW. ML, Catlg. Q638.1/4 (ML copy signed by the author), ISBN 0-646-16519-4, pp.30, A4. Contains author's own poetry pp.15-20, 26-28. A pity this work is relatively unknown, it deserves a wider readership because of its anecdotal history and humourous observations. eg., the "Gunna" beekeeper, who is always "gunna" do this or that but never does. Some independent editing would have assisted, but typos do not detract from inherent readability of the text. Based on my own historical publications I particularly liked the mix of typographical error, misplaced punctuation and historical inaccuracy in the following "Beekeeping history in Australia perhaps, commenced when Captain Wallis of the Isbell (sic) in 1822 brought hives of black bees to Botany Bay." Such minor eccentricities are more than compensated by the author's poetic efforts.

LEYDEN, Peter (1966) *The visual book of Australian bees*. Layout and art by Curtis, John L.. Sydney, Peter Leyden Publishing House. 8 p. illus. (part col.) 28 cm. His Visual books of Australian nature study, ser 1, 10. SLV

LUMSDEN, G. W. (1974, reprinted 1976) *Notes on Bees and Bee Diseases*. Department of Agriculture, South Australia.. Lumsden was Senior Apicultural Adviser. pp.36, s/c, Bulletin no.2.74. Chapters: Races and Anatomy; Stings, nature & treatment; Digestion of foodstuffs; Reproductive system; Relationship between nectar & honey; mead making; Bee diseases; Plural forms & derivations of anatomical terms; Intermediate & senior apiarists' syllabus. Bibliography refers to book possibly of Australian origin *Infectious Diseases of the Honey Bee* by "Bailey", Land Books. n.d. possibly refers to Fred Bailey

MORRIS, Katherine (1978) *Buzzy, the story of a honey bee*. Great Western Press, Sydney. pp.25, col. ill., 26cm. Juvenile literature

NORTON, Alf (2000) *A Beekeeper's Diary*, Pender Beekeeping Supplies. Chapters originally appeared in *The Australasian Beekeeper*, 1952 to 1958. Limited numbered edition of 200 copies, some in hardcover. Pp.185. Introduction by Bob Gulliford.

N.S.W. Department of Agriculture. *Notes on Eucalyptus Trees, from the point of view of the bee keeper.*, Pamphlet no. 542,

1902, pp.11, 24cm. spine title *Commercial Timbers NSW*, bound with other papers. NLA catlg N674.09944/M217

PRICE, Eva. (1994) ***Tall trees and honey bees: a selection of poems for children***. illustrated by John Hoye. Goulburn, N.S.W. pp.58, ill., 21 cm. SLV.

RAMM, Peter R. ***Historical Record of the Amateur Beekeepers' Association of N.S.W., Illawarra Branch Inc. 1961 - 1991***, c1991. Illawarra Branch - Amateur Beekeepers' Assoc of N.S.W., pp.77, s/c

<u>Notes</u>: well known names mentioned include Colonel G. (Guy) Pulling, Alan Clemson, Warren Taylor, Morris Morgan, Neville Cutts, Elizabeth Mocatta, Keith Doull, Bruce White. In Waratah Park, Sutherland, the Illawarra Branch maintains a Bee Garden, beekeeping museum and educational centre. This is the story of the foundation and day to day activities of a unique band of beekeepers.

Colonel H.G. Pulling and bees, Turramurra, N.S.W., 1957
Image at State Library NSW

REDPATH, N. *Keeping Your Own Bees*, 1978, 1st ed., Thomas Nelson Aust., pp.128, illus, gloss s/c, 13.5x20.5cm. $20 to $30

REDPATH, N. *A Guide to Keeping Your Own Bees in Australia*, 1981, Nelson. ISBN 0 17 005964 2. 1st ed., 1981, Nelson, reprinted 1983, 1985. pp.137, 15.5x23.5cm, colour illus h/c (maroon), index, biblio, glossary. Notes: photographs of Aust. beekeeping scenes (revised edition 1990, Penguin, ISBN 0 670 90277 2, 142p, blue h/c). 2nd ed. $10 to $28. Chapters: The Honeybee, The Bee Colony, Floral Sources of Nectar & Pollen, Obtaining Your Bees, Hives, Locating your Hives, Handling your Bees, Managing your Apiary, Requeening & Breeding,

Keeping Healthy Bees, Collecting your Honey, Products of the Hive, Some Regulations.

ROFF, C. Department of Primary Industries, Queensland. *Beekeeping Information* (1973) pp.12. Flowering calendar, Useful contacts, Equipment suppliers, Queen bee suppliers, Honey marketing contacts, Publications.

ROFF, C. *Beekeeping in Queensland* Queensland Agricultural Journal, V.102 no.3 (May-Jun 1976) pp.265-268

ROFF, C. (1983) *A history of beekeeping in Queensland and the Q.B.A.*, pp.27

ROFF, C. (1983) *Beekeeping in Queensland* (1990) pp.48

RICE, Norman V. M.B.E. *Queens'Land*, c1985, Northern Bee Books, Scout Bottom Farm, Mytholmroyd, Hebden Bridge HX7 5JS, U.K, pp.132, illus, colour cover & rear, 1st ed. s/c, 14.5x21cm, in print. Notes: Named by author Ron Brown in his 'Great Masters of Beekeeping', this is a classic work for the package and queen bee producer. Chapters: Honey Bees "Angels of Agriculture", A beekeeping Business that Grew, Reading Bee Colonies, Progress to Small Colonies, Breeder Queen Management, Maintaining Records of Production, Queen bee Mailing Cage, Nucleus Colonies for Sale, Package Bee Production, Freighting Bees, Costs Associated with Marketing, The Sex Life of Honey Bees, Instrumental Insemination, Marking Queen Bees, Introducing Queen Bees, Wax Cell Cup Production, Feeding Bees for Queen Cell Production, Pollen and Colony Population, Hot Room for Extracting Comb Honey, Processing Beeswax, Moving Colonies to a New Location, Hot Wax Treatment of Woodware, Industry Affairs, Summing Up. $30

RICE, Norman V. M.B.E. *Stinging Tales of Adventure*, Ausbee, 5 Powis Place, Carindale 4152, Queensland. pp.184, s/c, in print, $18, colour front & rer cover, illus., Foreword by Bob Gulliford, editor *Australasian Beekeeper*, Chapters: Honey Bees and World Travel, Learning Visit to the U.S.A., Visits to the United Kingdom, Advisory Invitations - Indonesia, Argentina, Mexico, Advisory Invitations - Burma, Invitation to Iran, Invitation to Pakistan, Invitation to China, Invitation to U.S.S.R., Tibet, Canada, A Beekeeper's World. Notes: Norman's second book, a very readable biography. It concentrates on Norman's globetrotting, both to support and promote his queen bee and package bee business as well as to give freely of his unique talents on an international scale.

RICE, Norman V. M.B.E. ***Milk to Honey via the Sea***, 1997, Ausbee, 5 Powis Place, Carindale 4152, Queensland. pp.99, s/c, in print, limited edition, colour title page, poem "The Bee Hive" by the author (see page 5)

Chapters: Early life on our farm; New beginnings; Our new school; Growing up on the farm; School holidays; The birds and bees; City living; back to the bush; The navy years; Going to sea; Civilian life; Insecticide business; Beekeeping; Retirement. Notes: Another autobiographical contribution from Norman. I found it to be interesting reading. norman has taken up book binding, so a limited number of copies are available in cloth hardcover.

SLOANE, Howard. ***Beehive Management in Australia***, 1975, 1976. Selection of articles originally printed in the *Australasian Beekeeper*. Copies: NLA, SLV, Brisbane City Council library, Univ. Melbourne and others. Chapters: The Young Beekeeper (Becoming a Beekeeper, Preparing for Spring, Spring, Transferring to Frames, His First Queen; His First Honey); Introducing Mailed Queens; The Honey Room; Swarm Control Experiments; Snelgrove Modified; Honey Hives and Brood Hives; Swarm Control and Brood Hives; Brood Apiaries; Out Apiaries; Drifting; Producing Comb Honey (Preparation,

Operation); Combs, Spring 1962; Interesting Observations; Colour and Cold; Unusual Behaviour of a Queen; Fielders; Robber Bees; The Ideal Bee; Bee Breeding; Messmate Flows; Making the Best of a Bad Site; Flavours of the Flowers; Honey and Health; Our Friends the Birds; The Beekeepers Place in Agriculture. s/c, illus, pp.56, SLNSW. Notes: Sloane was an observant beekeeper and an experimenter. In reading this book I learned many new facets of beekeeping. He records many experiences from the 1960s, many, if not all of which are relevant to today. The section for young beekeepers adds value to this work. Many illustrations are hand drawn adding to the friendliness of its informative style.

SMITH, Francis G. *The Hive*, 1966, Department of Agriculture, W.A., Bulletin no. 3464, pp.56, paper wrappers, Preface, var. illus. and photos of hive components, Chapters: The Hive; Types of Hive; Parts of the Hive; Assembling Hives; Recommended Hives. Smith was then Senior Apiculturist. Copy located early 2010 $21.

SMITH, Francis G. *An Introduction to Beekeeping in Western Australia*, 1968, revised ed., by Senior Apiculturist, Department of Agriculture, W.A., Bulletin no. 3108, pp.21, light board wrappers, 6 illus., Chapters: Introduction, The Beekeepers, Races of Bees, Diseases and Pests, Geography Climate and Vegetation, Hives, Apiaries, Honey Extracting Plants, Honey and Beeswax Production, Marketing and Export, Legislation, Organisations, Extension Work and Research Information Sources. Extra editions 1978, 1982 and 1989, latter by by Lee F Allan and Robert J G Manning.

BENECKE, Fred (2007) *Honey Business: A short history of beekeeping in NSW in the second half of the 20th Century.* Klimpston Press, Nowra, NSW.

SMITH, Francis G. *Honey Plants in Western Australia*, 1969, Department of Agriculture, W.A., Bulletin no. 3618, pp.78, stiff wrappers, Preface, maps, illus., Chapters: Intro; The Important Families of Bee Plants; Bee Forage Zones (Karri forest, Jarrah forest, Tuart forest, Coastal heath and banksia wooded heathland, Wandoo woodland, York gum wooded grassland, Transitional woodland, Heathland, Mallee and thicket); Monthly Calendar of Bee Plants; Descriptions of Main Honey Plants (45 varieties, pp.34 – 78) Smith was then Senior Apiculturist.

SMITH, Francis G. *Three Cells of Honeycomb*, 1994, self published, 36 Vincent Street, Nedlands 6009, Western Australia, s/c, pp.248, illus, 14x20cm, index, ISBN 0 9587538 5 7, in print. $25. Notes: biblio of author's publications, notably *Beekeeping in the Tropics*. An interesting read. Reviewed in *ABK* Feb. 1995, p.335. Chapters: Pt. 1: England & Scotland, 1946 into Forestry, Introduction to Beekeeping. Pt. 2: Tanganyika, Adulterated Beeswax, The Search for Proof, Daily Grind, Bee Botany, Completed Projects, Last Tour. Pt. 3. Australia: 1962 A New World, Legislation, Extension Work, Extracting Plant, Refinements in the Honey House, Major Events, Eastern States Tour, Hives, Apiary Sites, Bee Breeding, Beeswax, Research, The Field for Improvement

SMITHERS, Courtney N. *Backyard Beekeeping in Australia and New Zealand*, 1987, Angus and Robertson, North Ryde. s/c, illus, index, pp.118. ISBN 0 20715 279 9

SMITHERS, Courtney N. *Backyard Beekeeping*, 1992, Kangaroo Press, Kenthurst. s/c, glossary, index, pp.80, illus. ISBN 0 86417 458 6. (pbk) Notes: Smithers was an entomologist in the Entomology Department of the Australian Museum, Sydney, during the 1960s. UWSH. Now retired he still maintains an interest in beekeeping. Chapters: Introduction to Beekeeping, The Life of the Bee, Basic Beekeeping Equipment, Where to Keep Your Hives, Examining the Hive, Where to Get

Bees, Harvesting Honey from the Hives, Taking the Wax Crop, Taking Care of the Bees, Swarming - Swarm Control & Absconding, Increasing the Number of Colonies, Uniting Colonies, Moving Hives, Re-queening a Colony, Getting Ready for Winter, Honey & Pollen Flora, Honey & its Uses, Diseases Pests & Ailments, Bee Stings, Legislation, Index of Honey & Pollen Flora. Copy seen on the net in 2011 $30, another on Ebay $

SOUTH AUSTRALIAN BEEKEEPERS' ASSOCIATION, South Australian Beekeepers' Field Club. (nd) *Honey Cookery Recipe Book*. s/c, 18 x 12 cm., pp.16, contains imperial measurements so pre 1966, picture of R. H. Magor, apiarist, Prospect, S.A.

STACE, Peter. STEDMAN, Michael. (1998) *A manual for the control of American Foulbrood*. Primary Industries and Resources, Glenside, SA. pp.41, ill. (some col.) ; 30 cm. Produced on behalf of the South Australian Apiary Task Force. SLSA

TENNANT, Kylie. (1912-1988) *The Honey Flow*, 1956. reviewed *ABK* May 1956, pp.260, at least one reprint in 1983, another 1991: 19x22.5cm, 347p, gloss s/c. $25 to $200, dust wrappers rare. Copy found in 2010, $70, later eds up to $160. Notes: Novel about migratory beekeepers, Kylie spent three seasons with migratory beekeepers to gain material for her work. I've read this book several times and will again, the characters in the book are full of colour.

The jacket blurb is as follows "Bees in Australia do not merely fly to the blossom. Often they are carried by the migratory apiarists for hundreds of miles on trucks or by rail to a spot where the trees of the great eucalypt forests are in flower - as is described most effectively in this typically spirited story by Kylie Tennant. Camped in the scrub in some lonely place, these men watch over their hives and their great trucks, extracting honey in a plant towed behind with the caravan.

The story of *The Honey Flow* concerns the grand-daughter of a Health Food magnate who has ambitions to become a 'boss' apiarist. Her mind is on bees, but naturally the minds of the men with whom she has to work turn in other directions – notably to romance. These men, who are the most picturesque, independent and daring type of Australians, make their own roads through the forests, and similarly take their own way round or over their problems of love or money.

Humorous and happy-go-lucky, and always on the verge of disaster or triumph, the crew of bee-keepers move over the mountains and plains with always the mirage before them of 'striking it extra good' or 'coming in on a flow'. Fire, flood and feuds are their daily portion, but theirs is a rich and spectacular life. There may be other apiarists who are more prosperous and peaceable, but there are none more entertaining than Blaze Muirden and his brother Joe. Kylie ... worked and travelled with migratory apiarists in New South Wales and Queensland for three seasons before writing the novel."

From an historical feature in The Daily Telegraph for 29 May 1998 "Kylie was one of Australia's most distinguished writers ... She has described in her lively and moving autobiography, The Missing Heir, how she found authentic backgrounds for her novels by experiencing the same lifestyles as her characters, in the same settings. ..."

From National Library of Australia: Kylie Tennant and Xavier Herbert on a BSA motorcycle, 16 March 1964

From *The Oxford Companion to Australian Literature* "(1912-1988) born Manly, NSW, had varied experience as a journalist, publicity officer foe the ABC, barmaid, church sister, reviewer and lecturer. She frequently tried to acquire first-hand experience for her novels, including taking to the roads with the unemployed in the 1930s Depression, living in Sydney's slums with Aboriginal communities, travelling with itinerant bee-keepers and even spending a week in gaol. ... A vigorous, versatile, high-spirited and witty writer, her fiction ranges from the satiric to the poetic and expresses a highly comic but sympathetic appreciation of multifarious humanity. The protagonists of her novels are usually the dispossessed and underprivileged slum-dwellers, juvenile delinquents, the unemployed, tramps and nomads of all descriptions. By no means an ideologue, she is more delighted with the spirited waywardness of her disparate outcasts than concerned to offer political or social remedies. ... she affirms the value of life in the face of a clear perception of the tragedy of the human condition, a vision that is implicit in her richly suggestive descriptions of the indifferent Australian landscape, both natural and urban. ... Tennant was made AO (Order of Australia) in 1980."

From *Australian Literary Criticism, 1945-1988, An Annotated Bibliography* "Although Kylie Tennant's best novels were written before 1945, she remained a significant force in Australian literature during the post-war period, continuing to write fiction and to exert influence as a critic and editor. She gained an international audience during the 1930s and 1940s with her gritty, funny, truthful novels of Australian life."

The ACT Beekeepers' Association published a short review in April 2010. Some useful notes may be found in *Wikipedia* and a most useful web page is nla.gov.au/nla.ms-ms10043 which contains a "Guide to the Papers of Kylie Tennant", National Library of Australia's manuscript MS 10043. This MS contains a catalog to a wealth of material on and about Tennant as well as pointers to reviews and some biographical notes. The biography *Kylie Tennant: a life*, by Jane Grant, is accessible via Google Book Search.

From Tennant's autobiography "Because I am not very accurate I write everything down in a notebook and double check. When I was getting the material for *The Honey Flow*, I was a pest to the friendly apiarists, the brothers Koina and Brogan, with whom I travelled. 'What's wrong with the girl! We told you that yesterday!' 'And "Bimble Box".' This was a species of eucalypt. 'How would you distinguish Bimble Box?' Bill Koina gave a scowl and the perfect answer: 'It's bimbley, of course.' "

apiary at Weranga among Bimble Box trees and prickly pear, ca. 1926 [139]

---

[139] From *Trove*, see http://trove.nla.gov.au/work/36894805
John Oxley Library, State Library of Queensland

The Honey Flow dust wrapper:
the original is in delightful colour pastels.

WARD, B.A. ***Beginning in Bees***, 1980s, Short staple-bound pamphlet. Author was District Livestock Officer, South Eastern and Illawarra Region, Department of Agriculture NSW.

WARHURST, Peter & GOEBEL, Roger ***The Bee Book: Beekeeping in the Warmer Areas of Australia***, Department of Primary Industries, Brisbane, 1995, illus: pp.16 colour plates, index. pp.xii, 244, 25cm, ISBN 0724259198 (pbk.): $55.00 (est.), held by 30+ Australian libraries. Includes index, Bibliography. <u>Notes</u>: Packed with the sort of basic data beginners and semi-advanced beekeepers need. Filled with short & pithy paragraphs, easy to read with two column spread, well illustrated, 136 b&w photographs, 59 colour plates, 17 tables. Gleaned from information and experience gained by the authors. Summary: Honey bees for hobbyists, a part-time occupation or a commercial operation; managing hives where, in contrast to cooler areas, bees often continue to breed and gather honey throughout the winter. Reviewed in *ABK* July 1995, p.30. The section on beekeeping history relies on Weatherhead's research and shows no knowledge of Barrett's *The Immigrant Bees* series, published from 1995.

WARHURST, Peter & GOEBEL, Roger *The Bee Book: Beekeeping in Australia*, (2005) 2nd ed. pp.295. ill. col. plates. 25 cm. ISBN:0724259198 Includes index, bibliography. Copy at UQ Gatton Library Department of Primary Industries and Fisheries, Brisbane. Chapters include: An introduction to bee and beekeeping; The honeybee colony; Beginning in bees; Hive construction and preservation; General management; Flora; Feeding and watering bees; Queen bees and package bees; Swarming; Removing the honey crop; Honey extracting; Useful machinery; Products of the hive; Pollination; Pests of bees; Endemic diseases of bees; Chemical poisoning of bees; Exotic diseases and pests; Australian native bees.

I located this blurb: "*The bee book* has been written and compiled by beekeepers who are also apiary officers of the Department of Primary Industries and Fisheries, Queensland. It draws on their personal experience and that of other beekeepers, as well as over 100 years of DPI&F research and experience. This practical, readable and comprehensive book contains detailed information on honeybees and on every aspect of responsible, successful beekeeping - whether as a hobby, a part-time occupation or a commercial operation. It also covers the special requirements of managing hives in Australia where, in contrast to cooler areas, bees often continue to breed and gather honey throughout the winter. The book has 196 pages, 61 colour plates, 137 other pictures and covers:"

WEATHERHEAD, Trevor *Boxes to Bar Hives, Beekeeping History of Queensland*, 1986, Int. Colour Productions, Stanthorpe, Qld. pp132, illus, 4 colour plates, 1st ed., Coloured montage cover & rear, s/c, in print (order from: Secretary, Queensland Beekeepers' Association, Mrs P. Dewar, MS 461, Kalbar 4309, Queensland) $10. Recommended reading, interesting photos, some back to 1897. Introduction: Written to coincide with the Centenary of the Queensland Beekeepers' Association. Notes: 15 pages of beekeeping history to 1900; interesting photographs – 1883 honey label, Jones Apiary 1933, Beekeeping in Tingalpa 1897, Norm Rice 1964, honey labels, Schutt Apiary 1925, George Fletcher of Warwick 1900, F Bestmann 1930, Joe Olley c1930, Herb Simpson apiary 1921,

Restdown 1917, D & H Jones, pre-war school children with hives, Herbert Simpson 1915. <u>Chapters</u>: Introduction of Honeybees to Australia, Introduction of Honeybees to Queensland, Races of Honeybees in Queensland, Early Beekeeping to 1900, Beekeeping in Qld 1900-1930, Beekeeping in Qld from 1930, Beekeeping Literature, Royal National Assoc., Exhibiting Bees & Bee Products, Beekeeping Groups, Dept of Primary Industries, Qld Agricultural College, Honey Flora, Equipment Manufacturers & suppliers, Queen Bee Breeding, Diseases & Pests, Bees Exported from Qld, Marketing, Beekeeping Identities, Memories, Intermission.

The following short review appears at web site dave-cushman.net/bee/crit.html "Read August 2005. Trevor gave me a copy of this book at Apimondia 2005, he thought that the historic information on Australian beekeeping associations, would be of little interest, but I enjoyed reading all of it. The book deals with individuals and companies and because of my beekeeping equipment manufacturing past I was able to draw parallels to the UK equipment trade. I await the next instalment with interest. I am not sure of the availability of this item through the book trade, but I believe that copies are available from The Queensland Beekeepers Association (QBA. The QBA can be contacted at qba@hypermax.net.au The history was published on the occasion of the 100th anniversary of the QBA in 1986."

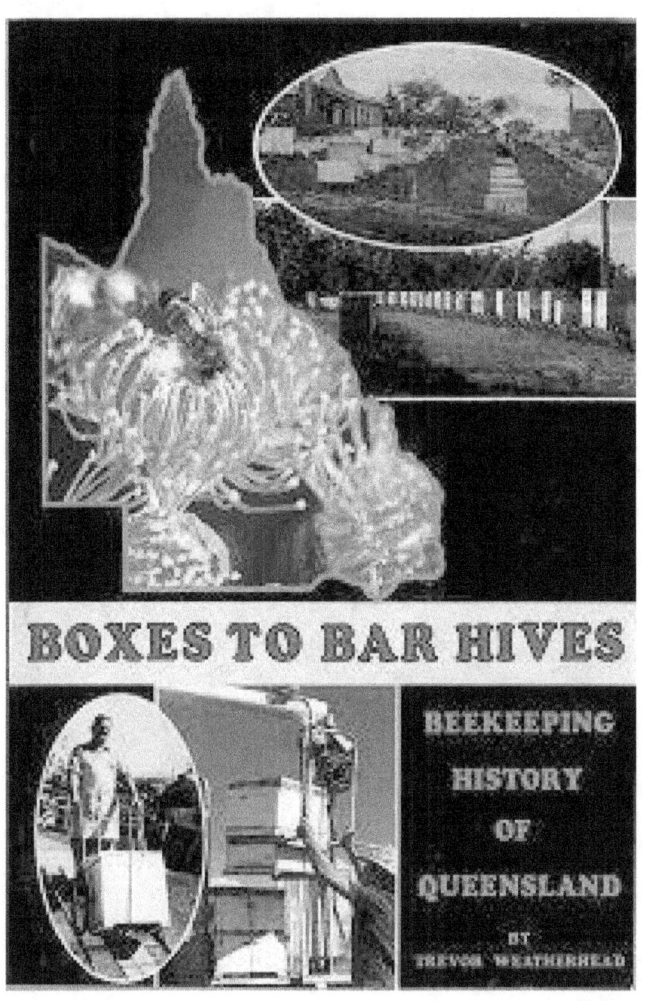

WILLSON, Mildred (1994) **Kangaroo Island Honey Cookbook**. Attractive coloured s/c, recipes, images of local honey labels. Chapter on 'The Ligurian Bee Story" contains inaccuracies, continues the confusion it attempts to clarify. ML

WILSON, Lorraine (1983) ***Catching the swarm of bees***. illustrated by MCALLAN, Marina. Melbourne : Nelson, 1983. pp.16, col. Ill, 14 x 22 cm. Primary reader for children

YOUNG, Lynette. ***The Melody Lingers On*** 1967, Hawthorn Press, Melbourne, h/c, pp.123, illus + 4 b/w plates, d/w, 14.5x22cm, index, SCL, $40 to $90. Copy found early 2010 $135. <u>Notes</u>: biography, portrait of Tarlton Rayment, biblio of his work (pp.29). Lynette was a very loyal assistant to Tarlton, and in his later years, protective. Many of his papers were lost in a bushfire that destroyed his home at Briagolong in Gippsland. For the intrepid researcher, two boxes of material that Lynette used for this biography may be found in a Sydney library. The CSIRO I believe holds some of his insect collection. The original drawings and plates used in the production of *A Cluster of Bees* are held at a library at Cornell University for no institution in Australia could be found to give them a home. Tarlton produced two manuscripts that were never published. *The Commercial Bee Farm* was initially delayed during the war years due to a paper shortage. The other was a successor to his prize winning novel *The Valley of the Sky*.

Beekeeping Journals

Rarely do copies of late 19th and early 20th century Australian beekeeping journals surface in the retail market - I've seen only two listed in the last 15 years. At times, issues of *The Australasian Beekeeper* and the *Victorian Bee Journal* dated from the 1920s have appeared on Ebay. The prime repository of these journals therefore are NLA and the State libraries. I'm unaware of any digitized issues.

Australasian Beekeeper 1899-present day, illus, Pender Bros., Maitland. 5/- per annum 1917.

Commonwealth Beekeeper Notes: incorporated into *Australasian Beekeeper*. SLV holds v. 2, no. 5-v. 3, no. 5; June 1, 1907-May 15, 1908. Monthly. "Official organ of the Victorian Apiarist's Association". Printed by: W.L. Davey, Melbourne. The *British Bee Journal*, Vol. 42, 1914, announced "The Australian Beekeeper has recently absorbed The *Commonwealth Beekeeper*, and the Bee Bulletin."

Robert Lewis John Ellery

La Trobe Picture Collection, State Library of Victoria. [140]

Victorian Bee-Keeper c1920, edited by F. R. Beuhne, revival of *Commonwealth Beekeeper* Notes: Melbourne Bee-keepers Association produced this monthly journal from ca. 1888.

Australasian Bee Journal. In *The South Australian Advertiser*, 8 July 1887 "A monthly journal intended for beekeepers has been started in Australia and New Zealand, entitled the *Australasian Bee Journal*, We have received the first number, which is full of matter interesting to apiarists. The beekeeping industry is making rapid strides in the Australasian colonies, and the journal is intended to supply a want which its conductors consider has been making itself felt for some time past. The proprietors of the journal have secured the services of correspondents in tin other colonies, and some valuable communications from them will be found in its columns, as well as general information useful to bee keepers." (p.5) In the *Rockhampton Morning Bulletin*, 4 August 1887 "Mr. J. Hopkins late of Matamata N.Z. has just issued the first number of a promising new journal, the *Australasian Bee Journal*; we trust the new venture will meet with success." (p.5) Opinion had firmed in the *Rockhampton Morning Bulletin*, 11 January 1888 "We are pleased to note that the last number of the *Australasian Bee Journal*, is a thoroughly practical one, and all persons interested in bee culture should read it; in fact all Australian beekeepers would do well to subscribe to the journal." *The Queenslander*, 28 July 1888 "The *Australasian Bee Journal*, published at Auckland, New Zealand, has lived through its first volume, and No. I of volume II has been sent to us. This is an admirable little paper, and should be subscribed to by all beekeepers no matter in which of the Australian colonies they

---

[140] http://adbonline.anu.edu.au/biogs/A040137b.htm

may live. It is intensely practical, giving the actual experience of beekeepers in various portions of Australia."

Australian Beekeepers Journal Dec. 1885 - July 1890, Vols. 1-4. Notes: Much valuable research and interesting reading is offered to those who can travel back 100 years in Australia's beekeeping history. A short reading period revealed H. Petersen of Nuggety Hill Bee Farm, Wattle Flat (Bathurst region) who in 1878 was transferred his bees to moveable comb hives. Another, William Niven, had kept bees since 1853. Published in Melbourne by Fergusson & Mitchell. NLA holds Vol. 1, no. 1-v. 4, no. 5; Dec. 1885-Aug./Sept. 1890; SLNSW holds Vol. 1, no. 1 (Dec. 1885)-v. 4, no. 4 (July 1890). *The Supplementary Catalogue of the Public Library of New South Wales, Sydney* [forerunner of SLNSW] *for the Years 1901-1905*, listed the same holding: "Vols. 1-4, no. 4, Dec, 1885-July, 1890 [no. 3, vol, 12, missing]. 4 vols, (in 1)"

From the online *Australian Dictionary of Biography*, Robert Lewis John Ellery (1827 – 1908), astronomer and public servant, was the first president of the Victorian Beekeepers' Club. In 1885 he edited the *Australian Beekeepers' Journal*. This journal had a healthy run of years for in Adelaide's *The Advertiser*, 4 January 1944 stated "The editor of the *Australian Beekeepers' Journal*, is Mr. P.J. Markham. Whitehorse road. Mitcham, Victoria. There is no similar publication in South Australia." (p.5)

Australian Bee Bulletin 1894/95 (Vol.3) to 1911, published by E. Tipper, West Maitland and edited by W. Abram of Beecroft. Published throughout the Commonwealth of Australia, New Zealand and the Cape of Good Hope. Notes: Author has a bound copy, with index, of Vol. IV, April 1896 to March 1897, pp.330; also a bound copy of Vol. VII, April 1898 to March 1899, pp.314; paid $160 & $200 in Sept. 2006. Rare in retail market place, ML has various early copies; copies also at University of Qld; Guelph Univ Canada; 3 libraries in USA;

Web page archive.org/details/cu31924058937115 lists "U.S. Department Of Agriculture. Library — Bulletin, Josephine A. Clark, Librarian. Catalogue of Publications Relating to Entomology, 1906" lists this holding: Apr. 28, 1896-Mar. 28, 1898; Apr. 30, 1898-Dec. 29, 1904. v. 5-6, no. 10; v. 7-13, no. 9.

An obituary appeared in the *Sydney Morning Herald*, 4 March 1910. "West Maitland, Thursday. Mr Edwin Tipper, editor and publisher of the Australian Bee Bulletin, died at his residence Wallabadah, [141] on Tuesday in his 76th tear. Deceased, who was a native of Bath, England, resided in Maitland about 40 years, where he built up an extensive job printing business. In the early sixties he was foreman in the office of the Maitland *Ensign*, which newspaper he took over and carried and carried on for some years. A few years ago he handed over the job printing business to one of his sons and devoted his time to bee-keeping and dairy farming. He leaves a family of five sons and three daughters." (p.10) *The Sydney Morning Herald*, 28 July 1927 (p.13) identified Tipper as a journalist and an agriculturist.

Victorian Bee Journal, Victorian Apiarists' Assoc., Tooborac, Vic. From 1930 published as ***Australian Bee Journal***. ill., 21 cm. SLV catlg states: Series date(s): Vol. 1, no. 1 (June 1918)-v. 11, no. 6 (June 1936); Vol. 11, no. 7 (July 1930) - Monthly CSIRO Black Mountain Library: Vol. 1, no. 20 (Dec. 1920)-v. 11, no. 6 (June 1930) (impf.) Copies also at SLQ. Publication continued as *Australian Bee Journal*.

Beekeeping, the official journal of the Southern Beekeepers' Association of Queensland; produced in Toowoomba, Qld. NLA

---

[141] Wallabadah is a village in the New England region of New South Wales, Australia. The town is located 50 kilometres south of Tamworth on the New England Highway.

holds Vol. 1, no. 1-v. 16, no. 1; Jan. 1958-Jan./Feb. 1973; [Incomplete]

The Bee of Australia, 8 issues, each pp.4. #1, 19 Oct 1844 - #8, 7 Dec 1844. This journal has nothing to do with bees or beekeeping, however its motto is worth recording:

"The 'Bee' still gathers sweets where flowerets spring;

But knaves and fools beware – our bee can sting."

The Bee Farmer, SLV catlg details: Title from cover. Devoted to the interests of beekeepers and the production of honey and wax. SLV holds Vol. 1, no. 1-v. 1, no. 9; Dec. 1, 1909-Sept. 30, 1910. From Mar. 1910: "with which is incorporated the *Federal Independent Beekeeper*" Printed for the Proprietor by Brown, Prior & Co., Melbourne

Beekeepers' Bulletin, Ferntree Gully, Vic. Holdings at SLV, NLA, Tamworth Agricultural Institute Library. Publ by Victorian Dept. Agriculture. Vic. Dept. Primary Industries holds Vol. 15, no. 3-vol. 18, no. 1 (1971)-(1974) Incomplete; Tamworth Agricultural Institute holds V 2 no 1 May 1957 - V 14 no 2 Spring 1969; NLA holds Vol. 7, no. 2 ; v. 15, no. 1-v. 19, no. 1 ; v. 19, no. 3-v. 22, no. 2; Aug. 1962 ; winter 1970-winter 1975 ; summer 1975/76-spring 1978; SLV holds v. 9 no. 2-v. 22 no. 2; May 1964-Spring 1978 .

Federal Independent Bee-Keeper c1908-20, edited by E. Penglase. Subtitled "a monthly journal devoted to bees, honey and the beekeepers' interests." Penglase and Armour. Fernbank, Vic. SLV holds v. 1, no. 1 (Aug. 1, 1908) - vol. 2 (1911, 10 copies Dec 1909 – Sept 1910. Copies also at UW Madison. v. 1 (no. 1-12) (1908/1909) v. 2 (no. 13-15) (1909:Aug. 2 - Oct. 1) v. 2 (no. 17-19) (1909:Dec. 1 - 1910:Feb. 1)

New Zealand and Australian Bee Journal 1883-?, <u>Notes</u>: one contributor was Queenslander Charles Fullwood (refer my

Immigrant Bees series), incorporated into *New Zealand Farmer* in 1885. SLV catlg details: Series date(s): Vol. 1, no. 1 (July 1883) Ceased in June 1885? Monthly. Printed by H.H. Hatr, Auckland. "devoted exclusively to advanced bee culture" NLA and SLV hold Vol. 1, no. 1-v. 1, no. 12; July 1883-June 1884

From the *Launceston Examiner*, 17 January 1885 "The *New Zealand and Australian Bee Journal* for January is to hand. This very interesting publication contains much valuable information to those who are fond of cultivating bees. It seems to have a very fair circulation in Tasmania, and in the present issue two letters from Tasmanian correspondents appear in its columns. A correspondent signing himself "A.G.G.," and a resident, writes about "Langstroth's Hives," for Tasmania, and Mr. Thomas Lloyd Hood gives a brief account of the introduction by him of Italian bees into Tasmania." (p.2)

From the *British Bee Journal*, 14 January 1886 "The *New Zealand and Australian Bee Journal* has ceased to exist. At the end of the second volume it has has been incorporated with the *New Zealand Farmer, Bee and Poultry Journal*, Although the new journal did good service and increased the number of members it never paid its way, and for this reason had to be given up."

Queensland Apicultural Journal. Official organ of the Queensland Beekeepers' Association. 2/6 per annum. I rate this journal as "the rarest of the rare." Issues include Vol.1 Oct. 1916 - Oct. 1921, qtrly, supplementary & last copy Dec. 1922. Only two known holdings: Univ. of California – Davis Campus (UCD), Catlg'd NRLF SF521 .Q4. University was approached by Caloundra Library to obtain article copies in April 2009 without success. They do not provide this service to satisfy overseas requests. This is a pity when only two institutions worldwide are known to hold copies of this rare journal. Copies once held by Qld. Dept. Primary Industries 1986 have disappeared from their collection from around 1997. A pity that no Australian library has any copies.

An article in the *American Bee Journal* for 1919 (p.229) refers to the April 1919 issue. The *Apicultural Journal*, the official organ of the beekeepers' association, is published at Brisbane under the editorship of H. L. Jones, … It is nicely "got up" and the printing generally is good. They are all practical men who control the subject matter. Queensland is blessed with many progressive apiarists and the State Association is a live one. At present there are three bee journals published in "Aussie," but the "*Australasian Beekeeper*," Editor W. S. Pender, is the oldest and enjoys the largest circulation. *The Queenslander* is very enterprising and spends a fair amount on illustrative reproduction. The *Victorian [Bee] Journal* is the newest, but more stodgy in its make-up. We like a good cover design, and the *Victorian [Bee] Journal* is lamentably deficient in that respect." By coincidence, this very issue is the one and only example held at the National Agricultural Library, a part of the U.S. Department of Agriculture, being vol. 1, no. 11, April 1919. Eventually, via Google Book Search, I identified that UCD holds at least Volumes 1 and 2, including issues dated Oct. 1916, Jan. 1918, Apr. 1920 and July 1920.

My Quest for this illusive journal: I first became aware of its existence in 1995 via Trevor Weatherhead's 1986 *Boxes to Bar Hives, beekeeping history of Queensland*. "In October, 1916, the Queensland Beekeepers' Association started a journal called the *Queensland Apicultural Journal*. The first copy was complimentary to Queensland beekeepers and after that the subscription was to be 2/6 per annum. This was published quarterly until October 1921. A supplementary copy was printed in December, 1922 and this, it would seem, was the last issue."

My quest to access copies began, hopefully directly or via an inter-library loan, to see if it had any contribution to make to my research efforts. A Google search in October 2006 pointed to a copy being held by the library of the Queensland Department of Primary Industries. However, my request to the DPI librarian revealed no current holding. I contacted Trevor, but, not surprisingly, then some eleven years later, he could not recall where he had sighted the journal. I then searched the catalogues of the State libraries of Australia, the British Library, and particularly, the "worldcat.org" online resource. [142] All failed to locate any holdings. The fate of the copy once held by the DPI remains unknown. Given the extreme rarity of this publication I must assume it was the DPI copy that Weatherhead saw. The DPI's "Beeline" web page, [143] still accessible in April 2009 (and still in March 2011), continues to list the QAJ amongst its resources, although the site seems to be frozen in time – apparently last updated in 1997.

Enter that invaluable research facility – Google Book Search. This indicated two volumes were held by the Davis Campus library at the University of California. My inter-library loan champion at my local Caloundra library, Maree Millard, made the approach, only to be told the University does not satisfy overseas requests. My next attempt found a kind hearted lady named Barbara Hegenbart, a librarian at UC Davis. She suggested some methods of approach and I passed these on to Maree again – more chance of success I thought by an institution to institution approach. "OK Peter, I'll do my best" said Maree. No go – Maree's request was from overseas. Dead end?

---

[142] "Worldcat is the world's largest network of library content and services."
[143] honeybee.com.au/Library/beeline/a97/Autumn97.html

While waiting upon a response from UC Davis, I continued my own efforts. Google's Book Search facility sometimes provides full text viewing of books, in other instances several pages are made available, or more frequently, what they call a "snippet" is supplied - about an inch / 25 mm high strip of viewable text. In other frustrating cases no text preview whatsoever is provided. The poor quality image of the title page of Volume I of the QAJ leaves the commencing year unclear but indicates the price, 5 shillings.

After many search attempts I managed to locate an article titled "The Introduction of Bees into Queensland", [144] the existence of which was hinted at by an earlier and almost forgotten research effort some years previous. Book Search indicated it existed in the Vol. 1 No. 1, October 1916 issue, page 1911, though I doubt the page number provided was correct. Book Search also stated there was another edition dated 1919 but no text searching on it is available.

Despite the limited text searching available in this instance I still managed to extract the following tempting but disjointed snippets from one article by repeated searches – "The study of beginnings is ever a fascinating one, especially in new countries such as Queensland. The question as to who first introduced bees here is as yet an unfathomed mystery, nevertheless, we trust that other writers in the columns of our new Bee Journal … This was in 1854, when this State was a part of New South Wales. ... remarkable, and is evidence that, if unmolested, the honey supply of Queensland would be much increased, had it not been for the attacks of the Bee Moth. Mr. A. J. Boyd informs

---

[144] Another article is a requim for Wilhelm Abram. Other subjects covered include Daniel and H.L. Jones; Goodna, West Maitland, Tewantin and other beekeeping centres; brood comb and other beekeeping topics.

me that in 1862, when starting his farm on Oxley Creek, the bush contained ... In 1864 the writer assisted in cutting out a large swarm of bees from a huge Eucalypt in the neighbourhood of Laidley, further proof that the old strain of bees was innately prolific and great workers. In those days, ... The writer's first contact with bees need not be set on record, for the very good reason that it was an experience the novice usually regrets on his first introduction. ... in 10-frame hives, also honey extractors, Langstroth pattern hives, etc. As early as 1872, Mr. Carroll was awarded a silver medal at the Ipswich Show, for bar frame hives; and in 1874, a medal in New South Wales ... and other modern appliances, the hives being for the most part gin cases or candle boxes. To Mr. J. Carroll, of Enoggera, belongs the distinction of establishing the first modern bee-farm in Australia. From 1872 to 1880 Mr. Carroll sent hundreds of ..." Disappointingly, that's all Google's Book Search would provide. With such tempting clues the QAJ appeared it would prove to be a gold mine of early Australian beekeeping history. But how to get access to it?

My request to NLA produced the following response from Julie Whiting, Manager, Serials Section "I agree that it is certainly an important source of information about the history of beekeeping in Australia and would definitely like to try and obtain copies for our collection. I have been in contact with the Queensland Beekeeper's Association and the President said that two members of the Association have copies of some issues of the journal and may be willing to provide photocopies of these for the National Library. He will check with them as time permits (probably a little later in the year when their beekeeping activities are a bit quieter). Ultimately he thinks their intention would be to donate their original copies to the John Oxley Library in Queensland. However, if I can obtain photocopies for our collection that would at least make some issues of this journal available in Australia in the near future. Regards, Julie."

To spread and stoke my search I wrote to the editors of *The Australasian Beekeeper* and the *Australian Bee Journal* in the following manner: "It is possible beekeepers who read your journal hold on their bookshelves old copies of the *QAJ*. Eventually I hope such holdings were gifted to the National Library of Australia or the Queensland State Library, either to be copied and returned or held as originals – firstly to insure their preservation, and secondly, to allow researchers to more fully tell Australia's beekeeping history. Would it be possible for you to place this request in an upcoming issue?" Des Cannon of *The Australasian Beekeeper*, produced the following prompt response: "Hi Peter, I have placed your letter in Letters to the Editor for the March issue, which will be posted to readers late in February. Regards, Des."

My query to SLQ was as follows "I've found tantalizing references to *Queensland Apicultural Journal* published by Queensland Beekeepers' Association between 1916 and 1922. 1997 *Beeline* website declares it held by Department Primary Industries Brisbane but is no longer listed. No Australian libraries hold copies. University of California Davis holds copies in a bound volume. UCD will not respond to overseas requests for extracts. Julie Whiting National Library Australia is aware of my interest. Would it be possible to lobby with NLA to request UCD to make copies available? Could you also contact the DPI library to see if they can investigate what happened to their holding?"

In January 2011 I sent the following request to NLA: "For 15 years I've been researching Australian colonial beekeeping history. You hold my books "The Immigrant Bees." An important resource in my research is the Queensland Apicultural Journal [note: "Apicultural" not "Agricultural"], no copies of which are held in Australian libraries. There were copies at the Qld DPI but they have disappeared. I believe copies are held by the University of California, Davis and the US National Agricultural Library. I've attempted to gain copies of some articles from UCD but they won't entertain private overseas requests. I believe it is in the interest of maintaining a full perspective on Australian colonial beekeeping history that NLA obtain full copies of this journal for their collection. Do you think you can assist?"

NLA was unable to help. However, Susan Langley, beekeeper to the Governor of the State of Maryland, came to my rescue in July 2011. Susan manages her hives and those of the Governor at Maryland's Government House. "I am going to try to make an early harvest of a super or two from my hives and the Governor's probably has 2 supers ready to come off. I am not allowed at the Residence on weekends as that's the family's time." This is her hobby; her day job as an underwater archaeologist makes interesting reading.

Kathleen, a friend of hers, is a graduate student at the University of California, Davis campus. Susan "sent her on a mission to find your volume to scan and email." Also in league was Bart Smith, another friend who works at the United States National Agricultural Library. Following are a few samples of the *QAJ* editions they located.

Queensland APICULTURAL Journal

Honorary Publishing Committee:
H. L. JONES, EDITOR; A. J. WHEELER; E. M. TARTE, SECRETARY.

Vol. 1.   JANUARY, 1917.   No. 2.

INTRODUCTION OF ITALIAN BEES INTO QUEENSLAND.

M. BLASDALL.

Long Pocket, Indooroopilly.

In regard to the controversy as to who first introduced Italian bees into Queensland, I unhesitatingly give the credit to Mr. James Carroll, of Milton, a number of years before he went to Enoggera. As far as my memory serves me, it would be about the year 1865 that I bought my first bar frame hive, and my first copy of "The American Bee Journal," which contained an article every month by "Novice" (A. I. Root). These articles were designated "Friendly Chat," or some such term, and were of such a charming character, that it was the first article I always chose to read in every number.

If my memory serves me right, Mr. Carroll imported his first colony of Italians from San Francisco in the year 1866, but the undertaking was a dismal failure, as the whole hive, on arrival in Brisbane, was a seething mass of moths and grubs, and was at once sunk in the river at the Old Company's Wharf.

Later on, Mr. Angus Mackay (then editor of the "Queenslander"), myself, and a few others, whose names I do not now remember, contributed £1 each, and succeeded in safely landing a colony, from which Mr. Carro'l subsequently introduced coloured queens to all his hives.

(Fancy Italian bees in Queensland in the 60's? We are certainly making history' and hope shortly to supplement Mr· Blasdall's interesting article by another from one of the oldest practical bee men in Australia.—Ed., "Q.A.J.")

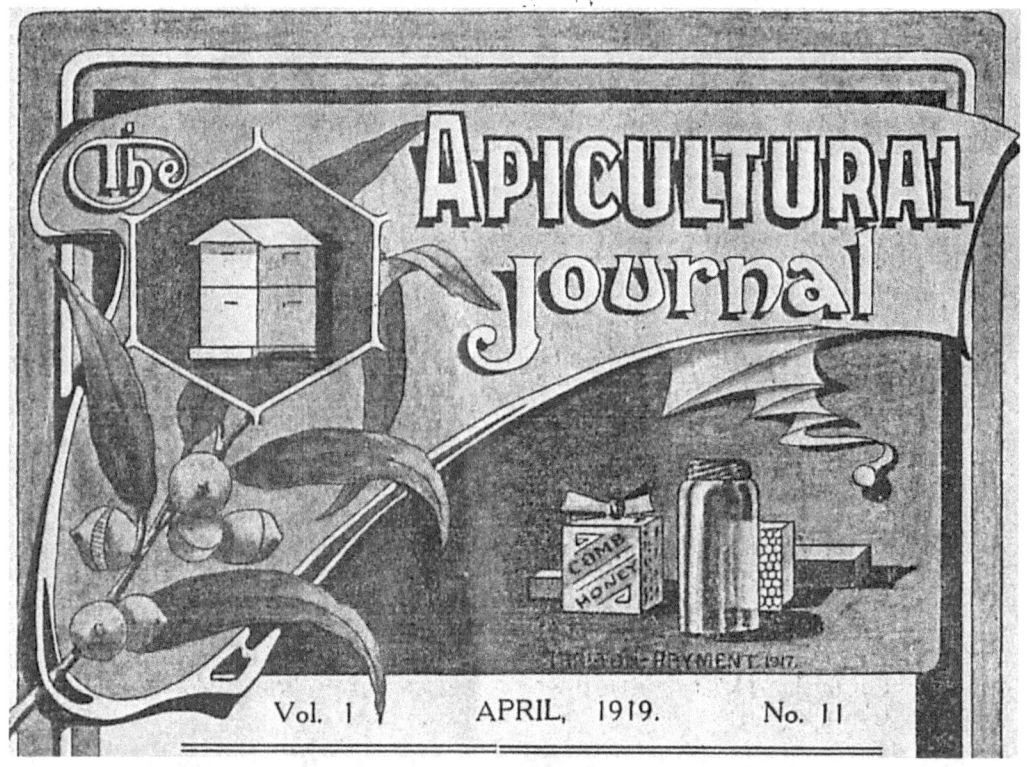

The *Queensland Apicultural Journal*'s banner page: artwork by Tarlton Rayment

Other Publications
Pamphlets & Bulletins & Course Notes

This section does not claim to be comprehensive and includes only those items that have come to my attention.

BINGHAM, G. *Beekeeping in Tasmania*, (1921) Dept. Agriculture, Tasmania. John Vail, Government printer. pp.8. Copy at Cornell University Lib. Author had kept bees for 35 years since 1886 "in the modern style and with modern methods". Gives typical equipment prices: a capping smelter 30s to 35s, cappings reducer £10 10s, other prices for smoker and veil 6s 6d. to 15s., hive tool 2s 6d., uncapping knife 7s. 6d., extractor – 2 frame 12 in. basket £7 to £8; hive with 8 frames, laying queen black or hybrid – 25s to 35s; around 40s with a tested Italian queen. Advice on how to capture and transport swarms. Full text accessible at

http://www.archive.org/stream/cu31924003054362#page/n8/mode/1up

Chapters: Site of an Apiary; Handling Bees; Hoe to Make a Start; Spring Management; Swarming; Honey and the Proper Time to Start Extracting; Implements Needed.

Hawkesbury Agricultural College, 1981 *Bee Breeding and Insemination Hawkesbury Agricultural College, Summer School 1981* pp.57., illus, s/c

Department of Agriculture, N.S.W, 1981 *Beginning in Bees*, illus, s/c. Notes: Course notes in A4 ring binder, *Agfact*

RAPHAEL, T.D. (Senior Horticultural Officer), Cunningham, D.G. (Stock & Apiary Inspector, (1954) Department of Agriculture, Tas., *Beekeeping in Tasmania, Bulletin no. 33*, pp.58, illus. First Edition. In the editor's copy, a pasted in owner's label provides Cunningham's name and address in

Devonport. Apparently given to a fellow beekeeper, the inscription reads "Your colony of bees is pathetically weak & will be lucky to survive the winter." Chapters: Introduction; Starting Up; The Bees; The Hives; General Considerations on the Handling of Bees; Considerations Regarding Queens, Swarming and Swarm Control; Production of Honey; Migratory Work, Winter Preparation; Causes of Loss; Honey Recipes.

RAPHAEL, T.D. CUNNINGHAM, D.G. *Beekeeping in Tasmania*, **Bulletin No. 42**. 1968, illus., pp.64, Government Printer. Chapters: Climate, Choice of district & site, Anatomy and life history of the bees, The Hives, The Handling of Bees, Swarming and Swarm Control, Food and Forage, Production and Handling of Honey, Migratory Work, Winter Preparation, Causes of Loss, Food and Health Value of Honey, Honey Recipes.

RAPHAEL, T.D. CUNNINGHAM, D.G. *Beekeeping in Tasmania*, c1970, illus., pp.64, Government Printer, reviewed *ABK*, Raphael was Senior Horticulturist, Cunningham was Stock and Apiary Inspector. Chapters: Starting Up, The Bees, The Hives, The Handling of Bees, Swarming and Swarm Control, Food and Forage, Production and Handling of Honey, Migratory Work, Winter Preparation, Causes of Loss, Food and Health Value of Honey, Honey Recipes.

Raphael,, T.D. Senior Horticulturist, Cunningham, D.G. Stock & Apiary Officer (c1967) Government Printer, Tasmania, *Beekeeping in Tasmania,* c.1974, pp.64, illus. This issue identifies 1954 as the first edition. Chapters: Introduction; Starting Up; The Bees; The Hives; The Handling of Bees; Swarming and Swarm Control; Food and Forage; Production and Handling of Honey; Migratory Work; Winter Preparation; Causes of Loss; Food and Health Value of Honey; Honey Recipes.

Department of Agriculture, Tas. ***Beekeeping in Tasmania, Bulletin no. 46*** Revised by D. G. Cunningham, Horticultural Instructor – Apiary. pp.66, illus. Chapters: Introduction; Starting Up; The Bees; The Hives; The Handling of Bees; Swarming and Swarm Control; Bees – Food and Forage; Production and Handling of Honey; Migratory Work; Winter Preparation; Causes of Loss; Food and Health Value of Honey; Honey Recipes.

Department of Agriculture, Tas. ***Beekeeping in Tasmania, Bulletin no. 58.*** 1981, Revised by Harold Ayton Apiary Officer. pp.40, A4 paperback, illus., makes effective use of tables. Chapters: The Tasmanian Industry; Starting Up; The Bees; The Hives; Handling Bees; Swarming and Swarm Control; Food and Forage; Production and Handling of Honey; Migratory Work; Winter Preparation; Causes of Loss; Apiaries Act. I found the following of interest in the section on "Races and Varieties" given the interest in English indigenous bees "There are many varieties of honey bees, but the two best known in Tasmania are the 'Blacks' (English Black or European Black) and the 'Italian' or 'Leather Italian'. The Blacks are hardy, industrious bees which visit a very wide range of indigenous and introduced flowering plants. They are capable of making a success of life where many other breeds would fail. Their main failing is a tendency to swarm, coupled with a nervous and excitable temperament. This not only makes them sometimes difficult to handle, but owing to their continuous racing round on the combs, makes the finding of the queens a very difficult operation. However, quiet strains do exist, and it is a pity that so far no bee-keepers here have concentrated on breeding them because after more than 100 years they have become particularly adapted to Tasmanian conditions." Revised ed. 1991, pp.76

Department of Agriculture, W.A. ***Apiculture in Western Australia***, A Journal for the Advancement of Beekeeping, published quarterly. Vol. 1&2 Autumn 1964, Vol. 3&4 Spring 1970. There may be other issues but these are the holdings at SLNSW.

Department of Agriculture, W.A. *The Hive* c1867/69

Hawkesbury Agricultural College, 198?. *Summer School in Apiculture,* pp.24., illus, s/c

DPI, Queensland (1997-) *Beeline: a Queensland perspective.* Brisbane. 25 cm. Periodical

Minister of State for External Affairs, *Undeveloped Agricultural Industries, No.6, Bee Farming.* Melbourne, 1915. pamphlet, illus, pp.16. Notes: Honey production figures expressed in $US, this publication intended for overseas consumption, possibly to induce beekeepers to relocate to or invest in Australia.

GOODMAN, Russell, HUNT, Peter;*Basic Beekeeping*, 1989, pp.27, bibliography. Victorian College of Agriculture and Horticulture (Distance Learning Centre), Warragul.st 3 impressions, SLVIC.

GULLIFORD, Bob , 1989. *Beekeeping for Pleasure and Profit* Paterson, N.S.W. Home Study Program, NSW Agriculture & Fisheries.

SOUTH AUSTRALIAN BEEKEEPERS' ASSOCIATION *Annual Report (1886 & 1887)*, 2nd 1886, 3rd 1887, Adelaide. Annual meeting and report. SLSA (catlg. 638.1 S726a Mortlock Periodicals)

WARRY, R. G. *Introduction to Bee Culture*, Department of Agriculture, N.S.W., . Farmers Bulletin no. 59, illus, pp.10, 1913

WARRY, R. G. *Rearing Queen Bees*, Department of Agriculture, N.S.W., . Farmers Bulletin no. 62, illus, pp.14, ill., 1913

WARRY, R. G. *Beekeeping for Farmers*, Department of Agriculture, N.S.W., . Farmers Bulletin no. 76, illus, pp.19, 19??

Catalogues & Ephemera

HAWCOCK, David. MONTGOMERY, Lee (1994) *A read-about, fold-out and pop-up bee*. Viking, Ringwood, Vic. pp.10 (3 folded) col. ill., 14 cm. Juvenile literature

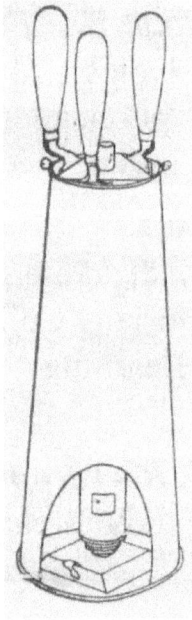

Knife Heater

Pender Bros. *Illustrated Catalogue of Beekeepers' Supplies* 9[th]ed. 1899 pp.5, (SLSA), 44[th]ed., July 1936, pp.32, illus, price lists, 15.5x34cm. $40

Pender Bros. Ltd. (1946) *Appliances for the treatment of honey & beeswax*. Pender Bros. Ltd., West Maitland, N.S.W. pp.23, illus, 21 cm. NLA. At least one reprint in 1953. I came across an identical knife heater set at an antique shop in Windsor. I've used it and it works very well. The other two knifes heat in a reservoir of simmering water. When the knife in use cools it is immersed and one of the other two hot knives put to use.

Pender Bros. Ltd. (1953) *Australian-made Honey Extractors and Pumps*. Pender Bros. Ltd., West Maitland, N.S.W. pp.30, illus, 21 x 14 cm.

Articles in Other Works

A catalogue of these items would run into the thousands. These are the few I've lately come across.

B-HERD, *Home Beautiful*, Aug. 1958. 79:16 June 1958 ***The Flying Toolbox***

HADOW, Lyndall. Walkabout, March 1966. ***Where the Bee Sucks***, pp.24-25, 2 illus, story of W.A's 'Honey Man of Bradford'

MILES, T. Geographic Magazine, 31:53-9 June 1958

MUTCH, T. D. 1921. ***The Farm and its Industries***, Department of Education, pp.260, illus, limp printed cloth, 8vo. section on bees pp.244-259. Mutch was Minister for Education, contributions by a variety of authors. Beekeeping section by H. G. Smith of Hawkesbury Agricultural College. $50

PARK, Andy Australian Geographic, No. 31, July-Sept. 1993 ***Chasing the Honey Flow***, pp.32-49 Notes: excellent colour photos, tables, fold out poster.

STEWART, Gerald. Home Beautiful, Aug. 1958. ***Honey of a Hobby***, pp.8 centre section, "H.B's Guide to Backyard Beekeeping" Notes: illustrations & advice by Colonel G Pulling.

Bibliography

1. Aitken, Richard and Looker, Michael, editors (2002) *Oxford Companion to Australian Gardens*, Oxford University Press, South Melbourne, Vic.
2. The *Australian Dictionary of Biography*
3. *Brett's Colonists' Cyclopaedia*, 1883
4. *Castner's Monthly and Rural Australian, A Family Journal, For the Farm, Garden, Poultry Yard, Dairy, Apiary, Household and Kindred Subjects*, May, Sept. 1895; January 1888
5. *The Cyclopedia of New South Wales* (1907)
6. *The Cyclopedia of Victoria, Vol. II* (1904)
7. *Dictionary of Australian Artists Online*
8. Doyle, Arthur Conan (1921) *The Wanderings of a Spiritualist*, Hodder & Stoughton, London
9. *Harper's Weekly*, New York, April 1881
10. *Journal of agriculture and industry of South Australia (1902)*
11. *Journal of the Department of Agriculture of Western Australia, Volumes 1-2* (1899)
12. Marks, E.N., 1973. Henry Hacker (1876-1973) *Ent. Soc. Qld News Bull.* 100:13-16
13. Muir, Marcie, (1970) *A Bibliography of Australian Children's Books,* Andre Deutsch Ltd., London
14. Musgrave, Anthony. *Bibliography of Australian Entomology 1775-1930*
15. Newspapers & Journals: *The Queenslander; Brisbane Courier*; The *Sydney Morning Herald*; *The Daily Telegraph*; Adelaide *Advertiser*; *Bush Advocate*; The *Australasian Beekeeper*; *The Rural Australian*; *The Australian Bee Bulletin*; *Australian Bee Journal*,

September 1933

16. O'Neill, Terrance & Frances, *Australian Children's Books to 1980, A select bibliography of the collection held in the National Library of Australia*, NLA, Canberra, 1989

17. *The Oxford Companion to Australian Literature* (2nd ed., 1994)

18. Pownall, Eve (1959) *Mary of Maranoa, Tales of Australian Pioneer Women*, F. H. Johnston, Sydney

19. Rayment, Tarlton (1935) *A Cluster of Bees*, Endeavour Press

20. Ritchie, John (General Editor) *The Australian Dictionary of Biography*, Melbourne University Press, 1990

21. Ross, Robert L. (1989) *Australian Literary Criticism, 1945-1988, An Annotated Bibliography*. Garland Publishing, New York. ISBN 0-8240-1510-X

22. Sim, Jean Constance Robertson (1999, 2007) *Designed Landscapes in Queensland, 1859-1939: experimentation – adaptation – innovation*. (A thesis submitted in partial fulfillment of the degree of Doctor of Philosophy in the Queensland University of Technology, November, 1999) See http://eprints.qut.edu.au/10835/1/wholePHDsim1999.pdf

23. *Sphecos*, a magazine on wasps

24. Tennant, Kylie. (1986) *The Missing Heir, The Autobiography of Kylie Tennant*, Macmillan, Melbourne.

25. *Trubner's American and Oriental Literary Record* (1865)

26. Weatherhead, Trevor. (1986) *Boxes to Bar Hives, Beekeeping History of Queensland*, International Colour Productions, Stanthorpe, Queensland

27. Wilde, William H; Hooton, Joy; Andrews, Barry. (1994) *The Oxford Companion to Australian Literature* (2nd. ed.) Oxford University Press Australia, 253 Normanby Road, South

Melbourne, ISBN 0 19 553381 X

28. YOUNG, Lynette (1967) *The Melody Lingers On*, Hawthorn Press, Melbourne

Index

A Beekeeper's Diary 215
A Dictionary of Scientific and Practical Beekeeping 193
A Few Words about Bees and Bee-Hives 141
A Fortune for the Brave 185
A history of beekeeping in Queensland and the Q.B.A. 218
A manual for the control of American Foulbrood 222
A read-about, fold-out and pop-up bee 252
ADAMS, S. G. 174
An Australian Beekeeping Bibliography 181
  Volume II 181, 182
An Introduction to Beekeeping in Western Australia 220
Annual Report, 1886 & 1887, S. A. Beekeepers' Assoc. 251
Apiarian Society of Victoria 10
APIARIST 11
APIMONDIA 174
Appliances for the treatment of honey & beeswax 252
Articles
  Chasing the Honey Flow 253
  Honey of a Hobby 253
  The Flying Toolbox 253
  Where the Bee Sucks 253
AUGHTERSON, W. H. 175
Australasian Bee Keepers' Guide Book for Amateurs 79
Australasian Bee Manual 108
Australasian Beekeeper 219
Australasian Farmer, The 11
Australasian Queen Rearing .. 164
Australian Bee Lore and Bee Culture 83
Australian Geographic 253
Australian Honey Board 175
Australian Honey Cookbook .. 175
Australian Imperial Force - Education Services 157
Australian Stingless Bees: A Guide to Sugarbag Beekeeping 212
Australian-made Honey Extractors and Pumps 253
Autobiography
  Stinging Tales of Adventure 218
AYLING, Robert I. 176
AYTON, Harold 250
Backyard Beekeeping 221
Backyard Beekeeping in Australia and New Zealand 221
BAILEY, Fred 182, 215
BARRETT, Peter J. 177, 179, 181, 182
Basic Beekeeping 251
Bee Book, Beekeeping in the Warmer Areas of Australia 227, 228
Bee keeping as a Business in Australia 134
Bee keeping for business & pleasure 192
Bee-culture 114
Beehive Management in Australia 219
Beekeepers I Have Known 192
Beekeeping 185, 190, 191, 218
Bee-keeping (Land Book No. 13) 157

Beekeeping and honey production in South Australia 92
Beekeeping in Australia 182
Beekeeping in Queensland.... 193, 218
Beekeeping in Tasmania 248, 249
Beekeeping in Tasmania, Bulletin no.33 248
Beekeeping in Tasmania, Bulletin no.46 .... 249, 250
Beekeeping in Tasmania, Bulletin no.58 250
Bee-Keeping in Victoria . 11, 158, 190
Beekeeping Thoughts of Springtime 214
Beeline
a Queensland perspective .. 251
Bees and Honey 159, 189, 191, 214
Bees and Honey in Australia.. 131
Bees as connected with horticulture 117
Bees of the Portland District .. 169
Beginner in Bee Culture, The 158
Beginning in Bees 227
BENECKE, Fred 183, 220
BEUHNE F. R. 11, 158, 235
B-HERD 253
Bibliography of Commonwealth Apiculture: from the databases of the International Bee Research Association 210
BINGHAM, G. 248
Biography
Melody Lingers On 232, 256
Biological and Technical Factors Affecting Profitability in Beekeeping 188
BLACKET, PENDRILL C. ... 158

BLAKE, S. T. 183
BOLTON, Prof. H. C. 183
BONNEY, A. E. 17
BORD, Janet 184
Boxes to Bar Hives, Beekeeping History of Queensland 229
BRAYBROOK, Laurie .. 184, 191
Bulletins
Beekeeping for Farmers 252
Beekeeping in Tasmania, Bulletin no.33 248
Beekeeping in Tasmania, Bulletin no.46 .... 249, 250
Beekeeping in Tasmania, Bulletin no.58 250
Introduction to Bee Culture 251
Rearing Queen Bees 252
The Hive 251
Buzzy, the story of a honey bee 215
CARROLL, James 22
Catalogues
Illustrated Catalogue of Beekeepers' Supplies 252
Catching the swarm of bees 232
CHAMBERS, L. T. 45
CHAPMAN-TAYLOR, Ray .. 184
CHAUNCY, Nan 185
Clemson, Alan 183
CLEMSON, Alan 186
Cluster of Bees, A 169
Colonial Beekeeper, The 45
COOK, S. C 187
Cotton
Rev. William Charles 255
William Charles 2, 66
Course Notes
Bee Breeding and Insemination Hawkesbury Agricultural College, Summer School 1981 248

Beekeeping for Pleasure and Profit 251
Beginning in Bees 248
Summer School in Apiculture 251
CRIBB, R.J. 78
Cumming, Dr. John 59
CUNNINGHAM, D. G. 248, 249, 250
Curtis, John L 215
DAVEY, Ivo 184
Department of Agriculture
& Stock, Qld 183
N.S.W. 189, 191, 215, 248, 251, 252
South Australia 156, 215
Tas. 165, 248, 249, 250
Vic. 157, 158, 184, 187, 188, 190
W.A. 250, 251
Department of Education 253
Department of Primary Industries, Qld 183
Department of Primary Industries, Queensland 190, 218
DICKINS, Charles 78
Diseases of Bees, Symptoms - Treatment and Control 175
DOULL, Dr. Keith 174
Doull, Keith M. 188
Doyle, Arthur Conan 203
DPI, Queensland 251
Durbridge, C. J. 188
Elements of Australian Agriculture 126
Ellery, Robt. L. J. 55
English bee 35
Filleul, Phillip V. M. 35
Fimmell, Norm S. 191
Firth, John William 188

Foote, Tom 188
Forty-two Years of Bee-keeping in New Zealand 116
Foul Brood, its symptoms and treatment 156
GALE, Albert 83
Geographic Magazine 253
GOEBEL, Roger 227, 228
Goldwing : the life story of the queen bee 165
GOODACRE
W. A. 159, 191
William Alexander 158
GOODMAN
R. D. 184, 188
Russell 191
Russell David 251
GROSSE, E. M. 83
Guide to Keeping Your Own Bees in Australia, A 217
GUILFOYLE, John L 192
Gulliford, Bob 251
GULLIFORD, Robert 192
GURR, C. G. 92
GUTH, Steven 193
HACKER, Henry 160, 164
HADOW, Lyndall 253
Handbook of New Zealand gardening: with a chapter on bee-keeping 142
Handy-Book on the Honey-Bee. How to manage the Honey Bee in New Zealand 96
HAWCOCK, David 252
Hawkesbury Agricultural College 248, 251, 253
HAWKINS, H.J. 96
HAY, David 96
Hints to beginners in beekeeping 164

Historical Record of the Amateur Beekeepers' Association of N.S.W., Illawarra Branch Inc 216
HOCKINGS, Harold J. 98
Holder, Margaret..................... 185
Holding on Beekeeping in Selected Melbourne Libraries 188
Home Beautiful 253
Honey and Pollen Flora . 165, 186
Honey and Pollen Flora of New South Wales 159
Honey Bee in Australia 125
Honey Book 172
Honey Business: A short history of beekeeping in NSW in the second half of the 20th Century 220
Honey Cookery Recipe Book 222
Honey Flora of
  South-Eastern Queensland . 183
  Victoria 158, 187, 188
Honey Flow............................. 222
Honey Plants in Western Australia 220, 221
Honey Without Stings............ 214
Honey, Natural Food and Healer 184
Honeybee............................... 193
Honey-bees............................. 188
HOPKINS, Isaac 99
HOWARD, A. W................... 117
HUNT, Peter 191, 251
Illustrated Australasian Bee Manual 114
Illustrated New Zealand Bee Manual 99
ILTON
  C. D. 190
  Claude 182

Immigrant Bees 1788 - 1898 .. 177
Immigrant Bees 1788 – 1898 Volume II 179
Immigrant Bees 1788 – 1898 Volume III 181
Immigrant Bees 1788 – 1898 Volume III 182
Immigrant Bees 1788 – 1898 Volume III 182
Introducing Queen Bees 164
Introduction to Beekeeping, An 160
JAMES, George...................... 164
JONES, H. Mervyn 193
Jones, Henry Lewis 194
JONES, Richard 210
Journals
  Apiculture in Western Australia 250
  Australasian Bee Journal .. 235
  Australasian Beekeeper 234
  Australian Bee Bulletin 236
  Australian Bee Journal 237, 238
  Australian Beekeepers Journal 236
  Beekeepers' Bulletin 238
  Commonwealth Beekeeper . 234
  Federal Independent Bee-Keeper 238
  New Zealand and Australian Bee Journal 234, 239
  Queensland Apicultural Journal 239
  The Bee Farmer................. 238
  The Bee of Australia 238
  Victorian Bee-Keeper 235
KACZYNSKI, Peter................ 191
KEEN, G. H............................ 164
Keeping Your Own Bees........ 217
KENEALLY, Thomas............ 210

Kill the pests, not the bees 214
KLUMP, John 212
LAMBERT, David 214
LANGRIDGE
    D. F. 190
    D. F. (Don F.) 214
LAU, Joy 214
LEE, John 214
LEYDEN, Peter 215
London 73
LUMSDEN, G. W. 215
MACKAY, Angus 117, 125, 126, 131, 134
MCALLAN, Marina 232
McMonigle, John 191
Melbourne 254
Melbourne Bee-keepers Association 235
Melody Lingers On 232, 256
MILES, T. 253
Minister of State for External Affairs 251
Modern beekeeping
    a paper 17, 57
MOLINEUX, Albert 141
Money in Bees in Australia ... 143, 166
MONTGOMERY, Lee 252
MORRIS, Katherine 215
MURPHY, Michael 142
MUTCH, T. D. 253
My life as a Bee-keeper 188
My life with the bees 187
My Little Bee Book 22
N.S.W. Agricultural Gazette 84
New York 35
NORTON, Alf 215
Notes on Bees and Bee Diseases 215

Notes on Eucalyptus Trees, from the point of view of the bee keeper 215
Notes on two Australian species of Trigona 98
Novels
    Golden City of the Bees 166
    Ned Kelly and the City of the Bees 210
Our Friends the Honey Bees, written especially for children. 191
Pamphlets
    Undeveloped Agricultural Industries, No.6, Bee Farming 251
PARK, Andy 253
Pender
    Bros. ... 164, 175, 234, 252, 253
    W. S. 143, 164, 166
Penglase, E. 238
Practical beekeeping 117
Practical Beekeeping, Handbook for Australia and New Zealand 184
PRICE, Eva 216
Proceedings
    First Australian Bee Congress 174
    XXVI International Congress of Apiculture 174
Products of the Hive 164
Profitable Honey Plants of Australasia 167
Queens'Land 218
Queensland Agricultural Journal 160, 183
Queensland Bee Book 78
RAMM, Peter R. 216
RAPHAEL, T. D. 165, 249
RAPHAEL, T.D. 248

RAYMENT
   Tarlton143, 157, 165, 166, 167, 169, 232
REDPATH
   N.217
Rev. John Ayling, Australian Pioneer: The Life of Rev. John Ayling, Clergyman, Educator, Beekeeper, 1825-1897 176
RICE
   Norman 229
   Norman V. M.B.E. 218, 219
ROFF, C 218
ROFF, C. 183
Rules and by-laws of the Apiarian Society of Victoria 10
Samson and the Bees 184
Scientific Bee Culture 108
Semi-Tropical Agriculturist and Colonists Guide, The 117
SLOANE, Howard 219
SMITH
   Dr. Francis 174
   Francis G. 220, 221
   H. Graham 159, 191, 253
SMITHERS, Courtney N. 221
South Australian Amateur Beekeeper 11
South Australian Beekeepers' Association 251
South Australian Beekeepers' Association 222
South Australian Beekeepers' Field Club 222
STACE, Peter 222
STEDMAN, Michael 222
STEWART, Gerald 253
Stinging Tales of Adventure .. 218
tale of Bridget and the bees ... 172

Talks to Beginners in Beekeeping 158
Tall trees and honey bees a selection of poems for children 216
TENNANT, Kylie 222
The
   Secrets from the Honey Pot 175
The Australasian, Staff Members 11
The Bee-Keeping Industry in Victoria 11
The honey bee 164
Three Cells of Honeycomb 221
Tipper, E. 236
Tips on Stingless Beekeeping 213
Tkomas Bolton, A Pioneer Beekeeper of Victoria 183
Truth About Royal Jelly 174
Victorian Apiarists' Association 172
Victorian Historical Journal ... 183
visual book of Australian bees 215
WACKWITZ, Susan 193
Walkabout 253
WALL, Dorothy 172
Wanderings of a Naturalist 203
WARD, B.A. 227
WARHURST, Peter 227, 228
WARRY, R. G. 251, 252
WEATHERHEAD, Trevor 229
WHITELAW, T. E. 156
WIGHTMAN, Bruce D 214
William Charles Cotton, Grand Bee Master of New Zealand, 1842 - 1847 177
WILLSON, Mildred 231
WILSON, Lorraine 232
wonderful story of Australian honey 175

YOUNG, Lynette.. 144, 151, 170,   232, 256

Abbreviations

ABK	Australasian Beekeeper
adv	advertisements
Anon	Anonymous
Ass	Association
Assoc	Association
b&w	black & white
bds	boards
biblio	bibliography
catlg	catalogue
cm	centimetres
col. ill	Coloured illustrations
d/w	dust wrapper
Dept.	Department
ed	edition
h/c	hardcover
illus	illustrated
imp	impression
Int	International
N.S.W.	New South Wales
nd	no date
NZBK	New Zealand BeeKeeper
Pbk	paperback
pp.	pages
p/c	paper covers
pp	pages
pts	parts
qtrly	quarterly
s/b	stiffened boards
s/c	softcover
Vic.	Victoria
Vol	Volume

DAO	Department of Agriculture of NSW, Orange
Lat	Latrobe Collection, Victoria
LISWA	See SLSA
LNT	Library of Northern Territory
ML	Mitchell Library, Sydney
NLA	National Library of Australia
OML	Oxley Memorial Library, Brisbane
PC	Private Collections
PLSA	Public Library of South Australia
SCL	Sydney City Library
SLNSW	State Library of New South Wales
SLQ	State Library of Queensland
SLSA	State Library of South Australia
SLTAS	State Library of Tasmania
SLVIC	State Library of Victoria
SLWA	Library of Information Services, Western Australia.
US	University of Sydney
UWSH	University of Western Sydney, Hawkesbury

www.ingramcontent.com/pod-product-compliance
Lightning Source LLC
Chambersburg PA
CBHW082057230426
43662CB00039B/2213